MAKING MARKETS WORK FOR AFRICA

# Making Markets Work for Africa

MARKETS, DEVELOPMENT, AND COMPETITION LAW
IN SUB-SAHARAN AFRICA

By Eleanor M. Fox
and Mor Bakhoum

OXFORD
UNIVERSITY PRESS

UNIVERSITY PRESS

Oxford University Press is a department of the University of Oxford. It furthers the University's objective of excellence in research, scholarship, and education by publishing worldwide. Oxford is a registered trademark of Oxford University Press in the UK and certain other countries.

Published in the United States of America by Oxford University Press
198 Madison Avenue, New York, NY 10016, United States of America.

© Oxford University Press 2019

First issued as an Oxford University Press paperback, 2020
ISBN 9780197540404 (paperback : alk. paper)

Library of Congress Cataloging-in-Publication Data
Names: Fox, Eleanor M., author. | Bakhoum, Mor, author.
Title: Making markets work for Africa : markets, development, and competition law in Sub-Saharan Africa / by Eleanor M. Fox and Mor Bakhoum.
Description: New York : Oxford University Press, 2019. | Includes bibliographical references and index.
Identifiers: LCCN 2018028059 | ISBN 9780190930998 ((hardback) : alk. paper)
Subjects: LCSH: Africa, Sub-Saharan—Economic policy. | Economic development—Africa, Sub-Saharan. | Antitrust law—Africa, Sub-Saharan. | Competition, Unfair—Africa, Sub-Saharan. | Africa, Sub-Saharan—Economic integration. | Markets—Law and legislation—Africa, Sub-Saharan.
Classification: LCC KQC738 .F67 2018 | DDC 343.6707/21—dc23
LC record available at https://lccn.loc.gov/2018028059

**Note to Readers**

This publication is designed to provide accurate and authoritative information in regard to the subject matter covered. It is based upon sources believed to be accurate and reliable and is intended to be current as of the time it was written. It is sold with the understanding that the publisher is not engaged in rendering legal, accounting, or other professional services. If legal advice or other expert assistance is required, the services of a competent professional person should be sought. Also, to confirm that the information has not been affected or changed by recent developments, traditional legal research techniques should be used, including checking primary sources where appropriate.

*(Based on the Declaration of Principles jointly adopted by a Committee of the American Bar Association and a Committee of Publishers and Associations.)*

You may order this or any other Oxford University Press publication by visiting the Oxford University Press website at www.oup.com.

*To my wife, Yacine, for her constant support and to my children,*
*Ibrahima and Aminata Aliyah*
*M.B.*


*To my children, Douglas, Margot, and Randall*
*E.M.F.*

# Summary of Contents

# Detailed Contents

# Foreword

THE ACADEMIC LITERATURE devoted to competition law has overwhelmingly and unsurprisingly concentrated upon developments in the United States and the European Union. Although, recently, there has been a growing interest in the developing world, sub-Saharan Africa has been left relatively unexplored by the competition law academy. That Eleanor Fox and Mor Bakhoum have collaborated to produce a sustained analysis of the role of competition law in this important component of the African continent is alone a pathbreaking initiative.

But their book goes far further than an examination of the existing legislation and jurisprudence in the 46 countries that constitute sub-Saharan Africa. The two authors set out their impressive ambition early in the text: "Our thesis is that Africa need more 'market,' but not the kind that simply works for powerful interests. It needs markets governed by rules that control the power of the powerful and unleash the talents and energies of the masses of people long left out of the economic enterprise."

The book notes how the Doha Round negotiations, which initially promised to help the developing world, virtually failed. Consequently, the developing world in general and Africa in particular were left to paddle their own policy canoe in hostile waters. What this book reveals in chapters that mine rare and often inaccessible information is how various African states have sought to adapt principles of competition law sourced in the main from the United States and the European Union to local conditions and the need for economic development that benefits more than simply the interests of the powerful.

The book extends beyond the traditional approach when it seeks to locate competition law and policy within the developmental challenges facing countries within this region. Here the authors lift their analytical gaze way beyond standard competition scholarship to discuss a competition framework that can help countries simultaneously meet the challenges of the local and the global. In particular, Part III of the book deals with the fundamental question for competition law and policy: countries need markets to ensure economic efficiency and distributional equity. But markets do not work themselves pure unaided by anything other than by market mechanisms themselves. Hence, some level of intervention is required, and thus the question arises as to the optimum regulatory system to preserve the idea of a market without it only working for the few.

The reader is left with a plethora of suggestions for a national law that seeks to meet the thesis they set out in their introduction together with a set of realistic ideas for international obligations. The impressive canvass of this book will stimulate debate among policymakers as, at the same time, it fills a significant gap in the existing literature that will be of great assistance to teachers of competition law and to adjudicative authorities seeking imaginative ways of developing a competition jurisprudence that will promote development in their countries.

Dennis M. Davis
Judge President, Competition Appeal Court,
South Africa, Cape Town
April 2018

# Preface and Acknowledgments

WE CAME TOGETHER to write this book because of our love for Africa, our continuing observations on how various sub-Saharan countries were progressively relying on markets and using them to achieve their development goals, and our hope that we could apply our competition law expertise and perspective to advance thinking about how markets and the chance to participate in them can help to enrich the lives of the people, especially the poorer population, in this most important, dynamic, and promising segment of the world.

When we decided to undertake this joint project, one of us (Mor), hailing from Senegal and currently based in Munich, had just completed a thorough survey of the West African countries' competition authorities, their accomplishments and challenges, culminating in a report, drafted at the Max Planck Institute, for the West African Economic and Monetary Union. The other (Eleanor), hailing from the United States, was expanding her expertise from a US/EU base to various African nations and was frequently visiting to advise, teach, and learn. We have learned much more from our research for the book and hope that the book will be a contribution to thought on markets, developing countries, and especially the countries and peoples of sub-Saharan Africa.

We owe an immense debt to so many people who have contributed to this project. Eleanor thanks her student Evan Gilbert, her principal research assistant on the book, who provided extraordinary research and editorial assistance through all phases of the project. She also thanks her former students Sophia Suarez and Elizabeth Yazgi for their excellent work on the manuscript, and she thanks her dedicated assistant, Brendan L. Heldenfels, for his invaluable contributions in preparing the manuscript. For inspiring conversations, some over the course of two decades, she thanks David Lewis, Dennis Davis, Simon Roberts, Norman Manoim, Tembinkosi Bonakele, Liberty Mncube, Francis Wang'ombe Kariuki, and Pradeep Mehta. She thanks Thomas Ross and Taimoon Stewart for helpful comments on the manuscript. She is grateful for the research support provided by the Filomen D'Agostino and Max E. Greenberg Foundation.

Mor thanks Felix Wahler, Dina Kagan, and Stella Wasielak for their invaluable research assistance. He also thanks Vincent Angwenyi for reading and commenting on some chapters. David Gerber has provided valuable insights during the process of drafting the book. Thank you, David. He is grateful to Josef Drexl, Director at the Max Planck Institute, for supporting this project since the very beginning and for his constant scientific support over the years. He also thanks Andreas Heinemann for introducing him to competition law.

Both Eleanor and Mor thank Michal Gal, Josef Drexl, and David Gerber, our collaborators and co-authors on the project Competition Law in Developing Countries that was supported by the Max Planck Society and the German-Israeli Foundation, for insightful conversations over the course of our joint work. Eleanor and Mor also thank Pradeep Mehta for many insightful conversations. This book takes inspiration from the 7Up projects of CUTS, the organization he founded and leads.

Eleanor M. Fox, New York
Mor Bakhoum, Dakar and Munich
July 2018

# Introduction

SUB-SAHARAN AFRICA CONSISTS of all of the African countries below or partly below the great Sahara desert. This is a large territory of 46 nations, different but with much in common, together facing a huge economic challenge: how to pull themselves up from cycles of poverty, corruption, and economic and political dysfunction, to meet the promise of better lives and inclusive growth.

This book makes a focused contribution to the grand problem. We deal with sets of nations in sub-Saharan Africa that have at least notionally embraced market solutions to lift up their people and their economies. To contain economic power and help make their markets work, almost all have adopted competition (or antitrust) law. This book continually relates this narrow-sounding specialty (competition law and policy) to the universe in which it is situated, including all restraints that subvert the market, keep the powerful powerful, and keep the markets from working for the people.

Our thesis is that Africa needs more "market," but not the kind that simply works for powerful interests. It needs markets governed by rules that control the power of the powerful and unleash the talents and energies of the masses of people long left out of the economic enterprise.

With our eyes on markets and their possibilities for the peoples of Africa, we look both inward and outward. We look at origins and demographics, at colonization and its legacies and later independence of nations and economic liberalization; at applications of competition law; at good work being done and yet to be done beyond the boundaries of competition law enforcement; and at the world competition system and the place of the sub-Saharan nations in it.

In this introduction, we take a quick look at the economic evolution of the sub-Saharan countries. We then introduce the contents of this book.

Modern human beings originated in sub-Saharan Africa some 100,000 to 150,000 years ago. Tribal settlements, kingships, and rival kingships developed, often with religious and spiritual bases. Economically, the kingdoms were dominated by agriculture, trade in commodities, and local extraction and production such as copper, iron, salt, and fabric. European colonizers eyed the vast economic potentials of Africa as early as the fifteenth century, leading to the scramble for Africa. Led by zeal for both economic and religious expansionism, the Portuguese, then the Dutch, the British, the French, the Germans, and the Belgians staked out colonial claims. The colonists had different styles. For example, the French typically took control over all facets of governance, treating the indigenous people as peons. The English mode was to delegate the duties of governance to local power holders, thus, as it turned out, collaterally nurturing leadership—a quality that would be of great significance when, much later, the territories won independence. Most of the region achieved independence from the colonial governors in the 1960s.

In sub-Saharan Africa today, most of the working people are employed in agriculture. This can amount to 60 percent to 70 percent of the population. Most agriculture is subsistence farming, and most of the farm families live below the poverty line. In many places, the farms are run predominantly by women. The farm small-holders need money to expand, but they typically have no collateral to put up, and they cannot get credit, especially if they are female. About 50 percent of the land mass of Africa is rural with little access to electricity and, where they have it, frequent shortages. The educational system is severely underfunded and deficient, health care is often unavailable, infrastructure—including routes to markets—is poor, and the government in power is often mired in corruption.

Africa needs investment. It is attracting investment, especially from China and India. From the start of the new millennium until the economic downturn of 2008, Africa was one of the fastest growing regions in the world; but growth has slowed. Despite dynamic growth at the turn of the last century, Africa is still one of the poorest regions of the world. Of the 48 poorest countries, 34 are African.

While sharing many characteristics, the countries of sub-Saharan Africa are diverse. They range from Benin, a small, very poor country on the west coast, to South Africa, a middle-class country and, until the recent financial crisis, one of the fastest rising economies in the world. In this book we explore several sets of African countries, what they do and what they can be expected to do in terms of opening their markets, incentivizing progress, and protecting themselves from economic abuses, by applying competition law and policy.[1] We relate the economic capabilities of the competition authorities to what has become known as the international standards of competition law and policy.

Part I begins with a statement on developing countries, economic development, and markets. It highlights some of the most daunting impediments to development, including economic and political conditions that close and capture markets. It identifies open markets and economic opportunity as major tools to achieve development that is sustainable and inclusive. We call this the microcosm.

Next we present the macrocosm. The book describes the global landscape. Focusing on competition law and policy, it traces the national roots of competition law, its original ambitions (moral, political, and economic), the internationalization of competition law, its technocratization, and the ongoing enterprise to formulate international standards. Finally, we portray the more homegrown cooperation within the African competition "family."

In Part II, the book takes a view from the microscope. It looks closely at the competition laws and policies of eight nations of French and Portuguese West Africa, eight nations of Anglophone and Creole Africa (central and eastern, and an island economy), and, separately, South Africa. We discuss how and why the competition laws were enacted and how they have been influenced by context and cultural heritage

The countries are all members of regional organizations, indeed overlapping ones. The book describes the common markets and other bodies for regional integration and cooperation in Africa. Regionalism is promising. In view of globalization and the technology revolution, markets transcend countries. The countries need local law, close to the level of the anticompetitive conduct that hurts them. They also need a level of integration, both for community and for efficiencies. Problems abound, however, and the book reveals the gap between the promise and the delivery.

In Part III, the book offers a normative analysis. It begins with a topography of four sets of sub-Saharan countries at different stages of development. It explores the countries' needs and aspirations for their competition systems, and asks what design of a world framework would fit them. Noting that the norms currently in play are essentially developed country norms, the book asks: What would a pro-development, pro-outsider competition law look like? If the standard competition law for the world were written from the experience base of developing countries rather than developed countries (where markets do not work well, monopolies and state ownership proliferate, barriers to market entry are high, and critical masses of people live near or below the poverty line), how would the "standard" law be drafted?

The concluding chapter integrates the threads of development, opportunity, markets, and competition in sub-Saharan Africa.

---

[1] We do not examine the important countries of Nigeria, Angola, Ghana or Congo. Ghana and Congo do not yet, at this writing, have a competition law in place. Nigeria and Angola have just adopted their laws.

# The Context

# 1

## DEVELOPING COUNTRIES, ECONOMIC DEVELOPMENT, AND MARKETS

DEVELOPING COUNTRIES, ESPECIALLY lower-income developing countries with low rates of growth, share key characteristics and challenges. Huge portions of their populations live below the poverty line. Millions of children do not have enough food or nutrition, they do not have access to clean water, they do not have adequate shelter, they do not have access to decent education, and their parents are likely not to have jobs, at least not in the formal sector.[1] If they beat the odds and have inventive ideas with commercial potential, they are not likely to get funding. If, again beating the odds, they are well qualified in mind and skill to enter the economic mainstream either as worker or entrepreneur, they are likely to be preempted by people with privilege and connections.

This is a view from the ground up. The handicaps are reinforced by economic and political conditions top down. The markets are generally highly concentrated with high barriers to entry. State ownership, with privileges granted by the state, is pervasive. Officials grant market favors to friends and compatriots in privilege and corruption, shrinking the channels open to market participation on the merits. Corrupt leaders and vested interests poison the economic well. Officials procure money for

---

[1] *See* ENDING EXTREME POVERTY: A FOCUS ON CHILDREN (UNICEF and World Bank Group 2016); POVERTY AND SHARED PROSPERITY 2016: TAKING ON INEQUALITY (IBRD/World Bank Group 2016). *See also* Editorial, *A Better Way to Fight Poverty*, N.Y. TIMES, May 5, 2005.

Making Markets Work for Africa. Eleanor M. Fox and Mor Bakhoum.
© Oxford University Press 2019. Published 2019 by Oxford University Press.

schools, housing projects, highways, and other infrastructure that are never built; the funds "disappear." Political leaders lavish money on construction projects for private gain and personal luxury. The people learn not to trust government and not to trust big corporations, which—they perceive—exploit all opportunities to bolster their power and to keep the weak weak.[2]

What tools can help? What do the people and the countries need? We would divide the needs into four parts. First, there are direct needs that could be satisfied by provision of material goods and services: food, water, housing, clothing, schools, medicines and health care, energy, and infrastructure. Second, there are services that empower the people to help themselves: teachers and training; information and communications technology. Third, there are channels of empowerment without cultivating dependence; in particular, opening markets to economic participation and thereby facilitating growth, and especially pro-poor growth. Fourth, there are values, without which a society may be restless, alienated, and unstable: dignity and respect for people, equity, and integrity of the system and its institutions. Programs and projects that enhance mobility and opportunity of the people increase both equity and efficiency. They enhance the vibrancy of markets and help to increase growth.[3]

This book focuses on prong number three: making markets work for people. Asked what can most help developing countries and their poorest populations, responders typically cite direct provision of necessities: food, medication, education, and training, which by definition are necessary. But more recently, policymakers add: in order to provide the people with the necessities of life, the countries need economic growth; in order to provide equity and spur development, they need inclusive, sustainable, economic growth,[4] consistent with equity.[5] Competition (or

---

[2] *See* Catherine Boo, Behind the Beautiful Forevers: Life, Death and Hope in a Mumbai Undercity (2011); Michela Wrong, It's Our Turn to Eat: The Story of a Kenyan Whistle Blower (2009); Editorial, *A Better Way to Fight Poverty, supra* note 1.
The paragraph in the text does not describe every developing country. Moreover, some are better positioned than others to move toward good governance and trustworthy institutions. But the conditions presented characterize at least a critical mass.

[3] *See* A Step Ahead: Competition Policy for Shared Prosperity and Inclusive Growth (World Bank Group and OECD 2017); Growth and Poverty: The Great Debate (CUTS 2011); Should Competition Policy & Law Be Blind to Equity? The Great Debate (CUTS 2013).

[4] *See* François Bourguignon, The Poverty-Growth-Inequality Triangle (World Bank 2004); Alfredo Saad-Filho, *Growth, Poverty and Inequality: From Washington Consensus to Inclusive Growth*, DESA Working Paper No. 100, ST/ESA/2010/DWP/100 (UN Economic & Social Affairs 2010); Poverty and Shared Prosperity 2016, *supra* note 1.

[5] *Id. See* Dr. C. Rangarajan—Indian deputy to prime minister, "*Growth cannot be chased at the cost of equity,*"speaking at launch of Growth & Equity, Essays in honour of Pradeep Mehta OneWorld South Asia, May 2, 2013.

market) policy, including removal of anticompetitive roadblocks placed by private and public power, is a critical tool to help achieve development and growth.[6]

How can market policy help? Market policy comes in many forms. The two forms at the heart of this book are: antitrust law, which prohibits and removes restraints by market actors who engage in harmful conduct such as conspiracies to raise prices and bar entry by competitors, and surrounding restraints that are not violations of law but do the same thing: raise prices, barricade entry, favor vested interests. In this larger, surrounding category, the barriers may have been constructed by government acts and measures that keep markets from working, either by excessive and anticompetitive regulations or by complicity with favored firms that get special privileges. Offenses of antitrust law are well documented. They often raise prices of necessities of life by 30 percent or 40 percent; they entrench dominant firms and keep entrepreneurs from contesting markets on their merits, often meaning that the indigenous populations are fenced out of a fair chance to engage productively in the economy. For the larger category (the one not limited to violations of law), examples are even more abundant, and if these barriers are not leveled, there is often little space for competition on the merits to work.

A number of the examples of success involve the World Bank Group, which teams up with competition authorities. The World Bank's mandate is to help improve the economic plight of the world's poorest countries.[7] It works with competition authorities in Eastern Africa. The missions of the World Bank and the competition authorities coincide. Here is a story of a Kenya–World Bank collaboration.

Francis Wang'ombe Kariuki is the executive director of the Competition Authority of Kenya. He approaches his job constantly aware that 43 percent of the people of Kenya fall below the poverty line, and more than 75 percent of the Kenyan workforce are farmers, mostly among the very poor. He looks for market projects that will do the most to help the Kenyan poor—and are politically feasible.[8]

The Competition Authority of Kenya and the World Bank identified the pyrethrum market in Kenya as a promising target of their attentions. Extract from pyrethrum flowers is used to make an ideal pesticide; one that is environmentally friendly and does not leave a hazardous residue on crops. Kenya's soil and climate are particularly friendly to the growing of pyrethrum. The local conditions produce the

---

[6] Growth and the factors that produce it are a complicated subject. Excellent essays, perspective, and debate are presented in GOOD GROWTH AND GOVERNMENT IN AFRICA (A. Noman, K. Botchway, H. Stein, & J. Stiglitz eds., 2012).

[7] *See* Investment Climate, World Bank Group, at http://www.wbginvestmentclimate.org.

[8] *See* module, International Competition Network, Developing Countries and Competition, http://www. internationalcompetitionnetwork.org/about/steering-group/outreach/icncurriculum/devco.aspx (at 30.03 minutes).

highest quality plant. Kenya was once the source of thousands of tons of the flowers a year, and sale of the flowers supported the livelihoods of some 200,000 Kenyan households. The industriousness of the Kenyan pyrethrum growers and sellers made Kenya the world's leading supplier of the insecticide made from the flower. Then the Kenyan legislature passed a law creating the Pyrethrum Board as the sole purchaser of the flowers and the sole processor and marketer of the extract. It required the farmers to sell their output to the Board. The Board delayed payment to the farmers and underpaid them, and was an inefficient processor and marketer besides. Most farmers were forced to abandon cultivation of the crop. The industry declined. Kenya's world market share fell from 82 percent in 1980 to 4 percent in 2009.[9]

The World Bank and the Kenya Competition Authority identified the problem and worked to remove the exclusive privileges of the Pyrethrum Board. The Bank helped stakeholders draft legislation. The competition authority helped publicize the barrier and its harms to stakeholders and legislators. In 2013, the legislature adopted a law repealing the monopoly of the Board. This action improved the incomes of more than 40,000 farmers. It induced farmers to re-enter the market, and induced both domestic and foreign investment in the market, lowering the price of crops by lowering the price of the critical input. And collaterally, the project promised to produce more jobs, a cleaner environment, relief from hunger, and a better chance for the people.[10]

In this case the monopolistic restraint was a government restraint, for the Board was a government board, and progress to dismantle its economic power required legislative action. Had the Board been a private monopoly, the Kenyan Competition Authority would have brought it to account directly by enforcing the competition law. Indeed, the competition law of some other jurisdictions allows the competition authority to sue government boards acting in the commercial marketplace, so in some jurisdictions these monopolistic practices would be an antitrust offense.

A story from Zambia involves both antitrust violations and rogue acts by state officials. It is a story of rigging bids for government tenders for the purchase of fertilizers. There were two big producers, Nyiombe and Omnia, and they dominated the market. Each of the big producers bid to supply the government with fertilizers, which the government would sell at subsidized prices to the farmers, and they typically won their bids. Curiously, the specifications written into the government

---

[9] For the plight of Kenya at the time of and involving the collapse of the pyrethrum market through bad economic policies, *see* PAUL FRANCIS & MARY AMUYUNZU-NYAMONGO, BITTER HARVEST: THE SOCIAL COSTS OF STATE FAILURE IN RURAL KENYA (2005), http://siteresources.worldbank.org/SOCIALANALYSIS/1104894115795935771/20938698/Bitter_Harvest.pdf.

[10] *See* Competition Policies—Open Markets in Kenya, World Bank Group, Investment Climate, Project Brief 91181.

request for tenders exactly matched what these two big producers offered, suggesting that they had an inside track to the government official in charge. (Indeed, Nyiombe and Omnia had personal links with the officials in charge of the procurement process, and they were accused of fraudulent relations with these officials.) Meanwhile, Nyiombe and Omnia not only monopolized the procurement segment (Zambian purchases) of the fertilizer market but they also divided territories between themselves, each refraining from bidding in the territory of the other and sharing with each other sensitive price information. As a result, smaller fertilizer companies were foreclosed from selling fertilizers to the government, which was one of the biggest buyers of fertilizer; the government overpaid for its fertilizer, by about US$20 million over four years, and in the monopoly territories prices rose. The competition authority uncovered the illegal cartel, sued the cartelists, and won their case. Then, the competition authority took another important step: it prevailed upon the government to reform its bidding process. By opening up the process to bidding on the merits and ending the conspiracies between Nyiombe and Omnia, prices of fertilizer dropped dramatically, smaller players had a chance to grow, the government saved millions of dollars, and the farmers were able to buy more fertilizer and were able to charge lower prices for their agricultural products.[11]

As the Kenya and Zambia stories illustrate, so many of the serious barriers that face the people, both as entrepreneurs and consumers, are a mix of public and private restraints, and the public restraints, such as strangely specific specifications set by government officials in procurement requests-to-tender, are often the result of lobbying and even bribing by big private firms.

There are countless stories of how a variety of artificial restraints entrench vested interests and keep the markets from working in the interests of the people. Many of these stories can be found in the collection edited by Simon Roberts, *Competition in Africa: Insights from Key Industries* (2016), and another collection edited by Imraan Valodia, Jonathan Klaaren, and Simon Roberts, *Competition Law and Economic Regulation: Addressing Market Power in Southern Africa* (2017), which especially highlight cross-border problems.

Competition law and competition policy deeply interact; they offer different tools to address substantially the same ills—unnecessary and unreasonable restraints on the market that hurt the people. Competition law and policy, together, can help make markets work for the poor; they can help make markets work for development.

---

[11] *See* Thando Vilakazi, *Undermining Inclusive Growth? Effects of Coordination on Fertilizer Prices in Malawi, Tanzania, and Zambia*, Chapter 4, sec. 4.4.1, *in* A STEP AHEAD, COMPETITION POLICY FOR SHARED PROSPERITY AND INCLUSIVE GROWTH (World Bank/OECD 2017). The case is on appeal.

The competition officials must—and in our experience usually do—choose their cases and projects carefully to pursue these goals. They are fortunate when they can enlist the aid of the World Bank, as in the pyrethrum example. They are constrained by scarcity of resources, including a scarcity of trained experts, and must choose their projects carefully. Moreover, they are confronted with a body of law—competition law—that has become increasingly technical, complex, and difficult to apply, often requiring armies of trained experts; and a body of law that may, but need not, favor entrenched big firms over clever and disruptive challengers. We may ask: Has the West overcomplicated this body of law? Has it built in a bias for the establishment?

With this background, we move to the world picture. What is happening in world competition law? Is there such a thing as "the world standard"? And if there is, is it the right one for poor, resource-starved developing countries with weak markets and high barriers to entry and only a handful of officials armed to enforce the law against well-resourced opponents?

# 2

# COMPETITION LAW AND THE GLOBAL LANDSCAPE

## The View from Above

DEVELOPING COUNTRIES' COMPETITION law and policy is a piece of a much larger picture. To understand its possibilities for developing countries, we must look at its place in the world.

Antitrust law originated (in its more modern form) in the United States with the passage of the Sherman Act in 1890 as a response to the industrial revolution, the growth of giant enterprises, and the great disparity of wealth that seemed to emerge overnight.[1] The Sherman Act is a lean statute. Its words are few. It prohibits agreements and combinations that unreasonably restrain trade, and monopolization and attempts and conspiracies to monopolize. The US Congress left it to the courts to interpret the law. For nearly a century US courts interpreted the antitrust law to protect the weak from the strong; although there was an increasingly vocal chorus of criticism that later took root that argued that the law was handicapping efficiency. Until approximately the end of World War II, the United States, almost alone, exalted freedom of competition as the way to promote economic democracy, to serve peoples' needs and material desires, to empower entrepreneurs, and in general to provide political freedom and economic opportunity. Antitrust law was enlisted to serve these goals.

---

[1] *See* HANS B. THORELLI, THE FEDERAL ANTITRUST POLICY 180–185, 226–229 (1955).

Making Markets Work for Africa. Eleanor M. Fox and Mor Bakhoum.
© Oxford University Press 2019. Published 2019 by Oxford University Press.

After World War II, Germany adopted antitrust law to disperse power and anchor democracy, drawing from the roots of the anti-authoritarian Freibourg School.[2] Several years later six European nations constructed the European Economic Community as an economics-based means for a lasting peace in Europe. The underlying Treaty of Rome incorporated competition law as a necessary underpinning of a common market. Enforcement of European competition law began in 1962 after enabling regulations were adopted. Little by little the European Union, now 28 nations but soon to become 27 with the exit of the United Kingdom, built a robust body of competition law with a special focus on openness and access to markets and a special concern with controlling state-sponsored restraints.[3]

The 1970s brought substantial economic change. Trade barriers were significantly lowered as a result of the Tokyo Round of the General Agreement on Tariffs and Trade (later folded into the World Trading Organization). Multinational firms grew. Famously, they located plants wherever they could get the cheapest labor, disregarding local context and needs. They built factories, exploited the workforce (while creating jobs), and displaced local suppliers and competitors through vertical integration, low-price transfers to their own local subsidiaries, and price squeezes on outsiders. They raised local firms' costs and chilled their innovation through restrictive terms in intellectual property licensing, exclusive dealing, tying, and territorial limitations on marketing. They commonly blocked the exports of their local joint venture to countries (including the United States) in which the multinational enterprise (MNE) had other plants; they influenced politics in favor of anti-socialist policies (bolstering dictators such as Chile's Pinochet); and, when they found better economic opportunities, they abandoned the country. So charged Jean-Jacques Servan-Schreiber in *The American Challenge*[4] and Anthony Sampson in *The Sovereign State of ITT.*[5] And so believed large segments of the world's population despite the goods, services, and jobs that the multinationals brought.

The developing countries complained about the MNEs' practices. On the antitrust side, they triggered talks under the aegis of the UN Conference on Trade and Development (UNCTAD), hoping to obtain world rules against the restrictive business practices of MNEs. Almost all of the practices of which they complained were then illegal per se under US antitrust law. Three groups of countries negotiated for the world rules: the industrialized countries, the developing countries, and the communist bloc. The nations reached agreement by the end of the 1970s, and in

---

[2] *See* DAVID J. GERBER, GLOBAL COMPETITION: LAW, MARKETS AND GLOBALIZATION 167–169 (2010).

[3] The competition law would prohibit member state policies of dealing only with nationals when purchasing supplies for the state, and building national champions.

[4] 1968.

[5] 1973.

1980 UNCTAD promulgated the Set of Multilaterally Agreed Principles and Rules for the Control of Restrictive Business Practices (RBPs) (also known as the Set or the UNCTAD Set). The United States signed the UNCTAD Set—but not before obtaining the concessions that it wanted the most: multinational enterprises were not singled out as enforcement targets; state-owned enterprises were not excluded from coverage; transfer pricing (pricing within one firm) was excluded from coverage; all restrictive business practices were subject to a reasonableness justification, and nations' adherence to the set of rules was voluntary, not mandatory; there were no sanctions for breach. Ironically, 1980—the date of agreement—was a turning point in US antitrust law; Ronald Reagan was elected president. The Reagan administration turned the dial of US antitrust law 180 degrees, away from economic democracy and toward efficiency.[6] The concern that had animated US antitrust for most of a century—to contain power and provide a better chance for the underdog—metamorphosed into a concern that antitrust not interfere with the efficiency of large enterprise. US antitrust became a blueprint for freedom of even dominant firms in the name of efficiency, as the United States turned its sights to competitiveness and economic power in the world.

Meanwhile, back in the 1970s, the world trading partners negotiated lower trade barriers under the aegis of the General Agreement on Tariffs and Trade (GATT), and, as a result, world trade soared. The technology and information revolution came on the heels of the trade reform. The winds of trade, innovation, and competition put pressure on firms to be cost-efficient. In the United States the pressure was felt in steel, cars, and electronics, among others. These forces of international competition were part of the changed landscape that brought Ronald Reagan to office in the United States in 1981. They continued to evolve.

The next major transformative event came in 1989–1990: communism had lost its grip. Masses of people in the Soviet Union and its satellite countries rebelled. Not only did they want political freedom, they wanted economic freedom. Russian communism's command-and-control economic system, which had promised a decent standard of living for everyone, had failed. The Berlin Wall fell at the end of 1989. The fall of the Berlin Wall was a major turning point. One by one, the previously communist countries adopted democratic political systems and market systems, albeit sometimes denominated socialist market systems to signal a continuing commitment of the nation to social equity. When the countries adopted democracies

---

[6] *See* Eleanor M. Fox, *The Modernization of Antitrust—A New Equilibrium*, 66 CORNELL L. REV. 1140 (1981). The Reagan revolution left in place, however, the persistently strong law against hard core cartels, principally, price-fixing.

and market systems, they began to adopt the set of laws that democratic/capitalist societies normally have. One of these was antitrust.

With the fall of the Berlin Wall, scores of countries adopted antitrust laws. Later events combined to trigger adoption of competition law by scores more countries including large numbers of developing countries. These later events included the successful conclusion of the Uruguay trade round in 1994, heralding globalization and a more integrated world, and the Asian financial flu of 1998. The financial crisis devastated a number of developing economies. They turned to the International Monetary Fund and the World Bank for help, and the financial institutions insisted on loan conditionalities that included adoption of competition law.

Beginning approximately with the end of the Uruguay Round and the ensuing birth of the World Trade Organization (WTO) as the umbrella over the GATT, policymakers and civil society encountered a dilemma: freer trade was encouraging competition, lowering prices, increasing availability of products, and increasing economic integration. Yet for all of its benefits, freer trade threatened to impair other goals and values. It could mean more aggregate wealth but with a skewed distribution and an impaired environment. Free movement of capital and freedom to move whole businesses abroad facilitated exploitation of workers, especially the unskilled. Free movement often heralded less social policy, including thinner welfare nets.[7] Moreover, the more open world markets facilitated world cartels and monopolistic practices across borders.[8]

Policymakers observed the socio-economic-political connections and proposed linkages of many fields with trade law in order to bring these new blights under control. For competition, the European Union was in the vanguard, for the European Union had always linked competition law with trade laws. As European officials observed, competition law was national, but transactions had become significantly international. The international impacts of business transactions seemed to require international principles of law; they required a holistic conception of the whole market, not just a view of successive national markets as if each were isolated. An international competition law could internalize externalities (hold companies accountable for price-fixing "even" to foreigners) and minimize disparities of legal rules among nations. Under an international conception, for example, Canadian potash producers would not be entitled to price-fix into Africa, and US multinationals would not be entitled to abuse economic power in Europe or South America. The European Union's proposal began with building blocks: information sharing and

---

[7] *See* Dani Rodrik, Has Globalization Gone Too Far? (1997).

[8] *See* Margaret Levenstein & Valerie Y. Suslow, *International Price-Fixing Cartels and Developing Countries*, 71 Antitrust L.J. 801 (2003).

cooperation among the competition authorities of each nation, technical assistance from developed to needy nations, and a requirement that national competition authorities incorporate international norms of due process, transparency, and nondiscrimination into their systems. A second stage would see the adoption of substantive rules such as those prohibiting cartels (price-fixing and dividing markets) and abuses of dominant firms' power. Eventually, the world framework could include the full panoply of substantive principles of antitrust and a mechanism for resolving disputes.

US officials and the US antitrust bar fought the proposal. They opposed an international antitrust framework of any sort, and they especially opposed the WTO as the forum for a world antitrust agreement. Americans argued that world antitrust would mean lowering standards to the lowest common denominator. Nations around the world bargaining table would (they argued) seek to protect *their* firms from the more efficient competition of outsiders rather than cultivate efficiency. Critics further argued that a world system would create a faceless, unaccountable bureaucracy run by a cadre of individuals who did not understand the technicalities of antitrust. They argued that the WTO was an inappropriate forum for world antitrust because it was run by trade officials, and trade officials bargain; they make concessions; they seek to protect their nation from economic inroads—of Chinese, Japanese, Koreans, Americans; whereas antitrust law is "principled" pro-market law; it entails application of "pure" and cosmopolitan rules of law, such as: You may not agree with your competitors to fix prices.

Developing countries, too, opposed the European proposal, but for different and sometimes opposite reasons. They did not trust the West. They feared they were being shortchanged by principles of efficiency (of multinationals) without equity; that they would lose their policy space; that they would be increasingly marginalized; that they would suffer a new economic colonialism.

American officials wanted to move the debate to another forum[9] and to shift the major concern of antitrust from abuse of dominant market power—the central concern in Europe—to cartels, the central concern in the United States. This would be a shift from equity for smaller firms to efficiency for consumers. Americans feared that the abuse of dominance violation left the door wide open for competition authorities to protect small businesses from efficient businesses. For a new forum, the Americans set their sights on the OECD—the Organization for Economic Cooperation and Development, which is an organization composed of the industrialized nations of the world and has no enforcement powers (as opposed to the WTO, which

---

[9] *See* JOHN BRAITHWAITE & PETER DRAHOS, GLOBAL BUSINESS REGULATION (2002), Chapter 5 (A state that cannot achieve its goals in one forum may adopt a strategy to shift to a more congenial forum).

welcomes developing countries and has enforcement powers). At the OECD, US officials introduced a recommendation against cartels—which largely meant, against competitor price-fixing. The proposal became the Recommendation of the OECD Council concerning effective action against Hard Core Cartels. It was adopted in 1998. The recommendation states that "Member countries should ensure that their competition laws effectively halt and deter hard core cartels"; that their laws should provide for effective sanctions and should include adequate provisions for document discovery and cartel detection; and that the member countries should cooperate in detection of cartels and enforcement against them while safeguarding confidential information. "Hard core cartel" was (peculiarly but pragmatically) defined to exclude anything the member country's law exempts. The recommendation advises that member countries continually examine their competition laws for unjustified exemptions and seek to eliminate them, and that they should make all exemptions transparent.

The adoption of the hard core cartel proposal, which was supported by studies showing the high cost to consumers of cartels, helped to shift world priorities from abusive practices of dominant firms to cartels. That the main problem of many developing countries was monopoly, not cartels, went unnoticed or unregarded. The proposal for an antitrust agenda in the WTO gradually lost momentum.

Meanwhile, the world was developing a consciousness of the plight of the very poor populations in developing countries. The *New York Times* ran a series of editorials, "Harvesting Poverty,"[10] showing how Western policies such as cotton subsidies derailed efficient small cotton producers in Africa, throwing tens of thousands of capable entrepreneurs and their families into poverty.[11] Consciousness of the ills and hardships of the billions of people in poverty led to the groundswell within the United Nations to adopt the Millennium Development Goals—which aspired to halve the number of people in deep poverty by 2015, and later to the Sustainable Development Goals—to end severe poverty and assure basic rights of humanity by 2030.

Meanwhile, in the United States, an international antitrust review committee (International Competition Policy Advisory Committee, or ICPAC) studied problems and solutions for international competition issues and recommended a new virtual forum for the competition problems of the world. This proposed new forum would have no secretariat or bureaucracy, and its recommendations would be entirely voluntary. It would be devoted only to antitrust issues (not trade and antitrust), and membership would be open to the *antitrust agencies* of all nations, not to

---

[10] *E.g., Harvesting Poverty; the Long Reach of King Cotton*, N.Y. TIMES, Aug. 5, 2003.

[11] *See also Harvesting Poverty; the Rigged Trade Game*, N.Y. TIMES, July 20, 2003.

nations themselves (thus contrasting with the WTO, the OECD, and UNCTAD, whose members are nations), and not limited to industrialized nations, as is the OECD. The ICPAC proposal became the International Competition Network (ICN), launched in October 2001 by 14 nations.[12]

One month later the WTO held its ministerial meeting for a new round of trade negotiations at Doha, Qatar, and the ministers adopted an agenda for the round—the Doha Declaration of November 14, 2001. This trade document recognizes that the developing countries had not shared equally in the gains from the prior trade rounds, and declared that this new round was to be the Doha *Development* Round. The Doha agenda contained three paragraphs on the interaction between trade and competition, "[r]ecognizing the case for a multilateral framework to enhance the contribution of competition policy to international trade and development" and the need of developing countries for enhanced technical assistance and capacity-building, and proposing work of the WTO Working Group on the Interaction between Trade and Competition Policy[13] to clarify "core principles, including transparency, non-discrimination and procedural fairness, and provisions on hardcore cartels; modalities for voluntary cooperation; and support for progressive reinforcement of competition institutions in developing countries through capacity building."[14] This would have been a start for a world framework for antitrust.

But the Doha antitrust agenda was not to see the light of day. The Doha Round negotiations, which began in Cancun, faltered on arrival. The United States and the European Union failed to offer sufficiently sizeable cutbacks in their agricultural subsidies (subsidies that particularly harm the developing world), and this was the main item on the agenda.[15] To help revive the negotiations, the nations agreed to remove several items from the more ambitious agenda, including removal of the item: competition law. Even so, the negotiations never became robust. The entire Doha Round—a round meant especially to help the developing world—has virtually failed.

The fate of the ICN was quite to the contrary. The ICN blossomed. It now has more than 130 member competition authorities and numerous nongovernmental advisers. Projects are under way on cartels, merger standards, technical assistance, regulated industries, and—the most challenging because of the most disparity—rules for unilateral conduct such as abuse of dominance. Through recommended

---

[12] *See* Eleanor M. Fox, *Linked-In: Antitrust and the Virtues of a Virtual Network*, 43 INT'L LAW. 151 (2009).

[13] This Working Group was launched in December 1996 in Singapore.

[14] Paragraphs 23 to 25 of the Doha Ministerial Declaration of Nov. 14, 2001. The Doha agenda item was developed principally by officials of the European Competition Directorate-General.

[15] *See Collapse in Cancun: The World Trade Agenda Gets Sidetracked*, KNOWLEDGE@WHARTON, U. of Pennsylvania (Sept. 24, 2003).

practices and almost infinite opportunities for personal interactions of officials and advisers throughout the world, convergence of law and analytical methodologies has occurred and is further occurring, and understanding and cooperation have increased albeit predictably on Western terms.[16]

The center of the international competition conversation shifted from the WTO to the ICN. It shifted from a more formal hierarchical and top-down project to informal horizontal networking. Within the national systems, the law, with the need for economic models and experts, has become increasingly complex and expensive and often beyond the capabilities of young competition authorities in developing countries to administer.[17]

Meanwhile, developing countries and regions are seeking out conversations and collaborations of their own that have particular relevance to *their* context and *their* state of development. Regional free trade areas and common markets have formed and are forming. The African Continental Free Trade Agreement (AfCFTA) entered into force in 2019 and negotiations on a competition dimension are in process. The more informal African Competition Forum is actively facilitating cross-fertilization, cooperation, better rules and standards, and discovery of modes of operation suitable to the African countries and peoples.[18]

---

[16] *See* Fox, *supra* note 12.

[17] *See* Neil R. Stoll & Shepard Goldfein, *Back to Basics: The (Over)Use of Economic Models in Antitrust*, N.Y. L.J. (July 10, 2012) (The models the experts introduce in court have gotten too complex even for the United States).

[18] *See* Chapter VI.

# The States, The Regions

# 3

## WEST AFRICA

### From State Control to Freer Markets

## I. Introduction

Clustered near the west coast of Africa just below the Sahara Desert are eight nations: Senegal, Mali, the Ivory Coast, Benin, Togo, Niger, Burkina Faso, and Guinea Bissau. Each country is a product of French colonization except Guinea Bissau, a former Portuguese colony. These nations with diverse cultural heritages but often similar political and economic trajectories are all trying to alleviate systemic poverty and cope with the forces of globalization.

This chapter tells a common tale: under colonial control, the political and economic governance of these nations was dirigiste, meaning that the state controlled the economy. As the nations began to win independence in the 1960s, barriers to trade were falling around the world, and more open markets and freer enterprise brought the promise of economic gains. The nations adopted economic-liberalizing reforms, often at the behest of the World Bank, with varying degrees of success. To complement economic liberalization, the states enacted competition laws to curb the power of an unfettered free market. However, the colonial system of law, which provides the foundation for most of the nations' political and legal structure, produced only weak domestic markets and political institutions.

Making Markets Work for Africa. Eleanor M. Fox and Mor Bakhoum.
© Oxford University Press 2019. Published 2019 by Oxford University Press.

This chapter describes the journey from government-controlled economies to market economies. It is the story of how and to what degree the nations freed themselves from their colonial pasts, how they adapted to markets, and how competition laws lent, or sought to lend, legitimacy to a market system that many feared could be captured by powerful players.

To tell this story, we examine the economic and cultural history of each nation (see Figure 3.1), highlighting the political economic context and the market obstructions still faced by each. We describe the competition law and policy of each nation and

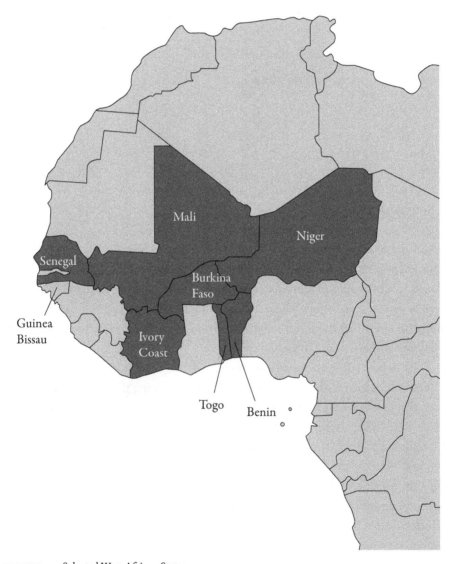

FIGURE 3.1 Selected West African States.

analyze the efficacy of these laws in addressing market problems. In doing so, we reveal an array of practical difficulties that limit the effectiveness of the competition authorities and the law. Finally, we examine the promise and limits of regional solutions, which we return in Chapter VI.

## II. Background: Socioeconomic Characteristics

### A. OVERVIEW

The eight West African countries range from Senegal, a relatively stable democracy on a rising economic trajectory with increasingly reliable institutions and a credible domestic competition law, to Guinea Bissau faced with political instability, a stagnant economy, and no national competition law. Although the West African states are striving to create more open markets, protectionist state intervention still plays an active role in their economies, hindering the development of markets.

When the West African states became independent from colonial control, they embarked on the difficult path of creating political institutions that would encourage economic development and foster competitive markets. After independence, most West African countries adopted single-party political systems. The governments were often democracies in name, but the political systems were not in fact democratic. Some countries, such as Senegal, transitioned peacefully to a more fully democratic multiparty system, and others experienced political turmoil, often with military coups.

The path to a development-friendly economy has been equally bumpy. As colonial states, West African economies were designed to feed Western states, principally France, with agricultural and mineral products. Until the mid-nineteenth century, they served as hubs for the slave trade. Little was done to foster local industrial development or to encourage the transformation of raw mineral and agricultural products to value-added goods. With an economic model stressing exports, little thought was given to development of diverse, competitive domestic industries. Instead, West African states suffer from undiversified economies that rely primarily on exports of agricultural and mining products. Industrial products are mainly imported.

West Africa suffers from high levels of poverty, corrupt political institutions, and increased inequality of wealth. Multinational enterprises (MNEs) dominate the economy and local entrepreneurism plays little role in the formal economy—although that role is beginning to expand. The informal sector is significant. It constitutes 41 percent of the gross domestic product in sub-Saharan

Africa.[1] On the one hand, this is beneficial because 72 percent of workers in sub-Saharan Africa are employed in this sector.[2] On the other hand, the economy suffers because informal firms do not pay taxes, their business activities and employment practices are unregulated, and the self-imposed limits (for example, informal firms cannot bid on public contracts or avail themselves of many other opportunities) means that the sector is not conducive to competitive and sustainable development.

These socioeconomic and political factors, explained further by the country profiles below, provide the backdrop for our later discussion of competition law and poverty.

## B. COUNTRY PROFILES

Using Senegal, the Ivory Coast, Mali, and Guinea Bissau as examples, this section tracks the economic and political trajectory of West African states. It concludes with a chart providing an overview of the socioeconomic characteristics of all of the states.

### 1. Senegal

Senegal is uniquely situated among African states due to its status as the economic center of French West Africa during the colonial period. Prior to colonization, Senegal garnered international attention as the hub linking African, American, and European trade routes. The French recognized Senegal's geographic centrality and established an administrative capital in Dakar, Senegal's current capital. This led to complementary infrastructure investment, the construction of economic institutions such as the West African Bank, and the modest, but not unimportant, integration of indigenous Senegalese individuals into the political sphere.[3] Senegal had a political elite capable of good governance even prior to independence.[4]

---

[1] MARC BACHETTA ET AL., GLOBALIZATION AND INFORMAL JOBS IN DEVELOPING COUNTRIES: A JOINT STUDY OF THE INTERNATIONAL LABOUR OFFICE AND THE SECRETARIAT OF THE WORLD TRADE ORGANIZATION, at 31 (2009).

[2] *Id.* at 26.

[3] *See* Gaye Daffé & Momar Coumba Diop, *Senegal: Institutional Aspects of Trade and Industry Policy, in* POLITICS OF TRADE AND INDUSTRIAL POLICY IN AFRICA: FORCED CONSENSUS?, at 284–285 (Charles Soludo et al. eds., 2004) (discussing the colonial heritage of Senegal and referencing the late-eighteenth-century grant of French citizenship to the population in Dakar, and 1914 election of Blaise Diagne, a Senegalese national, to the national assembly). *See also id.* at 271 (discussing the prominence of the Port of Dakar).

[4] Jean-Claude Berthélémy et al., *La Croissance au Sénégal: Un Pari Perdu?, in* ETUDES DU CENTRE DE DÉVELOPPEMENT DE L'OCDE (1996).

Senegal is considered the most successful postcolonial West African state. Upon independence in 1960, Senegal adopted a single-party socialist system under the direction of President Léopold Senghor. Senghor served as president for 20 years until he resigned in 1980 and was succeeded by his Prime Minister Abdou Diouf. The country embraced a multiparty system in the 1980s. Senegal experienced peaceful transitions of power, even electing an opposition party for the first time in 2000 with the democratic election of President Abdoulaye Wade. Most recently, the country elected President Macky Sall in 2012.

Even with the initial political and economic investment, Senegal has struggled to industrialize, diversify, or embrace a free market. In the 1960s, the state intervened heavily in the economy, emphasizing the agricultural and food-processing sectors, largely inhibiting the growth of national markets.[5] In the 1970s, the World Bank began encouraging Senegal to focus on industrialization with an emphasis on exports based on Senegal's comparative advantage.[6] That tack was initially promising, but Senegalese industry began declining in 1975 and has since struggled to recover in part due to an economic crisis in the 1980s.[7] The industries that thrive are almost entirely concentrated in Dakar and are largely owned by MNEs.[8]

Senegal still relies heavily on primary commodities, including phosphate mining and agriculture.[9] Agriculture alone employs 77 percent of the nation's workforce.[10] Because Senegal is located in a drought-prone area with variable rainfall, the weather is an important factor in the success of agriculture and thus its economic growth.[11] However, its services and tourism sectors are slowly expanding. The expansion is supported in part by Senegal's relative political stability.[12] Recent discoveries of important gas and oil reserves in Senegal led to the promise of greater economic development. However, the management of these resources has been strongly criticized, with the government signing one-sided contracts with international oil companies.

---

[5] *Id.* at 276.

[6] Daffé & Diop, *supra* note 3, at 277.

[7] *Id.* at 283.

[8] *Id.* at 283 ("[S]tudies of the Senegalese private sector . . . show that out of the ten biggest enterprises in business in Senegal in 1991, five were controlled by private foreign capital at more than 50 percent, against only three companies in which the government held majority interest and just one controlled by private Senegalese individuals.").

[9] CIA, *Senegal*, THE WORLD FACTBOOK (as of July 12, 2018).

[10] *Id.*

[11] *Id.* ("Senegal reached a [GDP] growth rate of 6.5% in 2015 and surpassed that in 2016–17, due in part to a buoyant performance in agriculture because of higher rainfall and productivity in the sector.").

[12] *See* Matthias M. Cinyabuguma et al., World Bank Policy Research Working Paper No. 831 (2017).

## 2. The Ivory Coast and Mali

Whereas France invested in Senegal in view of its geographic significance as a central trading hub, it did not give the same level of support to its other West African colonies. Most of these countries had a similar evolution. France set up their economies to serve as centers for raw resource extraction and export to support its own needs and industrial policies. The infrastructure continued to be underdeveloped, and the countries attracted little economic investment. The Ivory Coast and Mali are two examples. Although they adopted different political structures upon independence, their economic and political landscapes are similar.

Unlike in Senegal, where the French created domestic institutions, in Mali, the Ivory Coast, and other West African nations the French concentrated on political control and resource extraction. Most Africans, save for a few elite, were denied political rights and were subjected to a separate code of law called the *indigénat*. The French focused on the export of cash crops. In the Ivory Coast, for instance, the French established plantations for coffee and cocoa and relied largely on forced labor.

Upon independence, the newly sovereign nations pursued divergent political paths. Some countries, like the Ivory Coast, mirrored Senegal's trajectory beginning with the adoption of a one-party state and transitioning to multiparty democracy. However, the Ivory Coast did not enjoy the stability that Senegal did; it suffered a military coup and two civil wars.

Mali, like some other countries, underwent a bloodless military coup shortly after independence in the 1960s and remained a one-party state until 1991 when a popular uprising led to the adoption of a democratic constitution. The nation was largely stable until two coups in 2012 disrupted the region, requiring an international military intervention.

Both the Ivory Coast and Mali are slowly emerging from violent coups and civil wars and are coping with pervasive political and economic instability. It is a common story for West African nations. Constant disruption frustrates the states' ability to invest in infrastructure and to create stable institutions. This in turn leads to an undiversified economy primarily characterized by reliance on agriculture, a large informal sector, and an underdeveloped domestic market.

## 3. Guinea Bissau

Guinea Bissau is the only West African nation that was colonized by Portugal, and it was the first sub-Saharan African country to decolonize through guerilla combat. Its economic and political evolution has been markedly distinct from the other states.

Portugal faced significant barriers in fully colonizing Guinea Bissau: it was less technologically advanced than France or Britain; it was slower to industrialize than its peers; and it struggled to gain control over its colony due to both rivalry from other colonial powers and consistent resistance from strong African kingdoms.[13] Portugal engaged in consistent and brutal military operations to subdue the indigenous population.[14]

The Portuguese colonial policies were similarly harsh. Portugal relied heavily on the slave trade in Guinea Bissau to the point where the region became known as the Slave Coast. The Portuguese government focused on the cultivation of cash crops, frequently forcing the indigenous population to work the fields at gunpoint.[15] The colonial government was heavily centralized. Unlike other colonies, Guinea Bissau's governor formally ruled alone without even a token council to represent the indigenous population.[16]

Guinea Bissau achieved independence through armed conflict in 1973.[17] After independence, the conflict continued. There was an uprising and civil war in 1998; a coup in 2003; a military mutiny in 2004; an assassination of the president in 2009; another coup in 2012. While the country is democratic in name, no president has served a full term since 1974.[18]

Guinea Bissau is slowly gaining political stability, but it remains economically troubled. On the Human Development Index, Guinea Bissau is ranked as the least developed country in the world.[19] Like many West African countries, it still relies heavily on the export of raw resources with little industrialization or diversification. The development of domestic markets and local innovation has been stifled.

Given this background, it is not surprising that Guinea Bissau is the only West African nation to not have adopted a competition law.

## 4. Indicators

The following chart, Table 3.1, provides an overview of the socioeconomic characteristics of each West African state and the region as a whole.

The Human Development Index is a summary measure of average achievement in key dimensions of human development, including health, education, and standard of living. Health is assessed by life expectancy. Education is measured by mean years of schooling. Standard of living is measured by gross national income per capita. The

---

[13] *See* Barbara Harrell-Bond & Sarah Forer, *Guinea-Bissau Part 1: The Colonial Experience, in* AMERICAN UNIVERSITIES FIELD STAFF REPORT (1981).

[14] *Id.*

[15] *Id.*

[16] *See* Patrick Chabal, *National Liberation in Portuguese Guinea, in* AFRICAN AFFAIRS (Jan. 1981).

[17] *Id.*

[18] CIA, *Guinea Bissau,* THE WORLD FACTBOOK (as of July 12, 2018).

[19] *Id.*

sub-Saharan African average is .523—the lowest in the world. The West African average is below that, making it one of the least developed regions in the world.

The Ease of Doing Business Index, a World Bank Group publication, measures regulations affecting several areas of business life. For 2017, the following factors were included: starting a business, obtaining construction permits, accessing electricity, registering property, receiving credit, protecting minority investors, paying taxes, trading across borders, enforcing contracts, and resolving insolvency.

The Democracy Index, created by the UK-based Economist Intelligence Unit, ranks countries based on level of democracy. Countries are scored from 0 to 10 using 60 indicators. These indicators measure pluralism, civil liberties, and political culture. The countries are then categorized into four broad groups: Authoritarian Regime, Hybrid Regime, Flawed Democracy, and Democracy.

TABLE 3.1

Indicators for West African Countries

| Country | Population (in millions; July 2017 est.) | GDP (in billions) | GNI per capita | Human Development Index (HDI) | Doing Business Index (DBI) | Democracy |
|---|---|---|---|---|---|---|
| Benin | 11.03 | $25.29 | $1,979 | .485 (low) | 48.52 | 5.67 (hybrid) |
| Burkina Faso | 20.11 | $35.68 | $1,537 | .402 (low) | 51.33 | 4.7 (hybrid) |
| Guinea Bissau | 1.79 | $3.07 | $1,369 | .424 (low) | 41.63 | 1.98 (authoritarian) |
| The Ivory Coast | 24.18 | $96.27 | $3,163 | .474 (low) | 52.31 | 3.81 (authoritarian) |
| Mali | 17.89 | $40.98 | $2,218 | .442 (low) | 52.96 | 5.7 (hybrid) |
| Niger | 19.24 | $21.62 | $889 | .353 (low) | 49.57 | 3.96 (authoritarian) |
| Senegal | 14.6 | $43.07 | $2,250 | .494 (low) | 50.68 | 6.21 (flawed democracy) |
| Togo | 14.67 | $12.03 | $1,262 | .487 (low) | 48.57 | 3.32 (authoritarian) |
| West African Average | 15.44 | $34.75 | $1,833 | .445 | 49.44 | 4.42 |

## C. RELATION TO MARKETS AND COMPETITION

The West African nations faced the challenges of building political institutions conducive to economic development. Most countries adopted a single-party, socialist regime, but some, such as Mali, were ruled by a dictator. The economic powers of the states were left unchecked. National economies were planned from the top down with the state as the main actor. State-owned enterprises (SOEs) dominated the economy, especially in utility, energy, communications, transportations, and other strategic sectors.

The West African nations began moving toward democratic governance in the 1980s—some more successfully than others. Senegal, a relatively stable democracy, changed regimes three times in 30 years. The peaceful transitions of power, enhanced by strong political institutions, have created a more stable national economy. Other countries have had rough transitions to democracy. Guinea Bissau, for example, has experienced successive military coups since it became independent in 1974, hindering economic growth and specifically limiting the flow of foreign direct investment.

The economies inherited upon independence were not conducive to the development of competitive markets. The West African economies relied primarily on agriculture and mining, such as uranium in Niger and phosphate in Senegal. National infrastructure was focused on providing agricultural commodities and natural resources to France and Portugal. The transportation and communication networks, such as railways, were built to ensure efficient exportation of these raw resources. The industrial sector was underdeveloped, and industrial products were mainly imported. The industrial sectors that did exist were either owned by the state or dominated by MNEs. Local entrepreneurship primarily centered in the informal sector, and domestic industrial innovation was not incentivized.

Beginning in the 1980s in the wake of globalization and lowering barriers to trade, a new dominant understanding of political economy began to emerge. Following the fall of the Berlin Wall in 1989 and the wide embrace of markets in the 1990s, sub-Saharan African countries initiated a broad range of economic reforms that aimed to foster trade and to create a business environment hospitable to trade, influenced heavily by the Washington Consensus. The Washington Consensus principles,[20] widely circulated in 1989, reflected a course begun by the World Bank and applied through much of the 1980s requiring neoliberal reforms by beneficiary countries in order to receive state aid.[21] Aspiring to create a safe and friendly business environment for MNEs operating in developing countries, African governments embraced economic liberalization and privatization, this latter often as a precondition to receiving loans from international financial institutions.[22]

---

[20] *See* John Williamson, *A Short History of the Washington Consensus, in* From the Washington Consensus towards a New Global Governance (2004).

[21] *See* Introduction and Chapter 1 *in* The Politics of Trade and Industrial Policy in Africa: Forced Consensus? (Charles C. Soludo et al. eds., 2004).

[22] *See* Joseph Stiglitz, Globalization and Its Discontents (2002).

The economic reforms, combined with the liberal forces that felled the Berlin Wall, reflected a new and widespread appreciation of free markets and their potential for human development. The common belief was that people, in terms of both their freedom and economic well-being, are better off with democratic government and markets and that markets can be enhanced and safeguarded from abuse through competition law. Whether or not this message resonated with various developing countries, the countries needed financing from the international financial institutions. The funding came with market-related conditionality, including what is called "rule of law." This required nations to implement various sets of laws—such as property, corporate, and competition law—and to create institutions to enforce those laws.

## III. Evolving from Price Control to Freer Markets

Upon achieving independence in the 1960s and '70s, the West African nations began crafting economic identities separate from, although influenced by, their former colonial powers.

### A. PRICE CONTROL, LIBERALIZATION, AND LINGERING STATE INTERVENTIONISM

As we have seen, during the colonial period, the political institutions and regulatory frameworks essentially served the fiscal and trade needs of metropolitan France and Portugal. Mineral and agricultural resources were exploited to supply European industries, and regulatory frameworks were designed with little or no regard to developing local markets.

After becoming independent in the 1960s, the new sovereign states began refashioning their economies and crafting legal frameworks. The states faced hurdles. They had been molded by colonialism. Not surprisingly, the early postcolonial laws regulating competition bore the imprint of Gallic dirigiste policy: price control, predominance of SOEs, limited space for private initiative, and the subordination of the market to other concerns. This interventionist approach failed to provide better access to goods and services, and the SOEs were largely inefficient and did not enhance economic development.

In the 1990s, responding to the World Bank conditionality, the West African states eased regulations and began to make laws concerning pricing and firm behavior more market-friendly. The states passed competition laws and established competition authorities. These laws were designed to remove obstructions to competition (e.g., price-fixing agreements among competitors) and to let the market work to get better products and prices. But the national governments were reluctant to relinquish their active regulatory roles. They did not want to just stand by when they thought prices were too high. They could not resist intervention. Thus, they did not provide much support for independent competition authorities. The colonial history kept its grip, and the remnants of French dirigisme hindered a shift to markets. This halting move to markets does much to explain the patterns and trends of West African competition law and policy.[23]

## B. SHIFT TOWARD MORE MARKET-ORIENTED POLICIES

As mentioned, in the 1980s, the states began to adopt the principles laid out in the Washington Consensus due to pressure from the World Bank. These initiatives have spurred the development of competition law and policy in sub-Saharan Africa since the 1990s. Countries as advanced as South Africa and as small as the Gambia now have a competition act and a competition authority. The national policies developed within the broader context of both global and domestic reform. Wealthier European and North American nations were influential in prompting West African legislatures to retreat from their older welfare state approach. In many ways, developed nations "disseminated" free-market policies through political dialogues, the terms of international trade agreements, and the extraterritorial application of their laws. The United States and the European Union, for example, both tend to require that their partners in trade agreements adopt competition laws.

The liberalization of the 1990s, spurred on by World Bank conditionality and the influence of more developed states, led to the creation of more market-friendly competition laws throughout West Africa. Nations began accepting some measure of liberalization while not giving up state price control entirely. New competition laws were enacted, existing laws were reformed, and old price-regulation laws were made more market-friendly. Even though the new policies were less interventionist, the competition statutes contain significant exceptions to free market price-setting. Some contain "exceptional circumstances" provisions that allow the states to set prices or price ceilings for a limited time, in a limited number of sectors, or for certain products and services.

---

[23] Mor Bakhoum, L'Articulation du Droit Communautaire et des Droits Nationaux de la Concurrence dans l'Union Economique et Monétaire Ouest Africaine (UEMOA) (Stampfli 2007). *See also* Josef Drexl, *Economic Integration and Competition Law in Developing Countries, in* Competition Policy and Regional Integration in Developing Countries (Josef Drexl et al. eds., 2012).

Senegal's competition law, adopted in 1994, allows the government to monitor and control prices in certain situations. Article 42 reads: "When the circumstances so require, for economic and social reasons, the prices of certain goods, products and services may be determined by legislative or regulatory means." Article 43 provides that "measures against excessive price rises, caused by a situation of calamity or crisis, by exceptional circumstances or by a situation of clearly abnormal market in a given sector, can be issued by decree of the minister of commerce[;] duration of application may not exceed two months renewable once." Those two provisions set the legal foundations for price regulation in Senegal. Prices can be regulated by legislation, or the Ministry of Commerce may regulate the prices for a limited duration. The elastic exceptions—"situation[s] of calamity or crisis," "exceptional circumstances." and "situation[s] of clearly abnormal markets conditions in a given sector"—provide the government with significant leeway for market intervention.

Pursuant to Articles 42 and 43, the Senegalese government often intervenes to establish fair prices. It sets the prices of goods such as oil and gas and their derivatives. The government puts price ceilings on housing rentals.[24] Companies must receive authorization to set the prices of pharmaceutical products, sugar, flour, and bread.[25] For example, in 2006 the cost of bread sharply increased. The government called together all bread producers to negotiate a lower price. The negotiations resulted in a written agreement, a legal cartel.

Similar modes of price-setting can be found in other West African nations. Burkina Faso's national competition law, adopted in 1994, recognizes both the principle of competition and the possibility of price regulation. Article 1 provides that "[t]he prices of products, goods, and services are freely and solely determined in the whole territory by competition. However, in economic sectors or in localities where competition by price is limited because of monopoly situations, difficulties of sustainable supplies or by regulatory provisions, the Ministry of Commerce may regulate the prices under the conditions set by Decree." This provision embodies contradictory principles. On one hand, it establishes the freedom of competition and the free determination of the prices of goods and services. On the other hand, it empowers the Ministry of Commerce to control prices. The provision provides for price regulation when monopoly situations impact the free determination of prices, when there are

---

[24] *See* Loi n° 2014-03 du 22 Janvier 2014 portant baisse des loyers n'ayant pas été calculés suivant la méthode de la surface corrigée.

[25] *See* Décret 2006-1246 du 14/11/2006 modifiant l'article 3 du décret n° 95-77 du 20 janvier 1995 portant application des articles 44 et 64 de la loi n° 94-63 du 22 août 1994 sur les prix, la concurrence et le contentieux économique, JORS du 15/11/2006. Arrêté du 15/11/2006, portant application des dispositions de l'article 1 du décret n° 2006-1246 du 14 novembre 2006 modifiant l'article 3 du décret 95-77 du 20 janvier 1995 sur les prix, la concurrence et le contentieux économique, JORS, du 15/11/2006.

difficulties to supply the market, and when legislative provisions restrict the determination of the prices by competition. These broad categories—specifically the final provision, which allows for the legislature to set prices in seemingly any situation—create consistent potential for state intervention.

The Ivory Coast's competition law, adopted in 1991, allows the government to intervene and regulate the prices of necessary or widely demanded goods and services "when competition by prices is limited by monopoly situations or by legislative or administrative provisions." The government may also set prices in exceptional circumstances, such as situations of crisis or when the market of a given product or service is not functioning normally. Two important safeguards are provided: first, the government has to receive approval from the competition commission. Second, the government cannot set the price of a good or service for longer than six months. Additionally, in practice, the government consults the business community before regulating the prices, specifically with regard to the price of staples like sugar and rice.

Mali's competition law, enacted in 2007, follows the same interventionist bent. Article 3 allows the government to fix prices "in economic sectors and in areas where price competition is limited by any reason, in situations of crisis or in cases of excessive price hike in the market." The provision is similar to those of Senegal, Burkina Faso, and the Ivory Coast. The power to regulate prices is limited in three ways, but even the limitations may play into the hands of competitors prone to conspire when the regulation ends. First, price regulation for exceptional circumstances must be limited in duration. Second, the government must consult with stakeholders before regulating prices. Third, regulation fixing prices must detail how the prices are calculated, considering production costs and selling prices.

Togo follows the same approach in its competition act, adopted in 1999. The government may regulate prices in "exceptional circumstances" in the case of price hikes, during a crisis, or when market conditions require. These "exceptional" measures cannot exceed six months in duration.

In the late 1960s, Benin adopted a law on price regulation that allowed the government to regulate prices in certain circumstances, including in the case of "necessity."[26] The act did not define what a situation of necessity entailed nor how the government was to regulate prices. Moreover, the government actively regulated the prices of pharmaceutical products, oil-related products, water, electricity, school supplies, and bread. In 2016, Benin adopted a modern competition law, which applies to both private corporations and public entities that participate in the market.[27] It prohibits

---

[26] Ordinance No. 20/PR/MFAEP of 5 July 1967.

[27] Law No. 2016-25 of 4 November 2016 on the organization of competition in the Republic of Benin.

anticompetitive practices and unfair competition. However, the national authorities may still regulate the price of strategic goods and may intervene if the market conditions are non-competitive. Under this authorization, Benin currently sets a price floor for ground nuts and price ceilings for bread, petroleum products, and medicines.[28]

\* \* \*

In short, West African nations' competition laws are hybrid—on the one hand protecting markets and on the other regulating them by price control. Vague concepts such as "exceptional circumstances," "situation of crisis," and "in monopoly situations" keep the door open for unmonitored state intervention.

## IV. Regional Integration, WAEMU, and National Law

The West African Economic and Monetary Union (WAEMU) has preempted member states' domestic competition laws, and it has not filled this void with regional or local enforcement.

WAEMU was established in 1994 with the signing of the Treaty of Dakar. The treaty provides for common trade policy, a common currency (the CFA franc), a common market, and a regional competition authority. The treaty also provides for a regional accounting system, a stock exchange, and a framework for a regional banking system. Seven French-speaking West African nations are the founding members. Guinea Bissau joined in 1997, increasing the membership to eight.

The goals of WAEMU, as stated in the treaty, are to heighten the competitiveness of member states in an open market within a unified legal structure; establish a multilateral oversight mechanism; create a common market based on the free movement of people, goods, services and capital; institute a common external tariff; and harmonize member state laws in the areas of business, sectoral regulation, and taxation.

In 2002, WAEMU established a regional competition law. In 2007, it created an office within the WAEMU Commission in charge of competition matters across the eight member states and the common West African market.[29] It further created the Advisory Committee on Competition composed of representatives from the member states.

The legislation provides exclusive jurisdiction to the regional competition authority in matters regarding anticompetitive agreements, abuse of a dominant position, and state aids, such as subsidies by member states. Uniquely, the regional

---

[28] *Benin*, WORLD TRADE ORGANIZATION, *available at* https://www.wto.org/english/tratop_e/tpr_e/s362-01_e.pdf.

[29] *See* MOR BAKHOUM, ETUDE SUR LA RÉVISION DU CADRE INSTITUTIONNEL DE MISE EN ŒUVRE DES RÈGLES DE CONCURRENCE DE L'UEMOA (2012).

competition authority's exclusive jurisdiction extends even to cases affecting only national markets with no cross-border trade. There is little room for the states to enforce their national competition policies.

WAEMU's competition policy includes no provisions concerning unfair competition, providing member states with a small gateway for pursuing domestic restraints. Although unfair competition law mostly concerns offenses to individuals rather than to the market, such as trademark misuse and deceptive practices, it may include some matters within the competition law realm, such as refusals to supply and resale price maintenance. Thus confined, the national competition authorities focus on unfair competition practices and the monitoring of prices. Enforcement of competition law is nonexistent.

Beyond the limited room for enforcement in unfair competition, national competition authorities are also required to collaborate with the WAEMU Competition Commission in national investigations. However, the defanging of the national authorities has dampened their incentive to play a robust cooperative note.

WAEMU was both a blessing and a curse. On one hand, it provided a sense of economic unity to the eight member states. On the other, it took away the powers of the member states to protect themselves from major market restraints such as price-fixing cartels. The preemption by WAEMU eviscerated national enforcement, as we discuss below. While a project exists to restore the powers of the member states, to attack anticompetitive conduct, a successful outcome is not assured.[30]

## V. Modern Competition Laws in West Africa

By 2016, the Western African states other than Guinea Bissau had all adopted competition laws and had begun to create institutions to enforce them. This legislation is largely preempted, and the enforcement institutions are mostly idle. We summarize some of the limited enforcement, including before the preemption.

### A. PROHIBITION OF ANTICOMPETITIVE PRACTICES

### 1. Introduction

West African competition laws prohibit cartels, abuse of a dominant position, and abuse of economic dependence. They do not regulate mergers. A prohibition against cartels, especially agreements limiting price competition, is the hallmark

---

[30] *See* Chapter VI for a more thorough discussion of WAEMU.

provision of modern competition law and is both efficient—by removing a market impediment—and fair to consumers who are overcharged for their products. Also a mainstay of competition law, abuse of a dominant position prohibits monopoly or dominant firms from excluding or marginalizing rivals by strategies other than competition on the merits, and it prohibits excessive prices (usually only in extreme cases). Both cartel and abuse of dominance provisions seek to protect the market and facilitate competition.

Abuse of economic dependence focuses on protecting individual competitors, suppliers, or buyers that are in a position of dependence rather than protecting competition in the market. To run afoul of the law, the defendant need not be a monopolist or dominant firm. The concern is the unfair use of bargaining power. No analog is found in the antitrust laws of the United States or the competition laws of the European Union, although it can be found in the competition laws of a number of Eastern European and Asian countries and some others such as France and Italy.

## 2. Anticompetitive Practices: Cartels and Abuse of Dominant Position

All West African competition laws prohibit cartels and abuse of a dominant position, the two core categories of antitrust. However, the WAEMU Commission has the exclusive authority to prosecute such conduct, preempting enforcement by the national authorities, even with respect to local cartels with effects only within national borders. For example, construction cartels and bid-rigging on state procurements jobs, which are rampant in so many economies, cannot be challenged by the national authority.

Before WAEMU preemption, the more developed West African countries were beginning to enforce their national competition laws.

In Senegal, the Central Insurance Broker Agency (CIBA) had failed to pay certain premiums to two insurance companies. The two insurance companies referred the matter to the insurance industry federation (a trade association) FSSA. FSSA, after meeting with members, advised all members to break off business relations with CIBA. The member insurance companies followed FSSA's advice and signed on to a letter of boycott, even though some of them had no dispute with CIBA, and some had never even dealt with it. CIBA complained to the Senegalese Competition Commission, which took up the complaint and found that the companies' joint refusal to deal with CIBA was a blacklisting or boycott with the intent to exclude CIBA from the insurance market. The commission found that this action was an illegal boycott. On appeal, however, the Conseil d'Etat reversed, holding that the refusal did not involve competition or anticompetitive practices because it was not intended to affect prices in the market.[31]

The Senegal Commission had waded into a very modern debate: Are concerted boycotts of just one market actor, depriving it of its lifeblood of access to the market, illegal in themselves under competition law, or should a violation require proof that the action had an effect on the market and consumers? US law took the first position in the 1960s when it had concerns about exclusions of outsiders, but reversed itself in the 1990s, when it retreated to a laissez-faire model. [32] The Senegal Commission may have made the right choice for Senegal, but the important point is that Senegal was on the path to an active enforcement of the law.

### 3. Unfair Competition and Abuse of Economic Dependence

Most West African states also prohibit unfair competition or restrictive business practices. While some offenses labeled unfair competition, including certain resale price-fixing, are prohibited by the US and the EU competition laws, most of these offenses are outside of the scope of competition regimes because they harm "only" particular actors, not markets.

The line between conduct constituting an abuse of a dominant position (harming the market and usually consumers) and that amounting to a restrictive business practice that is "only" unfair to a player is often unclear. Because West African national competition laws condemn both anticompetitive acts and unfair competition, the agencies and the courts often do not distinguish between them. A Senegalese competition case against Air France illustrates the point. A group of travel agents alleged that Air France had abused its dominant position by unilaterally reducing agents' commissions from 9 percent to 7 percent. They based their claims on abuse of economic dependence: Air France dominated the market, and travel agents had to deal with Air France. The commission ruled in favor of the travel agents stating that Air France abused the travel agencies' economic dependence by "imposing on the agencies a rate to which they were obliged to assent in order to survive and which

---

[31] Syndicat des Assureurs Conseils Africains (SACA) and Central Insurance Broker Agency (CIBA) v. Fédération Sénégalaise des Sociétés d'Assurances (FSSA). *See* Mouhamadou Diawara, President, Competition Commission of Senegal, Judicial Perspectives on Competition Law, OECD Global Forum on Competition, December 7–8, 2017, DAF/COMP/GF(2017)8, at 7–8, reaffirming his view that concerted boycotts should be illegal per se under the competition laws.

[32] Silver v. New York Stock Exchange, 373 U.S. 341 (1963), effectively overruled by Northwest Wholesale Stationers, Inc. v. Pacific Stationery and Printing Co., 472 U.S. 284 (1985).

they would not have accepted if they had enjoyed independence."[33] Defendants appealed the commission decision and settled before the appeal could be heard.[34]

This appears to be a case of unfair use of bargaining power—not a typical violation of competition law, which usually defers to contract bargaining.

As of now it appears that the West African authorities have largely gone idle and are not actively pursuing potential violations.

## B. ENFORCEMENT INSTITUTIONS

### 1. Introduction

For the law to be deterrent, it must be enforced. Violations must be detected and punished. Creating effective institutions for enforcement and decision-making in West Africa is a challenge. Some West African countries are struggling to set up strong institutions in general. The executive often exerts control over the legislative and judicial branches, and the checks on executive power are weak. Administrative institutions function poorly, and corruption is rampant. This is the environment in which competition authorities operate. The agencies are usually not sufficiently independent from government to assure nonpolitical decisions. Their institutions are usually underfunded and understaffed; they lack human and financial capital and may lack leadership, expertise, and access to information.[35] They lack partners for coordination. Further, WAEMU's preemption has defanged national enforcement and removed the incentives of the national governments to invest in domestic enforcement institutions. We shall say a few further words on independence and institutions, and WAEMU.

### 2. Independence and Other Institutional Issues

Independence of the competition authority is especially important in sub-Saharan Africa because of the high levels of corruption and perhaps higher than usual

---

[33] Syndicat des Agences de Voyages et de Tourisme du Sénégal (SAVTS) v. Compagnie Air France. *See* Daniel P. Weick, *Competition Law and Policy in Senegal: A Cautionary Tale for Regional Integration?*, 33 WORLD COMPETITION 521, at 531 (2010).

[34] The travel agents sued for damages in the Dakar District Court. The District Court awarded them damages based on the differential between the commissions they were paid and should have been paid. The Court of Appeal reversed the award on grounds that the travel agents had not produced their tax returns and other documents necessary to show their real financial prejudice. Commission President Diawara criticizes the Court of Appeal reversal, noting that the Court of Appeal did not even give the travel agents the presumption of prejudice based on the violation, which is required by EU law. *See* Diawara, *supra* note 31.

[35] *See* William Kovacic, *Distinguished Essay: Good Agency Practice and the Implementation of Competition Law*, *in* EUROPEAN YEARBOOK OF INTERNATIONAL ECONOMIC LAW, at 14 (2013) ("The successful agency of the future is one that invests heavily in building knowledge and refreshing its intellectual capital.").

tendencies of officials to sue their enemies and privilege their friends. Firms may be able to bribe their way out of lawsuits, undermining the legitimacy of the competition authority—a pathology more likely to be entrenched when the executive controls the agency. Moreover, SOEs often dominate the markets. When SOEs, the government, and the enforcers are closely intertwined, the SOEs are often treated as above the law.

West African enforcement institutions are largely influenced by the French civil approach. As a civil law country, France has an administrative rather than a litigation-style model. Competition authorities may be part of the general governing administration, or they may be independent from it. Normally, in West Africa, the enforcement authority is placed within the Ministry of Commerce or trade, which is part of the executive. In some cases, however, the authority may have more structural independence and separation from the administration. The later model is referred to as the "independent administrative authority" (*autorité administrative indépendante*).

In Mali, Niger, Togo, and Benin, the enforcement authorities are not independent and do not have their own decision-making power. As extensions of the executive department, they combine competition law enforcement with price control. In Senegal, the Ivory Coast, and Burkina Faso, the competition authority is structurally independent, but in practice it is closely linked to the administration. For example, in Senegal, a representative of the government acts as a secretary general of the competition commission; in the Ivory Coast, the Ministry of Commerce reviews the decisions of the competition authority. Additionally, the competition authorities are financially dependent on the government, which allocates their budgets.

The administrative model is state-centric, and any independence is inevitably limited. For example, the model discourages investigations into anticompetitive practices originating from or endorsed by a state body, and those practices may be among the most harmful.[36] Moreover, the administrative model contemplates a narrow scope for rights to discover evidence and hearings in which the hearing examiner controls the proceedings, rather than broad discovery rights and parties' rights to cross-examine witnesses; and in many cases the investigative function is not separated from the decision-making function, producing claims (usually by Westerners) of lack of due process.

Still, the administrative model has procedural protections. This model, like adjudicative systems, protects the right to appeal a competition commission's decision to a court of general jurisdiction. Some states provide greater procedural safeguards

---

[36] *See* Eleanor M. Fox & Deborah Healey, *When the State Harms Competition – The Role for Competition Law*, 79 ANTITRUST L.J. 769 (2014).

aimed at making the decision-making process transparent and fair to the defendants. In Senegal, for instance, the agents who are involved in the investigation of a case may not take part in the final decision.

### 3. WAEMU Preemption

To understand the limits of national enforcement, we must return to the WAEMU framework. WAEMU adopted a community-wide competition law with a centralized approach, and the law was interpreted by the WAEMU Court of Justice to give exclusive competence to the WAEMU Commission to enforce competition law in WAEMU territory. The WAEMU Commission's exclusive enforcement and decision-making power extends not only to cases affecting inter-member state trade but also to anticompetitive practices affecting only national markets. As a consequence, the national competition authorities lost both their ability to prosecute anticompetitive practices and their decision-making powers, even regarding conduct occurring wholly within their borders. We discuss WAEMU's system of enforcement in Chapter VI.

Examples from Senegal, Mali, and the Ivory Coast reveal how West African nations have approached the creation of enforcement institutions.

Established in 1994, the National Competition Commission of Senegal (NCC) is an independent authority in charge of implementing the Competition Act. The NCC has both advisory and decision-making authority. It has the power to initiate investigations, hear cases, and impose sanctions. Although the NCC is formally separate from the government, the administration maintains significant control over it in practice. For example, the budget of the competition authority depends on the Ministry of Commerce. The NCC must inform the Ministry of Commerce when it decides to hear cases, and it must allow for the presence of a government representative at hearings. The NCC is not tasked with price regulation, which is assigned to another office of the Ministry of Commerce.

The NCC is a striking example of the detrimental effect of regional preemption. The NCC had begun to develop competence in investigating and deciding cartel and abuse of power cases. However, since WAEMU assumed exclusive jurisdiction, the NCC has largely fallen dormant.

Mali's competition authority was established in 1998. The National Directorate on Competition and Consumption (NDCC) in Mali is a specific division within the Competition and Regulation Division. It is divided into "Regulation" and "Investigation" subdivisions. Its competence includes initiating policy proposals for trade, competition, and consumer welfare, assuring the functioning of the market, regulating commercial activities, and supporting the economy. It may issue sanctions to enforce competition law, price regulation, and consumer protection law.

The Mali competition authority is a hybrid authority. It is charged with pursuing cases of unfair competition and violations of consumer protection. The DNCC receives an average of 20 complaints a year and has issued approximately 100 decisions since 1999.[37] The most common offenses include those pertaining to quality standards, excessive pricing, fraud in bookkeeping, inaccurate or misleading product information, export control, and contraband violations. The commission has reported no case dealing with cartels or abuse of dominance.

In the Ivory Coast, the competition agency is the National Competition Commission. The NCC was established in 1991. It is formally autonomous but has limited independence in practice. The agency may issue nonbinding advisory opinions on proposed legislation, but it has no adjudicatory powers. It has limited authority to investigate monopolies, anticompetitive agreements, and abuses of a dominant position. After initiating investigations and drafting opinions, the commission must refer matters to the Ministry of Commerce, which has the power to confirm or overrule the proposed decision.[38] The Ivory Coast authority has issued opinions in numerous disputes relating to unfair business practices in the perfumes and cosmetics sector and art sector, and anticompetitive practices in passenger transportation and the distribution of petroleum products.

Despite structures in place, the competition authorities have been debilitated by the WAEMU preemption. While some of the competition authorities such as those in Burkina Faso and the Ivory Coast actively cooperate with the WAEMU Commission by bringing cases to the commission, most do not cooperate. At the national level, the West African authorities focus on dealing with unfair competition law and monitoring prices.

## VI. Conclusion

The French West African states have adopted laws to open markets and protect competition, often at the behest of the World Bank and the International Monetary Fund. The project has been set back by political and economic instability, the lack of human and financial capital, and regional preemption of domestic competition law. It is a striking fact that there is virtually no competition law enforcement in French West Africa and no merger control law. Yet, the project of making the markets work

---

[37] *See* Bakhoum, *supra* note 29.

[38] Article 17 alinéa 1 de la loi 1991/CI states in this regard, «*le Ministre chargé du Commerce peut, après avis de la Commission de la Concurrence, infliger par decision motivée, une sanction pécuniaire immédiate à toute entreprise ou à toute personne physique ou morale coupable d'entente illicite ou d'abus de position dominante tel que définis aux dispositions des articles 7 et 8 de la présente loi*». The Commission has the power only to issue an opinion.

for the people has become increasingly urgent and its importance increasingly acknowledged. The obstacles may ultimately be overcome with focus, leadership, will, and a reset of the institutional environment to allow national law to work hand in hand with regional law. The first, necessary step is repeal of WAEMU preemption, as we discuss in Chapter VI. Thereafter, progress may be slow but can be deliberate.

# 4

## EASTERN AND SOUTHERN AFRICA

### I. Introduction

We turn eastward. This chapter focuses on selected countries in Eastern and Southern Africa apart from South Africa, which we treat separately in the next chapter. As in Chapter III, we profile selected countries and discuss the history, evolution, and challenges of their competition policies. In particular, we feature Kenya, Namibia, Botswana, Zambia, Tanzania, Zimbabwe, the island of Mauritius, and Malawi.

All of these countries have competition laws that are more or less enforced. Similar to the French-speaking West African states, they are all former colonies with a history of domination, economic exploitation, and exclusion of indigenous peoples, and they all now have markets and, by some measure, democratic systems of government. The United Kingdom was one of the principal colonial powers. Although some of this set of countries had French heritage, on the whole they did not inherit a dirigiste economic system and were better positioned to adjust to and take advantage of markets.

Some of the countries in this set were governed by dictators before they established democracy. Some were socialistic and focused on social welfare benefits rather than private initiative. On the economic front, they faced and still face the challenge

Making Markets Work for Africa. Eleanor M. Fox and Mor Bakhoum.
© Oxford University Press 2019. Published 2019 by Oxford University Press.

FIGURE 4.1 Selected States of Eastern and Southern Africa.

to diversify their economies, adding industry and information and communication technologies to the traditional mainstays of agriculture and mining.

Why did these countries adopt their competition laws? Some did so in response to their own needs and context. In most, however, the competition law is a product of external influences and a part of broader economic reforms imposed by the international financial institutions. Competition laws were part of the menu of structural adjustment programs designed by the World Bank and the IMF in the 1980s and 1990s.

The countries studied in this chapter are part of regional economic communities, the main being COMESA,[1] SADC,[2] and EAC.[3] All have overlapping memberships.

[1] Common Market of Eastern and Southern Africa.
[2] Southern African Development Community.
[3] East African Community.

All are also members of the informal network, the African Competition Forum (ACF). Regional communities, which hold great promise for coordinated action, better detection of offenses, and a common vision, are the subject of Chapter VI.

This chapter is organized as follows: Section II provides a general background of the historical, political, and socioeconomic characteristics of each country. Section III presents the main features of the countries' competition laws. Section IV describes the enforcement and the competition authorities' varying degrees of commitment and success. Section V recounts special stories of freeing up markets. Section VI concludes with an assessment of the countries' challenges and the importance of cross-border vision and collaboration (Figure 4.1).

## II. Historical and Socioeconomic Perspectives

### A. BACKGROUND: HISTORICAL, POLITICAL, AND ECONOMIC CONTEXT

All countries in this set are former colonies. Most of them became independent in the 1960s from British colonial rule. Namibia became independent in the 1990s from South Africa and was previously part of German South West Africa. Most of the newly independent states were emerging from concentrated political and economic power, war, and instability. The nations also faced the challenge of creating stable democratic political institutions and of transforming economies that had long suffered from exploitation and exclusion.[4]

Political domination and economic exploitation gave way to a new form of dependence: "different, less direct, less transparent, but often no less conducive to instability."[5] The former colonizers continued to influence the political process and to keep a tight hold on the main economic activities. They commandeered minerals and agricultural goods and shipped them off to European markets.[6] Transportation infrastructure was built primarily to facilitate export of raw materials and agricultural produce to Europe by connecting interior sources with costal ports. Other infrastructure was neglected. As a consequence, transportation infrastructure in sub-Saharan Africa is poor. It serves primarily the north-south trade and not the south-south trade. Deficiencies in the transportation infrastructure remain a major impediment to economic development.

Many of the countries in this set emerged from statist backgrounds. State-owned enterprises dominated the strategic markets. State-owned enterprises' (SOEs) privileges, as well as price control, have hampered the movement to markets. Even

---

[4] DAVID J. GERBER, GLOBAL COMPETITION: LAW, MARKETS, AND GLOBALIZATION 250 (Oxford 2010).

[5] *Id.* at 249.

[6] *Id.* at 251.

now, some of the nations' competition laws have exemptions or special rules for SOEs and give nontransparent protections to politically connected business.

Development normally entails moving away from reliance on agriculture and extractive industries and diversifying into manufacturing, adding value to the raw materials, and today, it may entail diversifying into internet and communications technologies and services. But most of the countries in this set still rely primarily on agriculture and minerals. Tourism plays a major role in their economies due to stunning game reserves. Lacking an industrial base, these states must rely on imports. Typically, primary-good exports are sold into competitive world markets at low prices, and the imports, often from large multinational enterprises (MNEs) in concentrated industries, are sold to the developing world at high prices. Still, some of the countries, such as Kenya, are taking a major role in innovating financial service systems (mobile money), pioneering a path to constructive development.

## B. INDICATORS

The following chart, Table 4.1, provides an overview of the socioeconomic characteristics of each state and the region as a whole. A description of the indicators

TABLE 4.1

### INDICATORS FOR EASTERN AND SOUTHERN AFRICAN COUNTRIES

| Country | Population (in millions; July 2017 est.) | GDP (in billions) | GNI per capita | Human Development Index | Doing Business Index | Democracy | Gini Index |
|---|---|---|---|---|---|---|---|
| Botswana | 2.29 | $39.56 | $16,680 | 0.698 (medium) | 64.94 | 7.81 (flawed democracy) | 60.5 |
| Kenya | 49.7 | $163.40 | $3,120 | 0.555 (medium) | 65.15 | 5.11 (hybrid) | 48.5 |
| Malawi | 18.62 | $22.50 | $1,140 | 0.476 (low) | 58.94 | 5.49 (hybrid) | 46.1 |
| Mauritius | 1.27 | $27.47 | $20,990 | 0.781 (medium) | 77.54 | 8.22 (full democracy) | 35.8 |
| Namibia | 2.53 | $27.02 | $10,380 | 0.64 (medium) | 59.94 | 6.31 (flawed democracy) | 61 |
| Tanzania | 57.31 | $162.80 | $2,740 | 0.531 (low) | 54.04 | 5.47 (hybrid) | 37.8 |
| Zambia | 17.09 | $68.90 | $3,850 | 0.579 (medium) | 64.5 | 5.68 (hybrid) | 55.6 |
| Zimbabwe | 16.53 | $33.87 | $1,810 | 0.516 (low) | 48.47 | 3.16 (authoritarian) | 43.2 |
| Average | 20.6675 | $68.19 | $7,589 | 0.597 (medium) | 61.69 | 5.91 (hybrid) | 48.56 |

is provided in Chapter III and in the appendix. For most of the indicators, higher numbers represent better outcomes (for example, Mauritius ranks highest of the set on the Doing Business Index and thus is regarded as having the most business-friendly environment in the region). The only exception is the Gini index, which measures wealth equality. The higher the number, the more unequally wealth is distributed.

## C. COUNTRY PROFILES

As the chart indicates, conditions vary significantly from country to country. They range from Mauritius—one of the most developed states in sub-Saharan Africa with strong democratic institutions—to Zimbabwe with a struggling democracy and weak economic prospects. We turn to a country-focused analysis.

### 1. Kenya

Kenya, extending to the east coast of Africa, is the largest and most advanced economy in Eastern and Central Africa and is industrially the most well-developed country in East Africa. The Portuguese were the earliest colonizers; they established trading posts at the end of the fifteenth century. In 1895, the British Empire established the East African Protectorate in roughly the territory that is now Kenya. Kenya gained independence in 1963, and the Independent Republic of Kenya was formed in 1964. It was ruled as a one-party state by an alliance led by Jomo Kenyatta until 1978. In 2010 Kenya adopted a modern constitution for a democratic republic. Kenya has been relatively stable, but has been blighted by fraud, corruption, and crises, notably at times of presidential elections, which have been struggles for power and spoils along ethnic lines—principally, the Kikuyu, the Kalenjin, and the Luo.

Kenya's major industries include agriculture, forestry and fishing, mining and minerals, manufacturing, energy, financial services, and tourism, including stunning game reserves (which exist also in most countries in this set). While Kenya is the economic hub of East Africa, inadequate infrastructure has frustrated economic growth rate averaging at 5 percent for the past eight years.[7] Most of the peoples' livelihood comes from agriculture, and some 70 percent of the agriculture-dependent population is very poor.

---

[7] CIA, *Kenya*, THE WORLD FACTBOOK (as of July 12, 2018).

## 2. Namibia

Namibia (then known as South West Africa) became a colony of Germany in 1884. The German authorities systematically killed more than 70,000 people in that period, and subjected the survivors to forced labor and segregation. In 1915, South African forces, fighting on the side of Great Britain during the First World War, occupied the colony. South Africa administered the territory under its apartheid regime until 1988. Namibia officially won its independence in 1990.

Namibia has had a relatively stable democracy. The founding president, Sam Nujoma, lead the country for 15 years. Since then, Namibia has been ruled by the same political party, the SWAPO. Opposition parties do participate in elections and have been gaining seats in the Namibian parliament.

Namibia's economy is dominated by the mining sector, including diamonds, uranium oxide, gold, and base metals. It is one of the largest producers of uranium in the world. The most important mine is Chinese owned. As in many African countries, agriculture plays a major role in the Namibian economy. It constitutes 7 percent of the gross domestic product (GDP) and 31 percent of employment. Commercial farming is dominated by white settlers, who sell their produce primarily for export. The services sector, primarily construction, provides 68 percent of the national GDP.[8]

Namibia is a lower-middle-income country with a GDP significantly above average for countries in sub-Saharan Africa. Although good economic management has contributed to economic growth and poverty reduction, Namibia is one of the most unequal countries in sub-Saharan Africa. Social and economic inequalities inherited from apartheid persist. Most native Namibians live in rural regions and rely primarily on subsistence farming.

## 3. Botswana

Botswana is a central southern land-locked country, one of the most sparsely populated countries in the world, and yet one of the world's fastest growing economies. The British established a protectorate in the region in 1885. During that time, Botswana (then known as Bechuanaland) was one of the poorest countries in the world. It won independence in 1966, adopting a democratic republic form of government and has since enjoyed over 50 years of political stability and peaceful transitions of power. Botswana is often called a model for African progress and prosperity. According to Transparency International's corruption perception

---

[8] CIA, *Namibia*, THE WORLD FACTBOOK (as of July 12, 2018).

index, Botswana has the cleanest government in Africa. However, like most sub-Saharan African countries, one party has remained in power since independence.

Diamonds were discovered in 1967 and have been an economic staple of the country, leading to significant economic growth until the recession of 2008. Recent increases in diamond exporting provide potential for economic growth. Tourism, subsistence farming, and cattle raising are other important sources of income. Two other elements limit the economic growth of the country. First, like Namibia, income inequality is among the highest in Africa. Second, Botswana has one of the highest HIV/AIDS infection rates, although the country does have one of the most advanced treatment programs in sub-Saharan Africa.

## 4. Zambia

Zambia is a land-locked country in Southern Africa. It was a British colony until 1964. Upon independence, Zambia was a multiparty republic. In 1972, the majority party adopted a one-party participatory democracy and banned all other parties. In 1991, a constitutional amendment provided for multiparty elections. A new party took power in the following election. Peaceful but contested elections have continued to this day.

Zambia had a fast-growing economy relying principally on copper supplemented by cobalt, gold, silver, and zinc. Agriculture, tourism, and the services sector contribute to the economy as well. Reliance on commodities leaves the national economy subject to global trends. When the price of minerals dropped in 2014, economic growth in the country slowed. Sixty percent of the Zambian population lives below the poverty line. Eighty-five percent of the workforce is employed in the agriculture sector. These difficulties are worsened by poor management of water and other resources, one of the highest birth-rates in the region, and a significant HIV prevalence rate.[9]

## 5. Tanzania

Tanzania is a politically stable but economically poor country in the Great Lakes region boasting renowned tourist destinations such as Mount Kilimanjaro and the Serengeti. Mainland Tanzania (then known as Tanganyika) was a part of German East Africa until the British took control following World War I. The nearby Zanzibar Archipelago was administered separately under Arab rule. The two

---

[9] CIA, *Zambia*, THE WORLD FACTBOOK (as of July 12, 2018).

territories gained independence in 1961 and 1963, respectively, and united to form Tanzania in 1964.

Upon independence, Tanzania adopted a socialist single-party regime. Mwalimu Julius Nyerere, a widely respected African figure, became president in 1961. His government pursued a policy of collective ownership of the country's economic resources and nationalization.[10] The goal was to facilitate redistribution of wealth to the indigenous people who had been left out of the economy during the colonial period. The country fell into economic decline beginning in the mid-1980s. The decline prompted a process for macro-economic change, moving to markets. However, the transition to a market economy is not entirely complete. The government owns all of the land (although it leases it), and is actively present in telecommunications, banking, energy, and mining sectors.

Tanzania adopted a multiparty system in 1992; the first multiparty elections occurred in 1994. Although the majority party remains dominant, opposition parties hold more than a quarter of the seats in parliament and received nearly 40 percent of the vote in the most recent presidential election. Zanzibar, on the other hand, which holds semi-autonomous status, has had contentious elections in recent years.

Tanzania has enjoyed GDP growth rates of 6 percent to 7 percent throughout the past decade, attributable largely to tourism, gold reserves, and financial services. The country has one of the fastest growing industrial sectors in sub-Saharan Africa, with an industrial growth rate of 8.8 percent. [11] Tanzania is one of the lowest-ranking countries on the Global Hunger Index, and it is among the lowest in the region on the United Nation's Human Development index.

## 6. Zimbabwe

Zimbabwe, a landlocked country, became a self-governing British colony of Southern Rhodesia in 1923. In the 1960s, the white minority government declared independence as Rhodesia, and the state became embroiled in a 15-year guerilla war with the indigenous population. A peace agreement eventually granted universal enfranchisement. Zimbabwe officially became independent in 1980.

Upon independence, Zimbabwe's economy was highly concentrated and was marked by significant government intervention. Robert Mugabe became prime minister in 1980 and then president in 1987; he was the country's only ruler for

---

[10] *See* Voluntary Peer Review of Competition Law and Policy: A Tripartite Report on the United Republic of Tanzania-Zambia-Zimbabwe, UNCTAD 2012, UNCTAD/DITC/CLP/2012/1, at 35.

[11] CIA, *Tanzania*, THE WORLD FACTBOOK (as of July 12, 2018).

30 years until he was forced to resign through military intervention in 2017. President Mugabe initiated economic change to centralize state power, including price control and nationalization measures. The government sought to grant economic opportunity to the largely disenfranchised black majority, including through land redistribution.

Poor economic performance and the global trend toward markets provoked strong opposition to Mugabe's economic policies. Black entrepreneurs pushed for liberalization and economic change. A major shift to market-friendly policies followed. The country is still poor. The CIA *World Factbook* states that nearly 95 percent of the country is either unemployed or underemployed. More than 70 percent of the people live below the property line. Droughts have led to low harvests and increased malnutrition. An extremely high debt burden drains resources and makes it difficult for the country to attract new financing.

## 7. Mauritius

Mauritius is an island in the Indian Ocean, east of Madagascar. It was discovered by Arab and Portuguese sailors and inhabited by the Dutch from the late sixteenth century until the early eighteenth century. Then the French settled the island. They brought slaves from mainland Africa, Madagascar, and India. The British took over in 1810. After abolition of slavery, more Indians arrived, mostly as indentured laborers. Chinese arrived as local traders. With this diverse population, the main language is Mauritian Creole.

The island achieved independence from Britain in 1968. Sir Seewoosagur Ramgoolam became the first prime minister, and Queen Elizabeth remained the head of state. The country has become one of the strongest democracies in Africa, with consistent free elections.

While the economy was initially dependent entirely on the export of sugar cane, Mauritius has been diversifying more successfully than other African nations. Tourism, textiles, and financial services contribute significantly to the economy. Mauritius is expanding into fish processing, internet and communications technologies, and property development. It ranks as one of the most business-friendly countries in Africa.

Mauritius is a middle-income country boasting one of Africa's highest per capita incomes. Only 8 percent of the population is below the poverty line.[12] A small French minority owns most of the island's business and are powerful politically.

---

[12] CIA, *Mauritius*, THE WORLD FACTBOOK (as of July 12, 2018).

8. Malawi

Malawi is a small, land-locked country that is among the world's most densely populated and least developed countries. It is a very poor country, facing chronic malnutrition, high rates of infant mortality, and a high HIV/AIDS prevalence rate that has left more than 1 million children orphaned.

In 1891 Malawi (then known as Nyasaland) was colonized by Britain and became a protectorate of the United Kingdom. It gained independence in 1964. It became a totalitarian one-party state until 1994, when it adopted a democratic, multiparty government. Since then, the country has enjoyed relative political stability and peaceful transitions of power. The political leaders, however, are often not trusted. The lack of economic growth has been blamed on corruption, poor governance, and inconsistent policy implementation.

The economy is based largely on agriculture, which comprises 30 percent of the GDP and employs 64 percent of the workforce. Eighty percent of Malawians live in rural areas, and they rely largely on subsistence farming. Recent droughts and flooding have resulted in consistently poor harvests and have led to increased malnutrition. Additional challenges include high population growth and a high HIV/AIDS prevalence rate.[13]

D. SUMMARY

All of the countries have a history of colonial rule and economic exploitation. Upon independence, most adopted interventionist economic policies with significant state involvement through SOEs. Zimbabwe, Tanzania, and Namibia included in their economic reforms the goal to redistribute wealth and provide opportunity to the deprived black majority.

The economies of these countries rely primarily on mining and agriculture, and export of these products. Export of minerals makes an important contribution to GDP, as in Zambia and Namibia. The economies lack diversification. In the countries other than Mauritius, poverty and inequality are systemic.

External factors produced important changes in the 1980s and 1990s. The World Bank and International Monetary Fund's (IMF) adjustment programs required most beneficiary countries to open markets and reduce state intervention. The required reforms came as a package, with competition law as an element. In most of the countries these external factors were the main driver of the adoption of their competition laws. Mauritius is an exception; its competition law is rooted

---

[13] CIA, *Malawi*, THE WORLD FACTBOOK (as of July 12, 2018).

in internal economic policy. Namibia adopted competition law as part of the process of independence from South Africa. South Africa also led by example for its neighbor Zimbabwe.

## III. Terms of the Competition Acts

What does competition law require? What can it do? We selectively summarize the statutes, which provide the basic blueprint. We start with more detail so that the reader can appreciate the text of key clauses, and proceed with highlights of other statutes, revealing similarities and some differences.

Of course there is a great deal of commonality. All of the statutes, with some nuances, prohibit restrictive agreements among competitors and buyers and suppliers. They all prohibit abuse of a dominant position, controlling a single firm's abuse of power. They all prohibit or allow conditioning of harmful mergers, and all but Malawi and Mauritius require pre-merger notification so that the authorities can examine mergers before they close. In their treatment of restrictive agreements, almost all of the laws flatly prohibit cartels (competitors' fixing prices or dividing up markets) per se; that is, without need of proof of anticompetitive effects, agreements of this sort are meant to have anticompetitive effects.[14] Bid rigging and collusive tendering to the government on procurement projects are usually explicitly listed as per se illegal, and concerted boycotts are often explicitly listed in the category. Most of the statutes also identify resale price-fixing agreements (suppliers' resale price agreements with their buyers) as per se illegal. Other agreements are analyzed for their competitive harms, and most systems allow for authorization by the competition authority of restrictive agreements that are nonetheless justified either by efficiencies or the public interest. Most statutes specify which public interests (such as employment and small business benefits) are admissible. For the abuse of dominance offense, most of the statutes contain a list of examples of prohibited forms of conduct. The lists were taken from EU law and often enlarged; for example, to specifically include more exclusionary conduct. Almost all of the merger control laws allow or require the competition authority to take public interest factors into consideration.

Many statutes also give powers to the enforcers to conduct market studies. This authority allows the agency to identify the market problems in sectors that seem not to be working well and to seek a remedy to correct the problems.

---

[14] Zimbabwe and Swaziland (a country not generally covered in this chapter) apply a rule of reason to cartels, making prosecution of cartels difficult.

A number of the statutes recite goals at the outset. The goals virtually all include efficiency, both static (lower costs, lower prices, higher quality) and dynamic (innovation), consumer interests, and competitiveness. Many also include economic opportunity, enhancing equality, protecting against too much economic concentration, and easing the path for micro and small business. Thus, the goals combine efficiency and equity, and generally include "inclusiveness" of people without power to engage in and benefit from the economic enterprise. The statutes do not reflect on the tensions and trade-offs between goals, leaving accommodation of efficiency and equity to the enforcers and the courts.

Procedurally, most systems have a competition commission with an executive director and a board of directors. The board, or Commission, makes decisions, which may be appealed to a specialized tribunal or to a court, from which further appeals may be possible; or the authority takes cases directly to a court. The first is called an integrated agency model; the second is called a bifurcated agency model. All statutes provide for investigative tools for enforcement, and imposition of penalties and other remedies on offenders, at least offenders in the "hard core" category. The tools are almost always woefully inadequate, and the authorized penalties are almost always so low and so long in coming, or practically impossible to enforce, that they cannot be counted on to deter even the worst violations. This means that much is left to the authorities to use their ingenuity in detecting market problems, publicizing them, persuading offenders to desist, working with the community to raise consciousness, and giving the stakeholders sufficient information to persuade them that they need competition, not collusion or monopolistic exploitation, to have better lives and more opportunity, and to assure their country's integration into regional and world markets.

What do the specific laws prohibit? And to what end? Our summaries are below.

## A. KENYA

Kenya's act, adopted in 2010, is typical in many ways. We present it first and in more detail than others to follow.

The Kenya Competition Act aims "to enhance the welfare of the people of Kenya by promoting and protecting effective competition in markets and preventing unfair and misleading market conduct. . . ." It aims to do so in order to:

(a) increase efficiency in the production, distribution and supply of goods and services;

(b) promote innovation;

(c) maximize the efficient allocation of resources;

(d) protect consumers;

(e) create an environment conducive for investment, both foreign and local;

(f) capture national obligations in competition matters with respect to regional integration initiatives;

(g) bring national competition law, policy and practice in line with best international practices; and

(h) promote the competitiveness of national undertakings in world markets.

The act prohibits restrictive trade practices, abuse of a dominant position, and harmful mergers and provides for market inquiries in order to control unwarranted concentration of economic power. Like a number of others (Malawi, Tanzania, Zambia, and Zimbabwe), the act covers consumer protection as well as competition. For example, it prohibits false and misleading statements and unconscionable conduct.

Under the heading of "Restrictive Trade Practices," the act prohibits anticompetitive agreements such as price-fixing and market division by competitors. (These are cartels.) Tracking language in the law of the European Union, the act prohibits agreements or concerted practices that "have as their object or effect the prevention, distortion or lessening of competition" unless they improve production or distribution or promote technical or economic progress, or (as additions to and unlike the EU list) promote exports or obtain a benefit for the public that outweighs the competitive harm. (The factors that go beyond those of the European Union and United States are public interest or industrial policy offsets.) The prohibitive language states, by way of example, that an offending agreement is one that:

(a) directly or indirectly fixes purchase or selling prices or any other trading conditions;

(b) divides markets by allocating customers, suppliers, areas or specific types of goods or services;

(c) involves collusive tendering;

(d) involves a practice of minimum resale price maintenance;

(e) limits or controls production, market outlets or access, technical development or investment;

(f) applies dissimilar conditions to equivalent transactions with other trading parties, thereby placing them at a competitive disadvantage;

(g) makes the conclusion of contracts subject to acceptance by other parties of supplementary conditions which by their nature or according to commercial usage have no connection with the subject of the contracts;

(h) amounts to the use of an intellectual property right in a manner that goes beyond the limits of legal protection;

(i) otherwise prevents, distorts or restricts competition.

Subsections (a), (b), (e), (f), and (g) track language of the EU Treaty. The other subsections are consistent with the EU Treaty.

A separate section on trade associations prohibits unjustified exclusions and making recommendations to members on prices and other terms of sales. A section on professional associations recognizes that some of their rules might be necessarily restrictive and invites applications for an exemption if the rules are "reasonably required to maintain (a) professional standards; or (b) the ordinary function of the profession."

Parties whose agreements may distort competition may apply to the competition authority for authorization (often called exemption) on grounds stated above, such as improving production or distribution, promoting exports, or serving an outbalancing public interest. This filing-and-authorization procedural model was part of the EU system at the outset of its competition regime; but the European Union has since abandoned it; in the European Union, agreements do not need to be filed and authorized.

The second common category of offense is abuse of dominance. First, for a violation, the firm must be dominant. The statute defines a dominant undertaking as one that "produces, supplies, distributes or otherwise controls not less than one half [the goods or services in the market]." Second, the conduct must be abusive. The section on abusive conduct, like the section on restrictive agreements, gives examples; and it provides for the authority to grant an exemption on the basis of the same criteria applicable to agreements. The list of abuses, by way of example, is:

(a) directly or indirectly imposing unfair purchase or selling prices or other unfair trading conditions;

(b) limiting or restricting production, market outlets or market access, investment, distribution, technical development or technological progress through predatory or other practices;

(c) applying dissimilar conditions to equivalent transactions with other trading parties;

(d) making the conclusion of contracts subject to acceptance by other parties of supplementary conditions which by their nature or according to commercial usage have no connection with the subject-matter of the contracts; and

(e) abuse of an intellectual property right.

The first four examples track the language of the European Treaty. The fifth is consistent with the EU case law.

A violation for either a restrictive agreement or abuse of dominance is punishable by up to five years in prison and a fine not exceeding 10 million Kenyan shillings (approximately US$100,000).

Mergers make up the third common category. The act requires the parties to notify their mergers to the authority before closing the transaction. The authority may approve or reject the merger, or approve it with conditions. It may base its determination on any factors it considers relevant, including

(a) the extent to which the proposed merger would be likely to prevent or lessen competition or to restrict trade or the provision of any service or to endanger the continuity of supplies or services. . . .

Other relevant factors specified include the extent to which the merger would be likely to create or strengthen a dominant position, the extent to which it would benefit the public to a degree outweighing competitive harms, and the extent to which it would be likely to affect the following: a particular industrial sector or region, employment, small firms' ability to gain market access or be competitive, the ability of national industries to compete in international markets, and the extent to which the merger would confer benefits from research and development, technical efficiency, increased production, efficient distribution, or access to markets.

A provision on unwarranted concentration of economic power gives the authority power to investigate "to determine where concentrations of economic power exist whose detrimental impact on the economy outweigh the efficiency advantages, if any, of integration of production or distribution." Interestingly, public interest in combating unwarranted concentration of economic power is defined only in market terms: price, profits, quality, which means this section is about making the market work, not overriding the market in the interests of (for example) workers or small business. After a negative finding, the authority may order divestiture or conditions.

## B. NAMIBIA

Namibia's Competition Act dates to 2003. The purposes are similar to Kenya's but the language is more emphatically inclusive of left-out people as well as more succinct. Inclusiveness aspects include goals to expand economic opportunity and achieve a greater spread of ownership among historically disadvantaged persons.

These goals can be traced to Namibia's apartheid history, shared with its occupier, South Africa, and the language is similar to the law of South Africa. The act states:

> The purpose of this Act is to enhance the promotion and safeguarding of competition in Namibia in order to—
> (a)  promote the efficiency, adaptability and development of the Namibian economy;
> (b)  provide consumers with competitive prices and product choices;
> (c)  promote employment and advance the social and economic welfare of Namibians;
> (d)  expand opportunities for Namibian participation in world markets while recognizing the role of foreign competition in Namibia;
> (e)  ensure that small undertakings have an equitable opportunity to participate in the Namibian economy; and
> (f)  promote a greater spread of ownership, in particular to increase ownership stakes of historically disadvantaged persons.

The provisions against anticompetitive agreements are, like Kenya's, derived from the European Treaty. Namibia's law on this point is identical to Kenya's,[15] except that Namibia also lists as a factor for exemption: the extent to which the agreement would be likely to enable small firms or those controlled by historically disadvantaged persons to become competitive. Like Kenya, professional rules may be exempted if reasonably necessary to maintain professional standards or the ordinary functioning of the profession.

On dominance and its abuse, the Namibian act provides that criteria for determining dominance "may be based on any factors which the Commission considers appropriate." The Commission has prescribed the criteria: a firm, or two or more firms, have a dominant position if they have (1) at least 45 percent of a market; (2) at least 35 percent unless the firms prove no market power, or (3) less than 35 percent if the Commission proves that they have market power. The list of illustrations of offensive conduct is taken directly from the European Treaty.

As to mergers, pre-merger notification is required. Factors for approval of a merger are the same as Kenya's except that, in the factor on relevance of small undertakings' ability to gain access or be competitive, Namibia includes, and Kenya does not, reference to historically disadvantaged persons.

---

[15] Kenya, however, adds as a listed example of an offense: using an intellectual property (IP) right in a manner that goes beyond the limits of legal protection. Note that both laws provide that the Commission may, upon application, grant an exemption in relation to the exercise of an IP right. Kenya art. 28, Namibia art. 30.

For offenses of the act, the Commission may approach the High Court to seek a penalty up to 10 percent of global turnover for the preceding years. The Commission may enter an agreement of settlement that includes a damages award to the complainant, with the complainant's consent. Otherwise, an injured party may sue for damages after the Commission has found an infringement or decided not to take action.

## C. BOTSWANA

Botswana adopted its competition act in 2009. The act has been amended, most recently in 2018. The act does not state its purposes.

Prohibited agreements fall into three categories: the first category is agreements among competitors that fix prices, divide markets, or bid rig. These are hard core agreements, prohibited per se and punishable criminally. A second category prohibits resale price maintenance (RPM) agreements, which are also punishable criminally but by a smaller fine. In a third category, the authority may prohibit an agreement "found to have the object or effect of preventing or substantially lessening competition in a market," and may prohibit an agreement that [taking language from the European Treaty]:

(a) limits or controls production, market outlets or access, technical development or investment;

(b) applies dissimilar conditions to equivalent transactions with other trading parties, thereby placing them at a competitive disadvantage;

(c) makes the conclusion of contracts subject to acceptance by other parties of supplementary conditions which, by their nature or according to commercial usage, have no connection with the subject of such contracts. Art. 28 (2).

Agreements of the third category may be exempted if there are offsetting benefits to the public in terms of lower prices, higher quality, greater choice, more efficient production or distribution (these are all efficiency benefits), or specific public interest benefits. The admissible public interest benefits are:

(d) the maintenance or promotion of exports from Botswana or employment in Botswana;

(e) the strategic or national interest of Botswana in relation to a particular economic activity being advanced;

(f) the provision of social benefits which outweigh the effects on competition;

(g) the agreement occurring within the context of a citizen empowerment initiative of Government; or

(h) the agreement in any other way enhancing the effectiveness of the Government's programmes for the development of the economy of Botswana, including the programmes of industrial development and privatisation. Art. 33.

Exemption is warranted only if the benefits are proportional to the harm, and the restriction does not eliminate competition completely in any market.

For the cartel and RPM offenses, victims may sue for damages, but only if the breach has been determined by the authority or court. No penalty is applicable for the other offenses—posing a challenge for deterrence.

*Dominance and its abuse.* The statute defines a dominant a position as one of such economic strength of one or more enterprises as to allow them to adjust prices or output without effective constraint from competitors or potential competitors. Regulations specify that dominance exists if one firm supplies 25% of the market, or three or fewer supply 50% . As for characterization of conduct as abusive (Section 31), the authority may, after investigation, determine any conduct to be an abuse of dominance. "Such conduct shall include" a list of eight practices: predatory conduct, tying and bundling, loyalty rebates, margin squeezes, refusal to supply and refusal of access, requiring or inducing a customer not to deal with competitors, discriminating in price or other terms, and exclusive dealing. In determining whether the conduct is abusive, the authority may have regard to the public interest factors applied to agreements ((d)–(h) above). No penalty is applicable for this offense.

The authority may conduct market inquiries where it has reason to suspect a restriction or distortion of competition. If competitive harms are identified that cannot be addressed by enforcing the law, the authority may make recommendations to the minister for further action.

*Mergers.* Mergers are subject to pre-merger notification. In its analysis, the authority must first determine if the merger is likely to prevent or substantially lessen competition, restrict trade, endanger continuity of supplies or service, or create a dominant position. It may in addition consider any public interest factors, including the extent to which:

(a) the proposed merger would be likely to result in a benefit to the public which would outweigh any detriment attributable to a substantial lessening of competition or to the acquisition or strengthening of a dominant position in a market;

(b) the merger may improve, or prevent a decline in the production or distribution of goods or the provision of services;

(c) the merger may promote technical or economic progress, having regard to Botswana's development needs;

(d) the proposed merger would be likely to affect a particular industrial sector or region;

(e) the proposed merger would maintain or promote exports or employment;

(f) the merger may advance citizen empowerment initiatives or enhance the competitiveness of citizen-owned small and medium sized enterprises; or

(g) the merger may improve the ability of national industries to compete in international markets. (Section 52)

In sum, in Botswana merger analysis, the authority may consider all factors including empowerment of people and small and middle-size enterprises (SMEs), employment, national economic strategy, and competitiveness.

\* \* \*

The reader will have noticed slight, but not substantial, differences in public interest factors relevant to exemption of agreements and merger analysis among the three statutes thus far examined. The factors include a mix of efficiency factors and public interest factors.[16] By way of contrast, neither US nor EU merger control law authorizes consideration of public interest factors, although an affected member state of the European Union is authorized to apply public security, plurality of the media, and prudential rules. The United States and the European Union count improvement of production and distribution, advances in research and development, and promotion of technical and economic progress as competition factors, as they rightly are.

## D. ZAMBIA

The Zambian law is the Competition and Consumer Protection Act of 2010. Thus, it combines the consumer protection function with the competition function. The act does not recite goals. The competition provisions are quite similar to the others described above.

As for the prohibition of restrictive business and anticompetitive trade practices, Section 8 prohibits any agreement, decision, or concerted practice that has as its object or effect the prevention, restriction, or distortion of competition to an appreciable extent in Zambia. Section 9 prohibits per se the hard core cartel categories (fixing prices, dividing markets, setting quotas, bid rigging, and collective refusal to

---

[16] Most of the public interest factors are similar to South Africa's, which we treat in Chapter V. Namibia, also being post-apartheid, tracks South Africa's language on helping historically disadvantaged individuals to become competitive. Botswana's language is most aggressive in including industrial policy: "the strategic or national interest of Botswana. . . ."

deal by competitors), and for these offenses it authorizes personal liability for fines and imprisonment as well as enterprise liability for fines. Section 10 prohibits resale price maintenance agreements per se. For other horizontal or vertical agreements, the agreement is prohibited if it has the effect of preventing, distorting, or restricting competition or substantially lessening competition in any market. If the agreement may have this effect, parties may apply for authorization. The Commission must grant an exemption if the agreement is likely to contribute to exports, efficiency, promoting competitiveness of micro and small business, or obtaining a benefit for the public that outweighs the competitive harm.

As for dominance, a dominant position exists if the enterprise has 30 percent or more of the market or not more than three firms have 60 percent or more. Abuse of a dominant position tracks the EU law for its first four examples. These include: imposing unfair prices, restricting production or outlets, discrimination, and requiring conditions not related to the subject of the contract. Zambia adds: denying access to an essential facility, charging an excessive price to the detriment of consumers (which is actually embedded in the European Union's first example), and selling goods below their marginal or variable cost. The offending enterprise is liable to pay a fine up to 10 percent of its annual turnover.

Mergers are subject to pre-merger notification. The Commission must determine whether the merger is likely to prevent or substantially lessen competition. The Commission must take into account all factors that affect competition, including concentration, barriers, "likelihood of the merger removing from the market an existing effective and vigorous competitor; dynamic characteristics of the market including growth, innovation, pricing...." The Commission *may* take into account "any factor which bears upon the public interest," including the extent to which the merger is likely to result in a benefit to the public that outweighs the lessening of competition, the extent to which it is likely to promote technical or economic progress, transfer of skills, or production or distribution, saving a failing firm, promoting exports or employment, enhancing competitiveness, or advancing the interest of micro and small business, "socioeconomic factors as may be appropriate; and any other factor that bears upon the public interest."

The Commission is empowered to initiate market inquiries. If the results suggest action that cannot be accomplished by competition law enforcement, the Commission must make recommendations to the minister.

Regarding coverage, the law states that the act binds the state acting in a commercial capacity. It states that the act does not apply to intellectual property, but then qualifies the exclusion: the Commission may apply the act where it reasonably believes that the agreement is a Section 9 or 10 (cartel or RPM) offense or "disproportionately restricts or prevents competition."

In enumerating the functions of the Commission, in addition to the usual tasks of investigating and assessing offenses, the act recites that the Commission is to "act as a primary advocate for competition and effective consumer protection in Zambia."

The minister is involved in many of the activities, appointments, and rule making for carrying out the act.

## E. TANZANIA

Tanzania's modern competition law, the Fair Competition Act, was adopted in 2003. Under "Restrictive Trade Practices," the law prohibits agreements with "the object or effect or likely effect to appreciably prevent, restrict or distort competition" but only if the acting person intentionally or negligently acts in violation of the section. Hard core violations—price-fixing, output agreements, collective boycotts, and collusive bidding and tendering—are prohibited without proof of effect and are void, but again only persons who intentionally or negligently contravene the provisions commit an offense. For agreements that distort competition but are not hard core, exemption may be granted if the agreement is likely to benefit the public by efficiencies—productive, allocative, or dynamic, the agreement distorts competition no more than necessary to attain the benefits, and the benefits outweigh the detriments.

As for the dominance offense, an entity is dominant if it "can profitably and materially restrain or reduce competition" in the market for a significant period of time and its market share exceeds 35 percent. The entity must not use its position of dominance "if the object, effect or likely effect of the conduct is to appreciably prevent, restrict or distort competition" (unless the conduct is exempted), and again the offense must be intentional or negligent.

Mergers must be notified. If the merger is likely to create or strengthen a dominant position (this was the test of the old EU merger regulation, which is now: significantly impede effective competition), the Commission may allow the merger (exempt it) if it is likely to benefit the public by efficiencies, including technical progress or by protecting the environment, the merger restrains competition no more than necessary to obtain the benefits, and the benefits outweigh the detriments to competition; or the merger is necessary to save a firm from imminent financial failure. The fact that the sole nonmarket public interest consideration allowed is the environment is noteworthy.

The Commission may make market inquiries, and the minister may direct inquiry. The Commission must conduct an inquiry before granting a block exemption—a device to exempt a category of cases from prohibition.

Regarding coverage, the act does not apply to exports. It explicitly applies to state and local government bodies, thus to SOEs, insofar as they engage in trade.

A separate part of the act (Part V) prohibits unconscionable conduct, and thus presumably would be an additional basis for prohibiting excessive pricing.

As penalty for offenses, the Commission may impose a fine of not less than 5 percent nor more than 10 percent of the firm's annual turnover. Uniquely, it may fine the offender two times the damage to persons harmed by the offense, which shall be paid to the victim.

Institutionally, a minister is involved in appointments, may require market inquiries, and may issue regulations.

While fairly exemplary of the competition laws of this set, the Tanzanian law has some advantages and some disadvantages. Explicit coverage of SOEs is helpful (also found in the law of Zambia), since so many of the market obstructions are by state and local governments operating in the market. Few laws are explicit in this regard, although silence can imply inclusion. The requirement of intentionality or negligence to warrant imposition of a penalty, also found in the law of Botswana, is a handicap. This requirement could impose an insurmountable burden on the authority. In merger assessment, Tanzania's confinement of nonmarket public interests to the environment is both interesting and rare. The cohort statutes typically specify as public interests SMEs and employment, and sometimes, expressly, whatever else the Commission deems relevant. The authorization for collection and payment of double damages to persons injured by a violation is unique and can be helpful and legitimating if the authority carries through.

F. ZIMBABWE

The relevant act of Zimbabwe is the Competition and Tariff Act, which means that the Commission deals with unfair trade as well as matters of competition. The trade mandate might incline the Zimbabwe authority more than others to consider unfairness to competitors in competition cases. The act was adopted in 2001, and therefore is older than most in its set. It is less precise in its prohibitions than the later competition acts. It basically prohibits any restrictive practice, monopoly situation (where one or more persons exercise substantial market control), and mergers contrary to the public interest. In determining whether the conduct or transaction is contrary to the public interest, the act states: "The Commission shall take into account everything it considers relevant in the circumstances, and shall have regard to the desirability of" promoting the interests of consumers, and promoting competition to reduce costs, procure innovation, and facilitate entry. In deciding whether a merger is against the public interest, however, the Commission is directed to consider a list of factors that are all market factors (plus a failing firm defense): likelihood of substantially lessening competition or creating a monopoly situation; and in doing so to consider factors such as ease of entry, concentration, dynamic characteristics of the market, and removal of efficient competition. As for a monopoly situation, the Commission must regard the situation as contrary to the public interest unless it results in a more efficient use of resources, it would deny benefits to consumers, it is reasonably necessary to enable the parties to negotiate fair terms of distribution, or its termination or prevention would have serious consequences for the level of employment or would substantially reduce export business.

In a section on exemptions and coverage, the act states that intellectual property is exempted "except to the extent that such a right is used for the purpose of enhancing or maintaining prices" or any other conduct that would constitute a consideration in a manner contemplated in the definition of "restrictive practice." (This is an exception that might swallow the exemption.) Moreover, "the Act shall bind the State to the extent that the State is concerned in the manufacture and distribution of commodities" (similar to Tanzania and Zambia), except that the state cannot be criminally liable. The minister is significantly involved in appointments, decisions, and policy.

Any person guilty of a hard core violation may be liable for a fine not exceeding approximately US$5,000 and may be sentenced to imprisonment for not more than two years. For other violations, fines up to approximately $2,000 may be imposed.

The Zimbabwe statute is confusing and imprecise in its prohibitions. Officials are seeking amendment.

## G. MAURITIUS

The Mauritius Competition Act, adopted in 2007 and proclaimed in 2008 and 2009, is aimed at protecting competition, efficiency, the market, and consumers. An exception is that the minister "may give written directions of a general character to the Commission relating to any additional public policy factors he wishes the Commission to have in regards to reaching its determinations."

As for agreements among competitors, the act prohibits any agreement that has the object or effect of fixing prices, sharing markets, and restricting supply AND "significantly prevents, restricts or distorts competition"; and it prohibits bid rigging and collusive tendering. The Commission may review other agreements among competitors where the parties have or are acquiring 30 percent or more of the market and "the Commission has reasonable grounds to believe that the agreement has the object or effect of preventing, restricting or distorting competition."

As for vertical agreements, the law prohibits resale price maintenance. The Commission may review other vertical agreements where one or more parties appear to be in a monopoly situation, defined below.

The Commission may also, in general, review a monopoly situation accompanied by offending conduct. A monopoly situation exists where one enterprise has 30 percent or more of the market, or three or fewer firms have 70 percent. The situation is subject to review in the case of conduct that has the object or effect of preventing, restricting, or distorting competition or otherwise exploiting the monopoly situation. The Commission must assess whether the enterprises have market power (can act without effective constraint) and whether the practices are "likely to have an adverse effect on the efficiency, adaptability and competitiveness of the economy of Mauritius, or are likely to be detrimental to the interests of consumers."

The Commission may review a merger where the parties together will have, or one alone has, 30 percent or more of a market and the Commission reasonably believes that the merger is likely to result in a substantial lessening of competition in a market. In practice, unlike most jurisdictions, pre-merger notification is deemed optional.

Where the Commission finds adverse effects on competition in any of the matters subject to review, before deciding on the remedy, the Commission must consider specified offsetting public benefits and the extent to which they should be taken into account. However, the listed benefits are all efficiency/consumer benefits with the sole addition of the safety of goods and services. In relation to restrictive agreements, the Commission may give directions on how to cure the violation but may "not impose a financial penalty unless it is satisfied that the breach of the prohibition was committed intentionally or negligently" (similar to Botswana and Tanzania). Where a financial penalty may be imposed, the penalty may not exceed 10 percent of the turnover of the enterprise in Mauritius during the period of the breach but covering no more than five years.

The statute exempts any agreement insofar as it concerns licensing or assignment of intellectual property rights.

## H. MALAWI

The Malawi law, adopted in 2000, is the Competition and Fair Trading Act. It provides for protection against deception and misrepresentation regarding consumer goods as well as protection of competition. As for the competition mandate, while it contains the three main categories of prohibition—restrictive practices, abuse of dominance, and unauthorized mergers—it leans on the side of fairness to competitors and expansion of entrepreneurial opportunity and would allow significant discretion of the Commission in balancing factors, market and nonmarket, efficiency, and competitor opportunity, in determining whether advantages to Malawi outweigh detrimental impact. Merger notification is voluntary.

## I. SUMMARY

In sum, the statutes of the set of countries are quite similar. On goals, they strive to make their markets work better and enhance the competiveness of their firms. They want to increase efficiency and equity; to prohibit exclusionary conduct and work toward inclusiveness, as well as to carry out public interest goals, including easing the path for small business, protecting workers from layoffs, and promoting exports. Most of the laws identify cartels, bid rigging, resale price maintenance, and sometimes concerted boycotts as hard core violations. The hard core violations are most heavily punishable, but even then, usually by fines that are not high enough to be deterrent and sometimes also only if the offending conduct is proved intentional or negligent. Inclusion of the vertical restraint (suppliers' instructing their customers to charge no less than a minimum price, or RPM) as a hard core offense is notable in view of the fact that a number of Western jurisdictions treat the practice as usually efficient and good for consumers—but still, it can be harmful, exploiting buyers directly or supporting cartelization, and keeping high prices high; thus the law of these nations reflects their choice to make the law simple where the usual observed consequence is bad for the people.

Most of the statutes follow the European format in prohibiting a wide swath of agreements in a first cut, and allowing justifications and exemptions. These statutes add public interest considerations whereas EU law does not; and they maintain a regulatory system requiring authorization of agreements that are not on balance anticompetitive, which EU law does no longer. All of the statutes also have abuse of dominance and merger control law, both of which also usually incorporate public interest factors.

This is the law on the books. Law on the books does not automatically translate into law that is obeyed. Is the law enforced?

## IV. Enforcement

### A. KENYA

The Kenyan authority was established in 2011. It is under excellent leadership and is enforcing its law actively, subject to economic and political constraints. Its budget has been growing. As of the start of 2018, it has 49 full time staff members, 6 of whom are lawyers and 23 economists.

In its early years, with no competition culture and huge challenges of enforcement, the authority embarked on a course of education and solicited cooperation. It devised a unique leniency program inviting trade associations in the financial services and agriculture sectors to voluntarily disclose contraventions of the act, for a limited time, in exchange for immunity from punishment.[17]

Increasing its proactive activity, the Kenyan authority has taken cartel decisions in cement, fertilizer, advertising, insurance, and the retail industry. Three of these decisions led to US$170,000 in fines. The authority recently denied a request for exemption by an accountants' professional association regarding audit fees. It has adopted a leniency program, inducing whistle-blowers to reveal the details of cartels, hopefully leading to criminal cartel prosecutions.[18]

In the areas of anticompetitive agreements and dominance, the Kenyan authority has been proactive in clearing the path for unique financial services featuring mobile money, and for distribution of cellular information services that help entrepreneurs—such as helping fishermen find the markets for their daily catches. Mobile money, allowing safe and easy transfers of small amounts of money by handheld devices, was pioneered by Kenya's Safaricom, which introduced the M-Pesa. And while it was a great innovator, having amassed power, Safaricom has tried to protect and exploit its power. In a victory of real practical importance, the authority forced Safaricom to drop its exclusivity clauses with agents, thus freeing up the agents to handle transactions from rivals such as Airtel. Safaricom protested that it had invested in its network of agents and had the right to their exclusive services (an argument that is often a winning one in the West), but agent exclusivity was an enormous barrier to entry of competition into mobile money services, and the elimination of the exclusivity clauses opened the market, thus enabling even the poorer population to have access to these financial services.[19]

---

[17] Joyce Karanja-Ng'ang'a, Competition Authority of Kenya flexes its muscles, BOWMAN'S LAW, Competition-Dealmakers (Aug. 2018).

[18] *Kenya's Competition Authority*, in EMERGING ENFORCERS 2018, GLOBAL COMPETITION REVIEW (Feb. 26, 2018).

[19] *See* Rafe Mazer et al., *Agents for Everyone: Removing Agent Exclusivity in Kenya & Uganda*, CGAP (July 22, 2016).

Still, people with no access to money cannot use money transfer systems. Access to credit is one of the thorniest problems for people with no money and no traditional channels for credit. Instant access to credit is one of the developing fields, with enormous benefits but also problems of needs for protection. Kenya, along with Tanzania, is one of the pioneering countries. *See* Greg Chen & Rafe Mazer, *Instant, Automated, Remote: The Key Attributes of Digital Credit*, CGAP (Feb. 8, 2016). *See also* Mayada El-Zoghbi, *Mind the Gap: Women and Access to Finance*, CGAP (May 13, 2015) (noting that women make up a dominant percentage of the unbanked, and that digital access has accelerated women's financial access in Kenya).

On the merger front, Kenya vets a number of mergers. Typically, the mergers are approved with conditions, often public interest conditions. For example, Kenya cleared Coca-Cola's acquisition of SABMiller's local subsidiary, making Coca-Cola the biggest water-bottling company in the area. The merged firm had less than 23 percent of the market, and the authority saw no competition problems. The authority approved the deal on the condition that Coca-Cola would continue producing the Keringet brand for at least three years, that the employees at a Keringet plant would be retained for at least two years, and thereafter the firm would retain at least 140 employees of the plant.[20]

The Kenya Competition Authority is a leader among its cohorts and reaches out across borders to collaborate with and assist neighbors in their joint enterprise in identifying and eliminating barriers to competition. Its Director General Francis Wang'ombe Kariuki was the inaugural chair of the African Competition Forum and plays an active role in bilateral cooperation, in the International Competition Network, and in free trade areas and communities such as COMESA. (See Chapter VI.) The Kenya authority is also active in competition *policy*: attacking serious barriers to competition that are beyond the reach of competition law enforcement. We gave one example in Chapter I, featuring Kenya's collaboration with the World Bank in destroying the power of a monopoly fertilizer board that had put tens of thousands of farmers out of business. At the end of this section, we describe some dynamic competition advocacy by the competition authorities of this set, including Kenya.

## B. NAMIBIA

The Namibian agency brings cartel and abuse of dominance cases, in addition to examining mergers. Mergers are its predominant focus. It issued its first-ever cartel fine in August 2016, by way of a settlement for a violation in the insurance industry, for N$15 million (US$1.2 million).[21] It conducted its first dawn raid (unannounced entry for search of evidence) in support of alleged excessive pricing of aviation fuel by Puma Energy Network in 2016.[22] It vets numerous mergers. As of the end of 2017, it had conditionally approved 39 and blocked 5. The agency has 17 staff members. It is challenged by a small budget, authority to impose only low statutory fines, and absence of a leniency program—which is a useful tool to incentivize whistle-blowers

---

[20] *See* Muthoki Mumo, *Coke now Kenya's biggest water bottler*, BUSINESS DAILY AFRICA, July 9, 2017.

[21] *Namibian Competition Commission, in* EMERGING ENFORCERS 2018, GLOBAL COMPETITION REVIEW (Feb. 26, 2018).

[22] NAMIBIA COMPETITION COMMISSION, Aircraft Owners & Pilots vs. Puma, Media Statement.

to report on cartels. Namibia is working to get a leniency program and also to get a specialized tribunal in order to sidestep long court delays.[23]

*Restrictive agreements and exemptions.* Namibia's competition statute, like several others in this set, has a special provision for professional associations whose rules may lessen competition. The association may apply for an exemption from the restrictive agreements prohibition, and the Commission may exempt rules "reasonably required to maintain professional standards or the ordinary function of the profession." Western statutes normally do not have such a specific provision but take account of exactly the same factors when analyzing association by-laws under general modes of analysis.

Namibia received an application from the Law Society of Namibia (NLS), which sought an exemption for rules on a broad range of subjects from fee-setting to marketing and touting legal services. The Commission's disposition provides a model blueprint: market-friendly while allowing proportionately limited exemptions where appropriate and necessary.

Here are some examples from the *NLS* decision. The Commission declined to grant an exemption for rules for developing fee guidelines. (Lawyers' associations' fee guidelines are effectively a euphemism for lawyers' fixing their fees.) The Commission recognized that not only was this function not reasonably necessary to maintain professional standards but it was price-fixing. Also, the Commission declined to exempt rules prohibiting lawyers from charging contingency fees, finding that charging contingent fees could not properly be equated with unprofessional conduct. It declined to exempt a rule that legal practitioners can hold themselves out as "consultants" only if they have been legal practitioners for 10 years, and declined to exempt rules prohibiting lawyers from sharing offices or practicing with a person other than a legal practitioner or from entering into a partnership or commission-sharing arrangement with a nonlawyer. It declined to authorize rules forbidding publicity or marketing stating a specific charge for certain legal work or criticizing or claiming to be superior to other practitioners, as being overbroad to protect against misleading information and hindering positive contributions to competition. But the Commission granted an exemption for a rule prohibiting lawyers from charging a fee unreasonably high in light of the circumstances, holding this rule properly within the category of rules necessary to maintain professional standards, and it also allowed a rule reserving to lawyers specialized work specifically reserved to lawyers by a statute. The Commission refused to exempt rules prohibiting touting and soliciting, deeming them too wide and possibly causing lawyers to be "reluctant

---

[23] *Id.*

to advertise or look for business legitimately due to the fear that they will be accused of touting."[24]

The Commission stated that its decision was informed by internationally applied norms, as the Namibia competition act requires. In fact, its decision is even more progressive than US and EU case law in drawing the line between unjustified restraints that harm people who need legal services and are not needed to maintain professional standards, and restraints in the interest of proper functioning of the legal profession.[25] For example, in the United States, most states authorize and federal law permits rules that prohibit lawyers' partnerships with economists or accountants.

*Mergers.* In view of its statutory mandate, Namibia is obligated to investigate a number of mergers a year. Most mergers are cleared, but a number—even those that pose no competition problems—are cleared with conditions. Conditions may require the merged firm to favor local content and not to lay off employees for a period of two years. The merger of Lewis Stores and Ellerine's is an example of a merger that, the Commission found, would have no negative impact on either competition or employment; indeed, absent the merger, 259 employees were likely to lose their jobs. However, the Commission was concerned that the merged firm's plans to reposition itself into a high-income customer segment might not work out in some towns and this eventuality might put some existing jobs at risk. For this reason, it conditioned clearance of the merger on a promise of no retrenchments for two years, with significant compliance and monitoring obligations.[26]

## C. BOTSWANA

Botswana's agency is small, having two to three lawyers and three to six economists in addition to about five interns who are also economists. The total staff numbers about 43.[27] Established in 2011, the agency got off to a strong start. It recruited as its first chief executive Thulasoni Kaira, the experienced head of the Zambian authority. By 2012 the authority had investigated its first cartel; it uncovered four more in 2013 and two more in 2014. It trained its sights on bid rigging in procurement. In addition to prosecuting bid-rigging cartels, it initiated a program to raise awareness of procurement officers and instructing the officers how to design tenders to avoid bid rigging and corruption.

Examples of the authority's investigation and enforcement activity include the following two, one from the procurement sector and one from industry. The authority

---

[24] *See* Hitjiua Tjiho, *Decision on Law Society of Namibia's Exemption Clarified,* 5 NACC COMPETITION NEWS 4, at 12–15 (2017).

[25] *See* California Dental Association v. FTC, 526 U.S. 756 (1999); Cipolla v. Fazari (C-94/04); and Macrino v. Meloni (C-202/04), ECLI:EU:C:2006:758.

[26] NACC COMPETITION NEWS, *supra* note 24, at 20–22.

[27] The numbers change but are in this range. *See Botswana's Competition Authority, in* EMERGING ENFORCERS 2018, GLOBAL COMPETITION REVIEW (Feb. 26, 2018).

detected flaws in a request-to-tender process for the provision of facilities management to Botswana International University of Science and Technology (BIUST). The investigation that followed revealed that the government had markedly failed to follow its established process for formulating tenders and providing specifications. (Failure to follow required tender procedures often implies that a complicit official purposely ignored the process in order to tip the contest to friends and cronies.) On the authority's intervention, the improper tender was canceled.

The authority also intervened in one of a number of cases in the concentrated and competitively challenged poultry and egg market. The dominant egg producer, Ross Breeders Botswana, had exclusive supply contracts with only two distributors, and it refused to sell certain low-grade eggs to any others. The company agreed to drop the exclusivity clauses, and seven new entrants came into the market.[28]

The authority vets numerous mergers. A typical recent merger outcome involved Bradleymore's Holdings acquisition of KFC franchises in Botswana. This episode is about public interest and is typical of how the authority applies public interest concerns in a value chain context. The authority found that the merger would cause no harm to competition, but it took "note of the commitment by Bradleymore's to develop a robust supply chain that is aimed at ensuring that local suppliers are capacitated to enable them to meet the supply requirements set by YUM i.e., adhering to the franchisors quality standards."[29] The authority approved the merger with conditions that:

i. Bradleymore's shall source a significant portion of their input requirements locally by continuing to source from existing suppliers that were engaged by VPB [the seller], provided they are ... accredited ... ;

ii. Bradleymore's shall ensure that local suppliers are assisted in penetrating or meeting YUM's standards of accreditation with the aim of sourcing from these suppliers; and

iii. The Parties shall not retrench any employees of the target entities as a result of the acquisition for a period of three (3) years from the implementation date. . . .[30]

On the cartel side, the authority has a leniency program but had not received a formal application at the time of this writing.

The authority has serious budget and staffing concerns and is seeking sources of funding.

---

[28] See BOTSWANA COMPETITION AUTHORITY, 2016/17 Annual Report, at 30.

[29] See BOTSWANA COMPETITION AUTHORITY, *Competition Authority Approves with Conditions the Acquisition of KFC Franchises in Botswana*, Feb. 7, 2018.

[30] *Id.*

D. ZAMBIA

The Zambian Competition and Consumer Protection Commission comprises 4 lawyers, 33 economists, and 67 staff. The authority investigates abuse of dominance cases and an increasing number of cartel cases. It vets more than 25 mergers a year.

For an example of cases, we mention one from the fertilizer industry. The market is highly concentrated. The government buys fertilizer for the farmer-support program and is a big buyer. The authority discovered and prosecuted a high-profile fertilizer bid-rig case in which it found the two leading firms, Omnia and Nyiombe, to have been colluding with each other and with government procurement agents to win virtually all the bids. We tell this story in Chapter I.

The Zambian authority has proceeded also against discriminatory and unfair pricing. Zambia Sugar is a super dominant producer of sugar in Zambia. It accounts for more than 92 percent of production in the country and is the second largest sugar producer in the world. A four-year investigation revealed that Zambia Sugar charged household consumers 28 percent more than industrial customers, although it incurred the same costs. It was charging household users in Zambia 41 percent more than export customers in the Great Lakes Region, where it faced competition. Even some high-volume industrial purchasers were charged higher prices than other high-volume industrial purchasers, which was found to be without justification. The Commission fined Zambia Sugar 5 percent of its annual turnover for price discrimination and unfair pricing, and ordered the company to formulate competitive prices for both industrial and household sugar in the domestic market. [31]

The Zambian authority clamped down on exclusivity clauses, even under the earlier unfair competition law. In the famous case of day-old chicks that were sold to be raised as broilers, Hybrid Poultry, which had 60 percent of the market, required Galaunia, the biggest buyer, to buy only from Hybrid and not from its competitors (the principal competitor being Tamba Chicks). Meanwhile, Hybrid facilitated a loan for Tamba Chicks and required Tamba to give it a right of first refusal if Tamba should be put up for sale. The authority invalidated the exclusive contract with Galaunia and, when Tamba was put up for sale, blocked the bid by Hybrid. Tamba was sold to a new entrant.[32]

Unfortunately, despite the enforcement, neither the sugar problem nor the poultry problem has been solved. Restraints in sugar, fertilizer, cement, and poultry appear to continue, in Zambia and its neighbors. The Zambian Competition Authority recently prosecuted an indirect cartel carried out through the Poultry Association of

---

[31] *Zambia Sugar fined K76 million*, ZAMBIA MAIL DAILY, Oct. 13, 2017. Zambia Sugar has appealed.

[32] *See* Thulasoni Kaira, *The Role of Competition Law and Policy in Alleviating Poverty—The Case of Zambia*, Part B, *in* THE EFFECTS OF ANTI-COMPETITIVE BUSINESS PRACTICES ON DEVELOPING COUNTRIES AND THEIR DEVELOPMENTAL PROSPECTS 133, 161–166 (H. Qaqaya & G. Lipimile eds., UNCTAD 2008).

Zambia, and it fined four hatcheries, including Hybrid and Ross.[33] The problems probably cannot be solved without integrated cross-border analysis and coordinated trade and competition enforcement,[34] for the leading firms are active in neighboring markets and may be cooperating with competitors across borders or enlisting government measures to raise barriers and dampen competition, as Professor Simon Roberts and his team at CCRED[35] and African Competition Forum studies suggest.[36]

Zambia has a leniency program, but as of the end of August 2017 the authority had received only one application, and that was not for a cartel but for a vertical (buyer-supplier) agreement. The players in the concentrated markets see themselves as fellow community members and are reluctant to report on one another. Moreover, it is reported: "Political interference results in lack of enforcement, as it gives the cartel members a feeling of comfort in not applying for leniency."[37]

Executive Director of the Zambian Authority Chilufya Sampa summed up the work and accomplishments of the Commission in year 2017: the Commission received 82 merger notifications (a large increase over the prior year), resulting in US$6 million merger investments, 4,430 jobs created, and 411 jobs maintained. It dealt with 13 abuse of dominance cases, including Zambia Sugar and a case against the ubiquitous Lafarge Cement company. It received and investigated 37 restrictive business practices cases. It handled 7 cartel cases, singling out a bread cartel that increased the price of bread by as much as 23 percent. Expressing outrage that the bread industry could take such advantage of the poorest of the poor, Sampa observed that the overcharge for this daily staple accounted for a considerable amount of poor people's income. Also in 2017, the authority made important information available to stakeholders, for example, by promoting school clubs in which students would write interactive essays, take quizzes, and hold debates about competition and consumer protection. In its informational mission, the authority uses local languages to bridge the language gap.[38]

Institutionally, the Zambian competition law gives power to the authority to conduct investigations, decide cases, and impose fines. This is an integrated agency

---

[33] *See* Charley Connor, *Zambia fines chick hatchery cartel*, GLOBAL COMPETITION REVIEW (Apr. 3, 2018).

[34] This means coordination of competition and internal market trade tools and is best accomplished in a regional common market with both free movement law and community competition law.

[35] Centre for Competition, Regulation and Economic Development at the University of Johannesburg.

[36] *See* Ernest Bagopi et al., *Competition, agro-processing and regional development: The case of the poultry sector in South Africa, Botswana, Namibia and Zambia*, Chapter 4, *in* COMPETITION IN AFRICA (Simon Roberts ed., 2016). For sugar, *see* Brian Chisanga et al., *Agricultural development, competition and investment: The case of sugar in Kenya, South Africa, Tanzania and Zambia*, Chapter 3, *in* COMPETITION IN AFRICA, *supra*. *See also* Chapter VI herein for regional cooperation.

[37] *See* Patrick Chengo, *Zambia: Competition and Consumer Protection Commission*, GLOBAL COMPETITION REVIEW (Aug. 11, 2017).

[38] *See* 2017 End of Year Media Briefing by Executive Director of CCPC Mr. Chilufya Sampa, https://www.ccpc. org.zm/index.php/media-releases/news/176-2017-end-of-year-media-briefing-by-executive-director-of-ccpc-mr-chilufya-sampa.

model, as distinct from a structure in which the investigative arm must present cases to an independent decision maker. The Zambian model has the virtue of expediency but the drawback of confirmation bias. Prosecutors tend to believe the hypotheses on which they launched the investigation.

## E. TANZANIA

The Tanzanian authority (the FCC) oversees not only competition but also consumer protection, including counterfeit goods. Mergers and counterfeit goods command most of its time. It has approximately 7 lawyers and 8 economists and a total staff of about 57. A slim staff and changes in leadership have hampered its accomplishments. In the year ending June 2016, it processed 42 merger applications and 2 applications for exemption of agreements, and it held 17 advocacy and awareness programs. Its subjects of investigation include suspected cartels in cement, sugar, petroleum products, and tobacco, and bid rigging in construction[39]—all usual suspects (through time and across countries).

In its formative days, the FCC established the applicability of the competition law to municipal councils. The municipalities had granted exclusive billboard rights along municipal roads, thus excluding outdoor advertising competitors from access to the market. The Commission declared the exclusive contracts void.[40] Establishing jurisdiction over municipalities is a positive development; many of the worst restraints are imposed by state or local governments.

Moreover, the FCC waged a strong advocacy fight to counter the lobbying and slanted public relations campaign of the cement oligopolists, who were trying to keep imports out of the market, as we recount in the next section.

## F. ZIMBABWE

Zimbabwe's authority is the Competition and Tariff Commission. The CTC comprises 3 lawyers and 12 economists, with 27 total staff. Even this small staff is dwindling, because of the country's desperate economic condition and freeze on new public hiring. In the three years 2014–2016, the Commission brought no cartel cases and 5 abuse of dominance cases, and it vetted 42 mergers.[41] The number of cases the CTC handles has significantly decreased over the last few years.

---

[39] *See* Annual Report of Tanzania Fair Trade Commission 2015/2016.

[40] *See* FCC Annual Report 2008/2009 and UNCTAD Peer Review (2012), overview at 4–5.

[41] *See* Mark Burke, Tamara Paremoer, Thando Vilakazi, & Tatenda Zengeni, Cross-*cutting Competition Issues in Regional Industrial Development*, African Industrial Development and Integration Research Programme (AIDIRP), University of Johannesburg CCRED Working Paper 20/2017.

Mergers have always been a mainstay of the Commission. Even under the predecessor law, mergers were vetted. They included big multinational mergers, which the authority cleared with conditions. The conditions were sometimes but not always helpful to competition, such as mandating price control or mandating continued operations of a plant or a brand that might not have survived in the market.[42] One sometimes has the impression that competition authorities of the developing countries are responding to a call to *do something* about an unpopular merger that they cannot practically enjoin.

For restrictive practices and abuse of dominance, targets of Zimbabwe's investigations have included cement and cigarettes. The cement industry behaved oligopolistically, but on investigation the authority found that the cause was market leadership, not collusion. Market leadership (and followership) without agreement is typically not an offense, and so no violation was found. The Commission did find the following conduct illegal as abusive practices: distribution of products in a discriminatory and unfair manner, imposing exploitative and unfair payment conditions, and withholding supplies in the formal market in favor of the informal market.[43]

In the *Cigarette Distribution* case, British American Tobacco Zimbabwe (BATZ) complained to the Commission that a new entrant Cut Rag was cutting corners by not complying with the required health warnings on the cigarette packages. BATZ surely regretted the complaint. Cut Rag was just trying to enter the market. Its regulatory default was not a competition problem, but BATZ's strategies *were*. The Commission found BATZ to have engaged in predatory practices, driving Cut Rag out of business.[44]

Economically, the Commission is facing harder times, along with its country.

G. MAURITIUS

In its nine years of enforcement, the Mauritius Competition Commission has been increasingly active and focused, despite scarce resources. Its first cartel infringement decision involved local beer manufacturers in Mauritius and Madagascar. One of the firms had agreed to shut down its operations in Mauritius and in Madagascar, restricting the supply of beer. The Commission imposed a penalty of approximately US$1 million. In the poultry market, the Commission has prosecuted and fined Panagora Marketing Company, which supplies Chantecler chicken to supermarkets and small retail shops, for imposing resale prices on retailers, preventing the retailers

---

[42] *See* Alexander J. Kububa, *Anti-Competitive Practices and Their Adverse Effects on Consumer Welfare: The Zimbabwean Experience*, EFFECTS OF ANTI-COMPETITIVE BUSINESS PRACTICES, *in* UNCTAD 2008, *supra* note 32, at 103–116.

[43] *Id.* at 118–119.

[44] *See* Bowman's Africa Guide—Competition, https://www.bowmanslaw.com/wp-content/uploads/2016/12/Guide-Competition.pdf.

from price-competing among themselves. (An appeal is pending.) In one of its first cases the Commission challenged retroactive volume-based discounts offered by Kraft for its popular processed cheese, and Kraft's tying the discount to preferred shelf space and display for various Kraft brands. Kraft had 90 percent of the processed cheese market and 70 percent of the cheese market in Mauritius. The Commission's prohibition led to the entry of two new brands and lower cheese prices.[45]

By mid-2017, the Commission had investigated a number of mergers. In most, no action was taken. In a few, the merger was cleared with conditions. Perhaps the highest profile merger was the huge international merger, with subsidiaries in Mauritius— Holcim/Lafarge Cement. The merger would have been a merger to monopoly in Mauritius. The Commission completed the case by settlement. The companies offered, and the Commission accepted, disposing of the Holcim Mauritius shares to Gamma, which was active in markets in which cement was used as an input (itself raising concerns, which the Commission addressed by undertakings.)

The Commission is also active in monopoly abuse cases. It brings enforcement actions against SOEs as well as private companies. It stresses leveling the playing field as well as serving consumers and promoting efficiency.

The Commission has a leniency program and has offered time-limited amnesty for both initiators of cartels and for resale price maintenance agreements, which are also per se illegal. However, in this small island economy, all market players know one another well, the competition culture is not deep, and the relationships are regarded as a factor in deterring whistle-blowing.

Perhaps being a small island economy has encouraged the Commission's international and cooperative outlook. The Mauritius Commission has memoranda of understanding for cooperation with the South African Competition Commission and COMESA. It gives technical assistance to neighbors near and far, including Ethiopia and Madagascar. It is active in the African Competition Forum and the International Competition Network; the Commission holds leadership positions in both.[46]

## H. MALAWI

Malawi has a Competition and Fair Trading Commission. While on the competition side the authority principally reacts to complaints and responds to a few merger filings—some referred for assessment by COMESA—it also launches investigations on its own motion. It has detected and put an end to price-fixing orchestrated by

---

[45] *See* Deshmuk Kowlessur, *Mauritius: The Competition Commission of Mauritius, in* THE EUROPEAN, MIDDLE EASTERN AND AFRICAN ANTITRUST REVIEW 2018, GLOBAL COMPETITION REVIEW (Aug. 11, 2017).

[46] *Id.*; Competition Newsletter, COMPETITION COMMISSION OF MAURITIUS, Oct. 2017.

trade associations, which often have limited awareness of the law. It has focused on critical products and services, such as school fees. It discovered that the Independent Schools Association of Malawi (ISAMA) had made fee recommendations to its members. It ordered ISAMA to issue a public withdrawal of the recommendations.[47]

The Malawi authority investigated the Insurance Association of Malawi for setting premium rates and recommending these rates to its members. It learned that the association's conduct followed the advice of the Registrar of Financial Institutions, who had become concerned that some insurance companies, were pricing below their costs and facing liquidity problems. The Commission found that the association had engaged in a cartel and ordered it to desist and to withdraw the recommended rates publicly. Then the authority engaged the Registrar in conversations and instruction on the competition law's requirements.[48]

The authority was alerted that the Blantyre Water Board disconnected citizens' water service for nonpayment of bills and would reconnect only three days after payment of the outstanding balance plus a penalty. The Commission held that the prolonged refusal to reconnect this essential life service was unconscionable conduct as well as a gross abuse of the company's monopoly, and was illegal as a misuse of market power. The Water Board complied with the Commission's order to cease this conduct and agreed to participate in a compliance program.[49]

A similar result befell ESCOM, the state electricity monopoly, when it disconnected power of a new tenant who refused to pay the outstanding bill of the preceding occupant.[50]

In other cases, in response to complaints or requests for authorization of agreements such as for restricted distribution, the Commission found that the conduct benefited consumers; it granted the authorization or dismissed the complaint.

The activity of the Malawi Commission is hampered by the intrinsic limits of a small staff.

\* \* \*

The following charts show: (1) the breakdown of competition cases brought in nine countries in southern Africa in three recent years (Table 4.2); (2) the institutional design (structure) of their competition systems (Table 4.3); and (3) the institutional design (staffing) of the competition authority (Table 4.4).

---

[47] Malawi Competition and Fair Trading Commission Newsletter, Oct.–Dec. 2013, at 15.

[48] See Charlotte Wezi Mesikano-Malonda, *Malawi: Competition and Fair Trading Commission, in* AFRICAN AND MIDDLE EASTERN ANTITRUST REVIEW 2017, GLOBAL COMPETITION REVIEW (July 22, 2016).

[49] Newsletter, *supra* note 47.

[50] *Supra* note 48.

**TABLE 4.2**

Analysis of Competition Law Enforcement, 2014–2016

| Contravention | Botswana | Malawi | Mauritius | Namibia | South Africa | Swaziland | Tanzania | Zambia | Zimbabwe | TOTAL |
|---|---|---|---|---|---|---|---|---|---|---|
| Abuse of Dominance | 20 | 6 | 22 | 4 | 33 | 2 | 7 | 2 | 5 | 101 |
| Cartel | 15 | 3 | 6 | 3 | 69 | | 6 | 3 | | **105** |
| Exemption | 3 | 4 | | | 6 | | | | | **13** |
| Failure to Meet Merger Conditions | | | | | | | 1 | 1 | | **2** |
| No Information | | 1 | | | 36 | | | | | 37 |
| Not a Competition Issue | | 1 | 1 | | | | | | | **2** |
| Prior Implementation | | | 4 | | 7 | 1 | 16 | | 1 | **29** |
| Retail Price Maintenance | | | | | 3 | | | | | 3 |
| TOTAL | **38** | **15** | **33** | **7** | **154** | **3** | **30** | **6** | **6** | 292 |

• South Africa accounts for 52.2% of cases and 67% of collusion cases, but abuse of dominance cases are more evenly spread in the relatively smaller economies of Botswana and Mauritius.

Courtesy of University of Johannesburg, Centre for Competition, Regulation, and Economic Development (CCRED).*

* This and the following CCRED charts are reprinted with permission from Mark Burke, Tamara Paremoer, Thando Vilakazi and Tatenda Zengeni, *Cross-cutting Competition Issues in Regional Industrial Development*, African Industrial Development and Integration Research Programme (AIDIRP), University of Johannesburg CCRED Working Paper 20/2017.

TABLE 4.3

Institutional Design: Structure

| Jurisdictions | Enforcement Model | Mandates | Leadership Structure |
|---|---|---|---|
| Botswana | Integrated Agency* | Competition | Multimember Board |
| Malawi | Integrated Agency | Competition & Consumer Protection | Multimember Board |
| Mauritius | Integrated Agency | Competition | Multimember Board |
| Namibia | Integrated Agency | Competition | Multimember Board |
| South Africa | Bifurcated Agency** | Competition | Unitary Executive |
| Swaziland | Integrated Agency | Competition | Multimember Board |
| Tanzania | Bifurcated Agency | Competition & Consumer Protection | Multimember Board |
| Zambia | Bifurcated Agency | Competition & Consumer Protection | Multimember Board |
| Zimbabwe | Bifurcated Agency | Competition & Consumer Protection | Multimember Board |

Courtesy of University of Johannesburg, CCRED.

Editors' note:

\* Integrated agency entails a commission or board within the agency that makes the first level determination.

\*\* Bifurcated agency means the agency goes to a specialized tribunal for enforcement.

TABLE 4.4

Institutional Design: Staffing

| Jurisdictions | Year Operationalized | Total Staff | Economists | | Lawyers | | Revenue (US$ million) |
|---|---|---|---|---|---|---|---|
| | | | No. | % | No. | % | |
| Botswana | 2011 | 33 | 5 | 15% | 4 | 12% | 2.2 |
| Malawi | 2013 | 19 | 7 | 37% | 2 | 11% | 0.8 |
| Mauritius | 2009 | 20 | 6 | 30% | 6 | 30% | 1.0 |
| Namibia | 2008 | 35 | 8 | 23% | 7 | 20% | 2.7 |
| South Africa | 1999 | 197 | 64 | 32% | 60 | 30% | 21.7 |

TABLE 4.4

*(Continued)*

| Jurisdictions | Year Operationalized | Total Staff | Economists | | Lawyers | | Revenue (US$ |
|---|---|---|---|---|---|---|---|
| | | | No. | % | No. | % | million) |
| Swaziland | 2010 | 17 | 4 | 24% | 5 | 29% | 0.7 |
| Tanzania | 2007 | 57 | 8 | 14% | 7 | 12% | 3.1 |
| Zambia | 1997 | 67 | 33 | 49% | 4 | 6% | 3.3 |
| Zimbabwe | 1998 | 27 | 12 | 44% | 3 | 11% | 2.6 |
| | | **472** | **147** | **31%** | **98** | **21%** | **38.1** |

Courtesy of University of Johannesburg, CCRED.

Regarding staffing, by way of comparison, the Antitrust Division of the US Department of Justice (one of the two US federal antitrust agencies) employs approximately 400 attorneys and, in the Economic Analysis Group alone, more than 50 PhD economists.

## V. Opening Markets with Competition Policy

The competition authorities devote some of their most productive time to competition policy other than enforcement. They do so in view both of the challenges of enforcing the law and the fact that there are so many market problems that cannot be solved by enforcing the law. Ideally, the competition authorities are not just responsive to complaints and merger filings, they are proactive. They identify the barriers and obstructions that hurt the people the most and the opportunities that can help them the most, and they tackle the problems alone or with partners, if they can do so practically and politically. The projects they choose reveal some of the main obstructions to free market competition in these countries. Here, we retell stories from Kenya, Zambia, Tanzania, and Malawi.

Kenya has identified access to mobile financial services as the main driver of financial inclusion in the country. In fact, Kenya leads the world in "mobile money." The system, M-Pesa, a safe and easy method for money transfers, was launched by the Kenyan firm Safaricom in 2007 and is now used by more than 30 million Kenyans. It started out as a method for microfinance loan repayments, and expanded to become a convenient way to pay for nearly everything from taxi rides to bills and to make deposits in savings accounts. The payment system is faster and easier to use than payment systems in most developed countries.

USSD (a communications data service) enables mobile financial services on any phone at low cost without a SIM card. The service is controlled by mobile network operators, the largest of which by far is Safaricom, with more than an 80 percent share. Small banks and other small financial institutions complained that they were overcharged for the USSD service—a necessary input—keeping their young mobile money systems from becoming competitive with Safaricom's M-Pesa. The Kenyan Competition Authority (CAK) opened a market inquiry. The inquiry found that Safaricom was probably favoring service providers (the big banks) with whom it shared financial interests. Also, the CAK found, Safaricom's pricing was not transparent, and neither customers nor competitors could know the base price and the additional costs of mobile service, making it harder for rival service providers to compete. The matter was resolved by Safaricom's signing an agreement with the CAK to cut prices to the overcharged smaller financial institutions and to publish its fees on its website.[51]

There was another serious problem: lack of interoperability of Safaricom with its emerging competitors in mobile money. This meant that M-Pesa users who received money from users of its rivals from Airtel or (soon to be mobile money competitor) Telkom, would not see the money go directly into their mobile money wallets. They would have to go to an Airtel agent to retrieve it—a big disincentive of people to patronize the rival. Lack of interoperability increased the market power of Safaricom. It shifted Airtel users to Safaricom. Both the competition authority and the communications authority (the telecoms regulator) sought solutions. One solution proposed was a breakup of Safaricom telecom services from M-Pesa to deprive the firm of its monopolistic incentives, but this drastic solution was opposed by both agencies as punishing success and also depriving Safaricom of integrative efficiencies. Both agencies agreed that interoperability was the solution. In the shadow of the agencies' publicizing their concerns, Safaricom and Airtel announced that they are implementing interoperability, so that transferred money will go directly into the users' mobile money wallets. Telkom, which has just launched its mobile money service T-Kash, expects to join the interoperability agreement.[52]

Problems in the taxi and taxi app market are common all over sub-Saharan Africa, where traditional regulated cab companies complain about the low prices of Uber and its ilk, and they test the countries' commitment to price competition. After Uber entered the Nairobi market, Little Cab, a Kenyan taxi-hailing firm (financed by Safaricom), complained that Uber was abusing dominance by its low prices. The CAK

---

[51] *CAK compels Safaricom to cut third party mobile banking Service Costs*, BUSINESS DAILY AFRICA, Mar. 16, 2017.
[52] *See* Saruni Maina, *Seamless Mobile Money Transactions Between Airtel and Safaricom to Begin Next Week*, TECHWEEZ, Apr. 6, 2018.

investigated. It found that Uber competed with all taxi services (i.e., there was no separate hailing service market), and that Uber had 28.6 percent of the market and was not dominant. Besides, Uber never charged prices below average variable costs (therefore its price was not predatory), and entry was easy so that Uber could never have priced high to recoup losses. Thus, the story was of competition, not abuse of dominance.

The CAK then had to fight on the legislative front, for Little Cab was seeking a regulation that would impose a mandatory price floor. A mandatory price floor would have raised prices to travelers. Collaborating with other regulatory agencies, including the transport agency and safety, revenue, and investment authority, and engaging sector players, the CAK recommended a market-friendly regulatory regime with no price floors. The National Assembly accepted the CAK's advice. Little Cab, meanwhile, had no option but to compete. It expanded its fleet and reduced its prices, all to the benefit of consumers.[53] It is now expanding across Africa.

Zambia's projects highlight an additional problem that is rampant in sub-Saharan Africa—government officials who, probably corruptly, skew the market in favor of their friends and patrons, excluding meritorious competitors and raising the prices of goods and services. In the story we retell here, people whose cars were damaged in accidents and needed a towing service had to pay exorbitant prices for towing. They complained to the Zambian Competition and Consumer Protection Commission (CCPC).[54] It turned out that police officers in Lusaka had a practice to designate which tow provider could go to which accident scene. The designated tow service providers, protected from competition, were charging $75 to $180 for towing cars a couple of miles, and since they would remove and sometimes "lose" the car wheels and battery of the towed vehicle, they were charging even more. The CCPC intervened. It decided that towing vehicles should be regulated and the vehicles should be licensed as recovery vehicles. The regulation is the jurisdiction of the Road Safety Agency. The police are no longer the gatekeepers assigning tow companies to accidents. The Road Safety Agency now sets prices at a fraction of the prices that were charged by the "monopoly" designees. The CCPC estimates that consumers now save $30 to $130 for one usage of a towing service.[55]

Zambia also tackles the persistently difficult problem of exclusionary practices by state-owned enterprises, which often are endowed with privileges from the state and

---

[53] March and April 2017. *See* Jake Bright, *In Kenya, Safaricom's Little Cab app goes head to head with Uber*, TechCrunch, Aug. 1, 2016.

[54] Zambia has seen increasing numbers of vehicle accidents, now amounting to about 50,000 per year. The average wage in Zambia is US$52 per month.

[55] *See CCPC opens probe into vehicle towing business at scenes of accidents*, Lusaka Times, Feb. 2, 2016. It is not clear why price regulation is needed after the monopoly assignments were prohibited.

often regard themselves as above the law. This example we cite is in the TV programming market. The Zambian National Broadcasting Corporation (ZNBC) is a state-owned monopoly operating in the free TV market. It had an exclusive agreement with MultiChoice Africa, meaning that it would accept programming provided by MultiChoice alone. MultiChoice owns a subsidiary in the pay-TV segment, GoTV, of which ZNBC owns 75 percent. A Zambian law requires that every commercial broadcasting service must provide at least 35 percent local content. To fulfill this requirement, a new entrant into the pay market, Wananchi Satellite Services, asked ZNBC if it would carry its TV1 and TV2 free-to-air channels. ZNBC refused on grounds of its exclusive contract with MultiChoice. The exclusivity foreclosed all competition in the pay-TV market because the local content requirement had to be fulfilled on free TV, and ZNBC was the gatekeeper. Zambia handled the problem by education and persuasion. It educated ZNBC, MultiChoice, and GoTV of the importance of competition as well as the requirements of the law. It persuaded ZNBC and MultiChoice to terminate their exclusive contract. In the aftermath, Wananchi and others have entered the programming market and are providing more variety and cheaper packages. For their cheapest package, the new entrants are charging about US$3.50 per month, as compared with MultiChoice and GoTV's charges of US$10.80 and US$8.50 a month. Thousands more subscribers have signed up. The agency said: "With more than 28.4 percent of the poor people currently having access to Television, they too are able to afford the cheaper alternative."[56]

Another recurrent problem in these countries is protectionism in trade. Local producers, often through their trade associations, prevail upon the government to keep out cheaper and often better products from across the border—sometimes from another continent but sometimes also from a neighboring sub-Saharan African country. Not unusually, the product is cement—as to which protectionist policies can be particularly devastating. Cement is a basic product needed for construction of schools, housing, office buildings, roads, and bridges—the infrastructure necessary for getting to market and ordinary living and learning under a roof, and critical for inclusive development.

The Tanzania authority tells this story: in Tanzania there were only three significant cement producers. Indian and Pakistani firms produced better and cheaper cement and were well positioned to compete in Tanzania, even with the high cost of transportation. The East African Community orchestrated high duties on cement in the EAC countries (of which Tanzania is one); the duties were 55 percent, later reduced to

---

[56] As reported by Patrick Chengo of the Commission. *See also* http://www.qfmzambia.com/2015/07/14/ccpc-terminates-multichoiceznbc-deal/.

35 percent. Then a great shortage occurred, leading the EAC states to agree to reduce the duty to zero. When prices fell, the East African Cement Producers Association went into action in Tanzania. They lobbied the government at the highest levels to reinstate the 35 percent tariff. They took their case to the press and thereby to the people, sounding the alarm that cheap cement from Pakistan and India was about to destroy thousands of jobs, rob the treasury of billions of shillings in import duties and taxes, and destroy the Tanzanian economy. The Fair Competition Commission responded to a particularly incendiary protectionist-favoring report in the leading newspaper, the *Business Times Economic & Financial Weekly*:

**To the Editor**

... Reading through the article, it is evident that the challenge to ensure the public understands fundamental principles of market economy ... remains enormous.... FCC ... would like to put the issues in context....

For the past one year, consumers country-wide were concerned about the rise of retail prices and the scarcity of cement in the market.

\* \* \*

Generally, the rationale for governments to protect an industry is to maintain employment and the attendant benefits in their countries. However, in the case of the cement industry which is capital intensive, such intended benefits have to be weighed against the high construction costs such a policy introduces in the economy. This situation is worse where our country is developing and therefore construction is a must and where the Government itself is using a high proportion of its budget in construction. It means the country is increasing the costs to itself and limits the growth of the downstream construction industry thus curtailing the employment benefits which the country was purporting to protect in the first place.

\* \* \*

It is against this background that The Fair Competition Commission would like to echo the Government move to ensure that the market remains open and contestable by allowing the interplays that discipline the market and lessen the consumer's burden. If cement produced thousands of miles from Tanzania can beat the production costs of our local cement industry, then the economists should think again on what we want to protect by re-introducing the suspended duty.

Michael Shilla
Acting Director-General
Fair Competition Commission
June 2009

The FCC's pro-competition arguments convinced Tanzanian President Jayaka Kikwete. Against the wishes of the trade ministry, Kikwete stood up for competition, announcing his decision to say "No" to a duty.

The *Business Times Economic & Financial Weekly* then changed its tone. Soon after the president's announcements, it carried a headline: "Locally manufactured cement: consumers' confidence wanes." Subhead: "Kikwete cautions on high prices; Pakistan cement better—Experts." The article reported the experts' opinion that Pakistan produced a higher quality cement than the Tanzanian producers, and it reported Kikwete's decision to reject a duty and his advice to the local producers to find the way to lower their prices for cement, which they apparently did.[57]

Malawi tells a similar story with a twist. The twist is that the Malawi producers wanted protection against cement from neighbors Tanzania and Zambia, all three being members of the common market COMESA. Common market rules ban internal market protectionism. In Malawi, as above in Tanzania, the cement market was highly concentrated. There were only three local manufacturers. The price was high. Then Dangote and Lafarge cement entered Malawi from Tanzania and Zambia, causing Malawi prices to drop and lowering construction costs. The local Malawi producers complained to the Ministry of Industry, Trade, and Tourism. They complained that the foreign cement was undercutting them, and they lobbied for an import ban or import duty. The Ministry of Industry, Trade, and Tourism asked the Malawi Competition and Fair Trade Commission (CFTC) to open an investigation. Noting that this was a cross-border matter, the CFTC reached out to COMESA. COMESA investigated and found no below-cost pricing, just competitive pricing. The CFTC used these findings to sensitize and convince the Ministry of Industry, Trade, and Tourism and the local cement producers about the need and virtues of open markets. The argument included the fact that Malawi had a growing population and increasing urbanization. It needed to build more buildings and roads, and thus needed more cement. The imports were necessary to give the government, individuals, and businesses access to more, higher quality cement at lower prices. The effort was successful. No import ban or duty was imposed.

These stories highlight industries and problems of the highest order for serving the people and building inclusive growth in sub-Saharan Africa. Industries of highest importance, and thus critical for fighting monopoly and opening doors to competition, include financial services, especially mobile ones, transportation, and

---

[57] This is a recurrent problem, and the Tanzanian FCC deserves credit for its courage. Press reports show that the large cement producers are continually raising alarms about low-priced imported cement, and as the cement industry grows more concentrated through mergers, the producers' political power to obtain protection from competition is likely to increase.

communications and media, and necessary inputs into infrastructure such as cement. Problems that must be tackled include SOE's privileged power, vested interest lobbying of government for protection from competition, often done through trade associations, and officials corrupted by (or with) business. All of these problems are addressed in the stories we have told.

## VI. Overlapping Membership in Regional Communities

We have noted that deeper regional coordination and integration is sometimes a better answer to market problems than national enforcement. The countries in the set of eight examined in this chapter have overlapping memberships in regional communities. Their memberships in COMESA, SADC, and EAC are shown below, in Table 4.5. The promise of and obstacles to regionalize are presented in Chapter VI. Alone or together, these regional communities might help to solve some of the bigger problems.

TABLE 4.5

Overlapping Membership in Three Regional Communities

| COMESA | SADC | EAC |
|---|---|---|
| Eastern strip | Southern | Great Lakes |
| 21 members | 16 members | 6 members |
| Kenya, Mauritius, Malawi, Zambia, Zimbabwe | Botswana, Mauritius, Malawi, Namibia, Tanzania, Zambia, Zimbabwe | Kenya, Tanzania |

Thus, the overlaps of these eight countries are:

Mauritius, Malawi, Zambia, and Zimbabwe are members of COMESA and SADC. Kenya is a member of COMESA and EAC. Tanzania is a member of SADC and EAC. South Africa, not included in the eight because it is the subject of Chapter V, is a member of SADC.

## VII. Conclusion

The eastern and southern countries' competition authorities span a range of functionality, from very high to almost inert. Even the highest functioning competition authorities face severe challenges in terms of financial and human capital, corruption, political pressure to favor government cronies and vested interests, and sometimes war and brink of bankruptcy. Ironically, the sub-Saharan countries (West African as well) face the highest barriers anywhere in the world to unleashing competition and realizing opportunities to compete in open markets, and have the greatest need for open markets, yet they face the highest hurdles to eliminating the restraints. Therefore, in the south and east, those countries and their authorities that have done well have done admirably well.

The authorities face innumerable challenges. We mention six.

1. *Priorities and proportionality.* The competition authorities are called on to do many things; too many things. They must ration their time and efforts. They *must* deal with mergers that are notified to them and complaints that are made to them, because their laws require it. These two tasks can easily overwhelm the authorities' workload and absorb their time and budget—and yet it is too bad if they do. More than 95 percent of the transactions and conduct are probably benign. It is so important for the authorities to set priorities and to apportion time to the most serious restraints and tasks, such as cartel enforcement, exclusionary monopoly tactics, and other restraints and barriers (including by mergers) that persistently keep outsiders out and raise prices.

Some of the authorities are extremely under-resourced, and their countries are extremely poor and volatile. For the heads of these authorities the challenge is even much greater. If their authorities spend all of their scarce time on routine must-do matters—assessing a merger that is on its face unproblematic or a complaint that is a personal squabble—they are missing an opportunity. They are, in their country, the voice of defense of the market for the poorest and marginalized citizens. They are doing their job if they raise that voice loud and clear wherever it can do the most good for their people. Competition authority heads are doing just that.

2. *SOEs, trade associations, and government procurement.* These are three vital areas for enforcement, and several of the authorities are doing a commendable job in these areas. State-owned enterprises are a significant source of market distortions. While some nations exclude SOEs from their competition laws or tread lightly on them, others expressly include SOEs in their coverage, and increasingly the authorities are calling them to account when they can. Similarly, trade associations are a common source of restraints. A number of authorities have trade associations in their sights. The Namibia action against the lawyers' association is one good example. The Kenyan amnesty program targeted at financial services and agricultural trade associations, and focused on educating these stakeholders in early days of enforcement, is another.

Government procurement represents a huge portion of the countries' budgets and affects the costs of vital necessities such as roads, schools, and children's meals. Procurement violations—bid rigging and complicit officials—lie at the intersection of antitrust and corruption. Botswana's observing and correcting deviations from the tender process is a good example of meaningful advocacy.

3. *Analysis: authorization of agreements.* The African competition agencies are developing their own brand of analysis. Parties seek authorization of an agreement (often called an exemption) presumably because they believe that the agreement

may distort competition (a broad, vague term), and the agency grants authorization, more often than not, on the basis of mixed economic and public interest grounds, intertwined. Here is the problem: in the usual case, it is not clear if the agreement is anticompetitive, for example, if, in the assessment of the agency, it increases market power, is not innovative, and harms the market and consumers. It is not clear how and how much the agreement helps the public interest and whether an anticompetitive agreement that hurts consumers is necessary to protect the public interest. Unbundling the issues would be useful and would be an immense aid to clarity and predictability.

4. *Merger control.* Mergers span a large range. Probably fewer than 3 percent are anticompetitive. Because review of mergers that meet the threshold is mandatory in most of the countries, merger review tends to take a disproportionate part of the agencies' time. Moreover, if the merger is large and is likely to create redundancy of workers, or is a value-chain merger and is likely to squeeze small suppliers, the agencies are likely to clear the merger with public interest conditions; no layoffs for two years has become almost boilerplate.

Downsizing staff might be one of the efficiencies of the merger, so the no-layoff condition can be expensive, pitting consumers' interests against particular workers' interests. The trade-off might be worth it, particularly in economies with huge unemployment. But this is not necessarily so. Perhaps authorities can initiate pilot programs wherein parties whose mergers create substantial layoffs are allowed to do so but must set aside a fund equal to two years' salaries of the laid-off workers for retraining, job placement, and seeding entrepreneurial ventures. The program would have to be personalized to the employees' needs and potentialities. The merger parties would be tasked with design of the program, and outcomes would be monitored.[58]

Regarding megamerger control, the sub-Saharan national authorities are handicapped. Huge anticompetitive mergers are not uncommon. The world may be better off without them, but they are cleared by the Western authorities, who settle for spin-offs of assets. Often, the biggest harms fall on developing countries, which are pressed to devise second-best remedies. The remedies often consist of weak conditions to alleviate any competition problem and to protect workers and SMEs. A regional voice might be necessary to protect the interests of sub-Saharan Africa.

5. *Institutional arrangements may raise problems.* There are trade-offs between expediency and due process. The integrated agency system in which the same board authorizes investigations and prosecutions and also decides cases raises a conflict

---

[58] The South African Competition Tribunal often imposes obligations of retraining laid-off employees on merging parties.

of interest. It is helpful for authorities to be aware of conflict situations and to take steps to minimize them, so that all people called before the institutions go away feeling that they had a fair shot.

There are other institutional challenges. In general, the authorities are living under conditions of scarcity. Their budgets are too low. Their staffs are too small. Their expert talent pools are too small. Their investigative tools are too weak, and the authorized penalties are either too low or conditions conspire against their imposition and enforcement. Everything cannot be cured at once; consciousness of the problems and the will to address them is the first step.

6. *Many restraints cross borders.* The actors are multinational, and predictably they have cross-border strategies. The supranational level of strategies conceals restraints, such as divvying up national markets. Only by deep collaboration of the national authorities with their neighbor authorities, transborder market research,[59] and eventually regional enforcement that combines the tools of internal market trade-and-competition can the authorities be in a position to identify and conquer some of the biggest market obstructions.

Through all of these challenges, a light shines. So many heads of the national competition systems follow their star to identify the most harmful market obstructions, to develop strategies to attack them, and to support the entrepreneurs who are trying to leap-frog over them. These dedicated leaders value inclusiveness and the need to develop sound substantive principles against harmful exclusionary restraints. The agencies they lead are deepening their cooperative relations with one another, increasing coherence of their laws and policies, building community, and gaining a view from the top.

---

[59] Significant cross-border research is needed and in process. Cross-border research is notably led by CCRED of the University of Johannesburg. Their work includes research in partnership with the University of Witwatersrand.

# 5

## SOUTH AFRICA

### Leaning in Toward Inclusive Development

## I. Introduction

South Africa, still recovering from the dark years of apartheid and still in need of laws and policies to integrate the cruelly excluded majority, has the most sophisticated system of competition law and policy in sub-Saharan Africa. It has a mission to expand economic opportunity and facilitate inclusive development. It is working on this mission in the form of proposed amendments to its competition law as this book goes to press. Despite South Africa's tribulations, its competition system has matured into one of the most outstanding and even pathbreaking in the developing world.

South Africa is a middle-income country with important industry especially deriving from diamond, gold, and other mineral wealth. It has a huge population below the poverty line. The Gini co-efficient is 0.68, making it one of the most unequal societies in the world. South Africa is a country of enormous energy and talent but extensive corruption and crime, and huge governance challenges. It is still fighting to eradicate the vestiges of apartheid, introduced by the Afrikaner government in 1913 with passage of the Natives Land Act and continued and expanded under British colonialism. In 1991, the apartheid laws were rescinded through a negotiated settlement between the state and the African National Congress (ANC), led by Nelson Mandela. The first multiracial democratic elections were held in 1994, when the people overwhelmingly endorsed

Making Markets Work for Africa. Eleanor M. Fox and Mor Bakhoum.
© Oxford University Press 2019. Published 2019 by Oxford University Press.

the ANC and Mandela became president. The country began reconciliation under Mandela's extraordinary leadership. But corrupt government asserted itself, especially during the presidency of Jacob Zuma, who finally resigned under pressure in 2018.

Virtually all of the New South Africa's laws require officials to take into account the historically disadvantaged people—those excluded by apartheid. Competition law is no exception.[1] Even now, the country despairs at the slow progress in spreading economic ownership and opportunity fairly.

In the wake of the UN Millennium and Post-Millennium Development Goals,[2] there is a new world consciousness of the need to combat deep systemic poverty and to reverse the tide of increasing inequality of wealth, income, and opportunity, the need to counter a Holy Grail of (short-term) efficiency that entrenches insiders with a model for more equitable, inclusive development.[3] If there is any nation in the world whose competition law mandates integration of equity and efficiency, it is South Africa, and its competition officials and policy people are intent to address this need.

In this chapter we first review the political and social context of South Africa, including the history, adoption, and implementation of the South African competition law. Second, we sketch the Competition Act, its structure and prohibitions. Third, we highlight selected cases to illustrate the law and its implementation, including the effort by the Competition Tribunal to give serious regard to the equality and inclusiveness values that animated the statute. Finally, we describe the amendments of 2018 and identify choices that the South African competition law presents.

## II. History and Context: Before South Africa's Modern Competition Law

In the years of apartheid (1948–1994), the economy of South Africa was controlled by a few diversified conglomerates doing business in mining, finance, and industry. The conglomerates were largely owned by a few very wealthy white families—for example, the Oppenheimers (who owned De Beers and Anglo American Corporation), producing gold, diamonds, and other minerals, and the Ruperts (who owned the Rembrandt Group), offering finance services and producing tobacco and luxury goods. The network of interrelations of the families that "owned" South Africa is strikingly documented in *McGregor's Who Owns Whom*.[4] Most of the strategic industries, including steel, oil, and telecoms, were run by state-owned enterprise.

---

[1] *See*, for the scope of the black empowerment program, Broad-Based Black Economic Empowerment Act 53 of 2003 (So. Africa), *amended by* Broad-Based Black Economic Empowerment Amendment Act 46 of 2013. *See also* Department of Trade and Industry, Broad-Based Black Economic Empowerment Strategy (2003).

[2] U.N. GAOR, *Millennium Development Goals Report* (2015). *See infra* note 81.

[3] *See, e.g.*, Christine Lagarde, Managing Dir., IMF, *Lift Growth Today, Tomorrow, Together* (Apr. 9, 2015).

[4] *See* Robin McGregor, McGregor's Who Owns Whom (1986).

Against the background of a high concentration of industry and a high degree of state involvement, the first competition statute—Regulation of Monopolistic Conditions Act—was adopted in 1955. This act had no teeth. It did not prohibit anticompetitive conduct. It did not cover mergers. It was administered by the Board of Trade, which had virtually no powers. At most, the minister could proclaim that certain conduct was criminally prohibited, which he did only in respect of resale price maintenance.[5]

The 1955 Act was replaced by the Maintenance and Promotion of Competition Act of 1979, which established the Competition Board and for the first time created merger control. Hard core cartels (price-fixing, market division) were specified as a violation of the act in 1986. Merger reviews were secretive and mergers were invariably approved[6]— until apartheid ended. Then began a new era of independence,[7] and eventually the 1979 Act was replaced by the Competition Act of 1998—a modern competition law.[8]

But let us go back to the mid-1980s. The protest against apartheid finally produced the world campaign for divestment from and boycott of South Africa. The campaign mushroomed and reputedly played a large role in the downfall of apartheid.[9] As an unintended consequence, the big businesses of South Africa were insulated from competition from abroad and grew into yet stronger monopolies.

On February 11, 1990, Nelson Mandela was released from prison. In 1994, the first free elections were held. The African National Congress won the elections, and its candidate Mandela became president. Transformation of business was essential; but how to do it? When Mandela was released from prison, he expressed his view that South Africa's big businesses had to be nationalized. He said:

> The nationalization of the mines, banks and monopoly industries is the policy of the A.N.C. [African National Congress], and a change or modification of our views in this regard is inconceivable.

But change they did. In 1992 Mandela went to the World Economic Forum in Davos. He had conversations with world leaders, including Communist Party leaders from China and Vietnam, and, the story is told,[10] they persuaded him to change his

---

[5] *See* DAVID LEWIS, THIEVES AT THE DINNER TABLE 18 (2012).

[6] *Id.* at 21–22.

[7] *Id.* at 25.

[8] Maintenance and Promotion of Competition Act of 1979 (So. Africa), *repealed by* Competition Act of 1998 (So. Africa).

[9] Lindiwe Mabuza, *The War on Apartheid Is Far from Over*, N.Y. TIMES, June 20, 1990.

[10] Andrew R. Sorkin, *How Mandela Shifted Views on Freedom of Markets*, N.Y. TIMES, Dec. 9, 2013.
   The collapse of the Soviet Union also reportedly influenced Mandela's views.

mindset. If South Africa wanted investment, if it wanted to be economically integrated into the commerce of the world, it had to embrace markets. Returning to South Africa, Mandela had to persuade the ANC. Despite significant opposition, Mandela's views prevailed.

The rejection of nationalization did not answer the question of how to control economic power and transform ownership. Might the answer be antitrust, with a breakup of the large monopolies and large conglomerates, putting the pieces into the hands of a new black business class? This route was seriously contemplated. But it did not happen. When the new competition bill was drafted, it was (as was usual for legislation) negotiated in NEDLAC—the National Economic Development and Labour Council, comprising business, government, and labor. The process involved, first, the drafting of a policy document. The policy document identified as the framework the alignment of the twin goals of competitiveness and development. Guidelines assured the public that " 'on the one hand competitiveness and efficiency are pursued, and on the other that this process will ensure access to many more people previously denied an equal opportunity to participate in the economy.' "[11] These aims, including the public interest in safeguarding jobs, promoting black empowerment, and facilitating the growth of small and medium-size business, became the backbone goals and framework of the new competition law.

## III. The Competition Act of 1998

The South African Competition Act was adopted in 1998.[12] The preamble recalls the history of apartheid and the aspirations of the people for a fair society.

### PREAMBLE

The people of South Africa recognise:

That apartheid and other discriminatory laws and practices of the past resulted in excessive concentrations of ownership and control within the national economy, weak enforcement of anti-competitive trade practices. and unjust restrictions on full and free participation in the economy by all South Africans. That the economy must be open to greater ownership by a greater number of South Africans.

---

[11] Department of Trade and Industry, Proposed Guidelines for Competition Policy para. 2 (1997) (So. Africa).

[12] Competition Act, act no. 89 of 1998.

That credible competition law, and effective structures to administer that law. are necessary for an efficient functioning economy. That an efficient, competitive economic environment, balancing the interests of workers, owners and consumers and focused on development, will benefit all South Africans

**IN ORDER TO—**

provide all South Africans equal opportunity to participate fairly in the national economy;
achieve a more effective and efficient economy in South Africa;
provide for markets in which consumers have access to, and can freely select, the quality and variety of goods and services they desire;
create greater capability and an environment for South Africans to compete effectively in international markets;
restrain particular trade practices which undermine a competitive economy;
. . . BE IT ENACTED . . . ."

The preamble thus presents a vision for a marriage of equity and efficiency. Was this a plausible scenario or an impossible dream?

The goals of an effective, efficient, and inclusive economy are repeated in Section 2: Purpose of the Act, which underscores the goals of promoting "efficiency, adaptability and development of the economy," ensuring that "small and middle sized enterprises have an equitable opportunity to participate in the economy," and promoting "a greater spread of ownership, in particular to . . . historically disadvantaged persons."

The act then enumerates prohibitions. We lay out the principal ones below, laying the framework for describing certain key cases, assessing how well the jurisprudence meets its ambitions, and suggesting a better alignment of the goals and the law.

## A. THE COMPETITION ACT

### 1. Sections against Anticompetitive Agreements

Sections 4 and 5 prohibit agreements and decisions that constitute restrictive practices. Hard core cartels[13] and minimum resale price maintenance[14] are

---

[13] Hard core cartels are agreements among competitors to refrain from competing on a term of trade such as price.
[14] Agreements for resale price maintenance are vertical agreements between a supplier and its distributors. They set the price—usually the minimum price—at which the product can be resold.

prohibited per se. Other agreements are prohibited if they have the effect of substantially preventing or lessening competition, unless a party to the agreement or decision can prove outweighing advantages through technology, efficiency, or pro-competitive gains.

Under Section 12, the Commission may grant an exemption for agreements that are in the public interest. These are agreements that promote exports and promote the ability of small businesses or those controlled by historically disadvantaged persons to become competitive, change productive capacity necessary to stop decline in an industry, or promote economic stability of an industry designated by the minister.

## 2. Sections against Abuse of Dominance

Sections 7 and 8 define dominance and prohibit abuse of a dominant position. A firm is defined as dominant if it has at least 45 percent of a market. If the firm has 35 percent to 45 percent of the market, the firm must show that it does not have market power. Even if the firm has less than 35 percent, the firm may be proved dominant if it has market power.

The conduct prohibitions are listed in Section 8. Dominant firms are prohibited to charge an excessive price to the detriment of consumers and to refuse to give a competitor access to an essential facility when it is economically feasible to do so. Dominant firms are prohibited also from doing a set of acts catalogued in Section 8(d) unless the firm can show outweighing technological, efficiency, or other pro-consumer gains. These acts are prohibited unless the firm proves outweighing advantages. The enumerated acts are:

(i) requiring or inducing a supplier or customer not to deal with a competitor,
(ii) refusing to supply scarce goods to a competitor when it is economically feasible to do so,
(iii) selling goods or services on condition that the buyer purchases separate goods or services unrelated to the object of a contract, or forcing a buyer to accept a condition unrelated to the object of a contract,
(iv) selling below marginal or average variable cost, or
(v) buying up a scarce supply of intermediate goods.

Other exclusionary acts are prohibited under Section 8(c) if the plaintiff can prove that the anticompetitive effect outweighs the technological, efficiency, or other pro-competitive gain.

For the acts singled out for condemnation in Section 8(d), the Competition Tribunal is empowered to impose high penalties, but for the "catch-all" 8(c) violations, fines are not authorized except for repeat violations.[15]

---

[15] Competition Act § 61(1).

In the case of hard core violations such as price-fixing, a leniency program induces whistle-blowers to come forward and tell all. Whistle-blowers who give the agency sufficient information to prosecute may be immunized from penalties.[16]

### 3. Price Discrimination

Section 9 prohibits price discrimination by a dominant firm if it is likely to have the effect of substantially preventing or lessening competition, unless the price discrimination is cost-justified or in response to changing market conditions.

### 4. Mergers

Section 12(a) prohibits mergers likely to substantially prevent or lessen competition unless outweighed by technological, efficiency, or other pro-competitive gain or justified on certain public interest grounds. For public interest, the Commission or Tribunal must consider the merger's effect on: a particular industrial sector or region, employment, ability of small businesses or firms controlled by historically disadvantaged persons to become competitive, and ability of national industries to compete internationally. Uniquely, the Competition Act provides that a merger may be prohibited or conditioned on public interest grounds alone whether or not it is anticompetitive.

### 5. Institutional Structure

South Africa has three institutions of enforcement and adjudication. They are: (1) the Competition Commission, which is headed by a Commissioner; (2) the Tribunal, a quasi-adjudicative body that holds hearings and decides cases—its members may be lawyers, economists, and others; and (3) the courts. The Court of Appeal has a dedicated panel for antitrust appeals. Where a constitutional issue is raised, the Constitutional Court may decide the case. The Commission investigates, does research, including market studies, brings cases before the Tribunal, and determines small merger cases. It brings large merger cases to the Tribunal with its recommendations. The Commission is administratively accountable to the Economic Development Department, currently led by Minister Ebrahim Patel. The office of Commissioner is currently held by Tembinkosi Bonakele. For its first 10 years, the Competition Tribunal was presided over by David Lewis. Lewis was succeeded by Norman Manoim. In the Court of Appeal, the chief judge of the

---

[16] *See* COMPETITION COMMISSION, CORPORATE LENIENCY POLICY § 3.1 (2004), http://www.gov.za/sites/www.gov.za/files/25963u.pdf.

competition panel is Dennis Davis, a competition law expert, who has held this position from the start of the enforcement of the 1998 Act. The Court of Appeal has powers of de novo review. It has often overturned the Tribunal's rulings.

The language of the act leaves a good deal of space for interpretation. While the Preface and Purpose sections of the act express the aim to bring the historically suppressed majority of the population into the economic mainstream and to open a path for small and middle-size enterprise, the prohibitory sections do not expressly incorporate the Preface or Purpose. A technocratic rather than teleological Court of Appeal has not read the purposes into the text of the prohibitions. Moreover, the different treatment specified for Section 8(c) and Section 8(d) offenses has created confusion. Section 8(d) is meant to identify particularly bad offenses, accordingly calling on the firms to explain and justify, but as litigation has revealed, the list is both overinclusive and underinclusive.[17]

Institutionally, the Commission is under the line of authority of the minister of economic development. The minister determines the budget for the Commission and approves the strategic plans of the Commission. The minister is concerned with industrial policy, including the plight of workers and small business. In the case of mergers, the minister may advocate for jobs (no retrenchments) (as do the unions), for small business, and for the development of black industrialists.

With this structure and framework in mind, we turn to selected competition jurisprudence of South Africa.

## IV. Selected Case Law

### A. INTRODUCTION

In this section we treat cases decided by the Tribunal and in some instances by the Court of Appeal. The cases span a range of substantive issues. Some of the Tribunal decisions have been reversed by the Court of Appeal.

In the South African Constitutional Court, advocates are encouraged to cite international authorities for guidance. If a US precedent is invoked and the US Justices have split, counsel in African courts may cite the dissenting opinion with as much authority as they cite the majority opinion.[18] Why? Presumably, both opinions are well thought out and rigorously argued, and the disagreement turns on policy perspective. One perspective or the other might be a better fit for South Africa, and

---

[17] In the case of mixed conduct, falling into both §8(c) and (d), the Court has lumped the clear offenses with the catch-all offenses and thereby raised the bar of proof and remedies to the 8(c) level. For difficulties caused by the textual dichotomy, *see* Ministry Background Note on Competition Amendment Bill, 2017 (Dec. 1, 2017).

[18] *See, e.g.*, State v. Makwanyane, 1995 (3) SA 391 (CC).

it is not necessarily that of the US majority opinion. We present certain reversed Tribunal cases in this spirit. The Tribunal may have made the more compelling case, giving regard to "inclusiveness" or making the law more manageable and thus more effective. Or the Court of Appeal may have made the more compelling case based on the technical language of the prohibitory section.[19]

South Africa's unique apartheid history might be considered a reason for African neighbors to discount South African law as a model for them. But the contrary is the case. The exclusionary element of apartheid produced the South African Competition Act. The South African competition institutions may have had greater incentives than others to invent the wheel of efficiency-with-equity.[20] The basic problem of deep systemic poverty without mobility in an economy dominated by a few privileged players resonates across sub-Saharan Africa.

## B. SELECTED CASES

Here are selected cases highlighting the competition problems and the legal principles. We begin with cartels and the *Pioneer* (bread) case. Second, we continue with market definition in the context of two mergers, *JD/Ellerines* and *Prime Cure*. Third, we address agreements involving standards set by the industry (*Netstar*). Fourth, we address abuse of dominance: (1) what is dominance; (2) excessive pricing—*Mittal* and *Sasol*; and (3) exclusionary acts—loyalty rebates (*South African Airways*) and price discrimination (*Nationwide Poles*). Fifth, we address mergers—public interest (*Wal-Mart/Massmart*).

## 1. *Pioneer*—The Bread Cartel

Cartels in basic, staple products that the poorest people need to stay alive are rightly and obviously a major priority of competition authorities, especially in developing countries. Breaking up the cartels can literally be a matter of life and death. And in a society with little antitrust consciousness, publicity that cartels are being caught and punished can be a major steppingstone toward developing a competition culture, people that demand their rights, and compliance.

---

[19] Of course there are other reasons for reversal, such as insufficient evidence to support a conclusion. Claimed errors of this kind have not been the principal reason for the reversals.

[20] Namibia shared the apartheid history. *See* Mihe Gaomab II, CEO of the Namibian Competition Commission, *Competition Commission can assist in reducing income inequality*, http://www.nacc.com.na/cms_documents/ b76_commission_can_reduce_income_in equality.pdf.

The catching of the bread cartel was such an event in South Africa. As told by David Lewis in his book, *Thieves at the Dinner Table*:[21] "The uncovering of the bread cartel was an early product of the Commission's corporate leniency programme." Premier Foods, one of the leading baking/milling companies, applied for and got leniency from the Commission—meaning that, if it exposed a cartel and faithfully assisted its prosecution (which it did), Premier Foods would receive immunity from punishment. In view of Premier's revelations, co-conspirators Tiger Brands and Foodcorp confessed to their price-fixing conspiracy, agreed to administrative fines, and agreed to set up compliance programs.[22]

Representatives of the South African Human Rights Commission appeared at the hearings before the Tribunal for approval of the settlements. They argued that basic food cartels not only violated the competition law but also violated the South African Bill of Rights. They testified: "When placing illegal corporate activities within their complete social context, anticompetitive practices become thieves at the dinner table."[23] Thus, the title of David Lewis' gripping book on the birth and evolution of the South African Competition Act.

Pioneer, however, held out. It did not settle. It denied its involvement. It was tried and held liable. The Tribunal decision in the *Pioneer* case reveals the inner workings of the cartels. Premier, Tiger Brands, Foodcorp, and Pioneer together held 50 percent to 60 percent of the bread milling and production market. They conspired for four years to inflate the price of bread, meeting at offices, pubs, and a game reserve, and sharing information on the extent and timing of their planned price increases and the limits on the discounts they would give to the big supermarkets.[24] At the remedy stage of the litigation, unmoved by Pioneer's request for leniency and indeed finding that Pioneer's witness lied at the hearing, the Tribunal imposed a fine of nearly 200 million rands (approximately US$15.5 million) for the cartels.[25] The Commission designed creative relief. Pioneer would invest 150 million rands (approximately US$12.7 million) in additional baking capacity.[26]

---

[21] LEWIS, *supra* note 5, at 205. For the right to food as a human right, *see* Tristan Feunteun, *Cartels and the Right to Food: An Analysis of States' Duties and Options*, 18 J.I.E.L. 341 (2015); and Smita Narula, *The Right to Food: Holding Global Actors Accountable under International Law*, 44 COLUM. J. TRANSNAT'L L. 691 (2006).

[22] *See* Press release, Competition Commission, Tiger Brands admits to participation in bread and milling cartels and settles with Competition Commission (Nov. 12, 2007), http://www.compcom.co.za/2007-media-releases; Press release, Competition Commission, Competition Commission settles with Foodcorp. (Jan. 5, 2009), http://www.compcom.co.za/assets/Uploads/AttachedFiles/MyDocuments/5-Jan-09-CC-Settles-with-Foodcorp.pdf.

[23] LEWIS, *supra* note 5, at 207.

[24] *See* Competition Commission v. Pioneer Foods Ltd., 15/CR/Feb 07, 50/CR/May08 [2010] ZACT 9, paras. 47, 106 (Feb. 3, 2010).

[25] *Id.* at para. 175.

[26] Consent and Settlement Agreement between the Competition Commission and Pioneer Foods, Ltd. (15/CR/Mar10) (Nov. 2010). *See* Tembinkosi Bonakele & Liberty Mncube, *Designing Appropriate Remedies for Competition Law Enforcement*, 8 J. COMP. L. & ECON. 425 (2012).

The case and its outcome were widely publicized in the press. The *Pioneer* case[27] is an important marker in building a competition culture in South Africa.

## 2. Relevant Market

Cartels are per se violations of the competition law, and thus there is no need to define the relevant market in cartel cases. The agreement is the offense.

In the case of alleged offenses that are not per se illegal, the plaintiff must normally define the relevant market. Market definition is a lawyers' instrument to isolate the area of affected competition and then to gauge the effect therein. The market must include all products whose prices provide good constraints on the price of the product sold by the merging parties (or of a firm challenged for abusing dominance). Drawing boundaries around an area and calling it a market does not change the dynamic of competition, but still, market definition is often the key to the resolution of an antitrust case. If, for example, there are major areas in which the businesses of the merger partners overlap, drawing the market narrowly around the area of overlap may lead to a conclusion that the merging firms have very high market shares and that there is high and increasing concentration. Conversely, drawing it widely to include many other players will dilute the attributed market share and may make the merger seem insignificant. Similarly for monopoly cases: Are smart phones and tablets in the same market as Microsoft's PC operating system, or is the PC operating system the market? Are banks including checking account services in the same market as mobile money transfer systems such as M-Pesa, or is there a mobile money transfer market in Kenya (featuring Safaricom)?

In many cases there is a dispute among the economists (and the parties who retain them) as to the boundaries of the market. Typically, competition authorities want to know: What firms and products are effective constraints on the prices of the merging firms that will prevent consumer prices from rising? All firms that are effective constraints should be included in the market. The South African Competition Tribunal has refined the question. It asks: What firms provide an effective constraint on prices *to the poorest consumers*? This inquiry could narrow the market and provide more protection for the poorer people.

The Tribunal's approach can be illustrated by two cases, *JD Group/Ellerines* and *Prime Cure*. In *JD/Ellerines*,[28] two of South Africa's best-known department stores proposed

---

The Constitutional Court later upheld the right of the overcharged bread distributors to bring a class action. *See* Children's Resource Centre Trust v. Pioneer Food Ltd., (50/2012) [2012] ZASCA 182 (2012) (Supreme Court of Appeal permits class certification). *See also* Mukaddam v. Pioneer Foods Ltd., 2013 (5) SA 89 (CC) (Constitutional Court confirms SCA judgment in *Children's Resource*).

[27] 15/CR/Feb 07, 50/CR/May08 [2010] ZACT 9.

[28] *JD Group Ltd. and Ellerine Holdings Ltd.*, 78/LM/Jul00 [2000] ZACT 35 (2000).

to merge. They both sold their goods to low-income customers. One of the merger partners, the JD Group, also had upscale stores. Under apartheid, credit was denied to black South Africans. Because no credit was available, masses of people were not able to buy furniture or appliances because they did not have the cash to pay the price. Ellerines pioneered a marketing approach that offered generous credit to "some of South Africa's poorest consumers, many of whom do not even have access to a bank account."[29]

In discussing whether the market was limited to credit purchases of furniture and appliances or whether it also included more upscale buyers and sellers, the Tribunal said:

> In this case . . . the parties to the transaction are the final link with the consumers, and, at that, the poorest, least powerful of South African consumers. In other words, the interests directly affected by this merger are represented by millions of atomized, disorganized individuals incapable of defending their economic interests except to the extent that they are able to exercise a preference for one retail outlet over another. This evaluation will seek to assess whether the transaction has the potential to increase the power of the parties over the consumers that they serve and who are the source of their prosperity.

Rejecting defendants' argument that the market included higher-end stores, the Tribunal said:

> The distinction [based on Living Standard categories] informs advertising strategy in very subtle ways as an amusing example alluded to during our proceedings shows. Ellerines in the LSM [Living Standard Measure] 3–5 market offer a free sheep worth R300 if goods above a specified amount are purchased. A graphic of a sheep is depicted in the advert. Bradlow's, the high end JD brand, also offers a free gift for customers purchasing above a specific amount. The gift, however, underlines the difference in social status of the LSM categories—Bradlow's offers not a free sheep, but a coffee table book on 101 ways to cook lamb!

The Tribunal found that the relevant market was the sale of furniture and appliances on credit to consumers in a low-end LSM category through national chains of furniture shops. The Tribunal enjoined the merger.

The second case involved the merger of two of three firms that offered capitated health care insurance coverage, Medicross and Prime Cure.[30] Capitated coverage

---

[29] *Id.* at 2.
[30] Medicross Healthcare Group Ltd. v. Competition Comm'n, 11/LM/Mar05 (2005), *rev'd*, 55/CAC/Sept05 [2006] ZACAC 3 (2006).

was an embryonic form of managed care. Millions of poor South Africans were not covered by medical insurance because they could not afford it. According to the Tribunal, significant coverage of the poorer population was not going to happen without the development of the capitated insurance product. The capitated product was in early stages of development when Medicross and Prime Cure decided to merge. The Tribunal found a market in the capitated insurance product for low-income persons. It concluded that the merger would stamp out in its infancy the innovation incentives to develop this promising option that could bring large numbers of the uninsured poor into the realm of insured health care.[31] The Tribunal said: "We have little doubt that a significant merger in this embryonic market will slow the pace of innovation, it will reduce the number of alternative modes of provision on offer, and it will likely slow the pace at which new forms and concepts of low-income healthcare insurance are introduced."[32] The Tribunal prohibited the merger.

The Court of Appeal reversed the Tribunal, rejecting a capitation market. It faulted the Tribunal for failure to introduce traditional evidence such as customer substitution tests. It concluded that the market must include primary managed health care products for low-cost medical plan options.[33] From the vantage of this larger market, it appeared as though the merger deprived the market of nothing of value, because concentration figures changed very little.

The Chair of the Tribunal, David Lewis, later explained: "We were dealing with a new product for which price data and evidence of consumer substitution were not available. [Evidence] was not going to come from the application of a simple arithmetic formula."[34]

### 3. Agreements—Horizontal and Vertical—Standard Setting

Typically, and in South Africa, agreements among competitors and among buyers and suppliers are illegal if they are anticompetitive and if the anticompetitive effects are not outweighed by pro-competitive, technological, or efficiency aspects, except for cartels, which are normally illegal per se or at least viewed through a very hostile lens. It is not always easy to determine whether agreements other than cartels are anticompetitive because they may have some pro-competitive effects. Assessment of effects may be greatly aided by information about intent or purpose, which can put flesh on the bones of what the firms were trying to do. (Were they trying to exclude rivals or exploit customers? Or were they just responding to the market?)

---

[31] *Medicross*, 11/LM/Mar05 at para. 203 (2005).

[32] Competition Comm'n v. Medicross Healthcare Group Ltd., 11/LM/Mar05, para. 194 (2005).

[33] *Medicross Healthcare Group Ltd.*, 55/CAC/Sept05 [2006] ZACAC 3, para. 39 (2006).

[34] LEWIS, *supra* note 5, at 110.

Some of the most harmful restraints have been erected under the aegis of a trade association, where competitors come together and talk to one another about their industry. The trade association easily and frequently becomes a forum for the competitors to fix prices, divide markets, and raise barriers to outsider entry.

Trade associations also serve neutral and good purposes. Setting standards or best practices, such as to make safe products, may be important to society and not harmful to competition. Still, competition law enforcers are appropriately on the lookout for excessively high standards that do more to keep entrants out of the market than to keep products safe. As the US Supreme Court observed even for standards set by well-meaning rivals:

> [E]stablished ethical standards may blend with private anticompetitive motives in a way difficult even for the market participants to discern.... [A]ctive market participants cannot be allowed to regulate their own markets free from antitrust accountability.[35]

In South Africa in the early 1990s, in the wake of unprecedented and escalating car thefts, a new technology was developed—the tracking and return of stolen vehicles (SVR, or Stolen Vehicle Recovery). Netstar emerged as the leader in the market, with Matrix as number two and Tracker further behind. The big three occupied more than 90 percent of the market.

The car insurance industry (SAIA, or South African Insurance Association) decided it wanted standards; it wanted to accredit trustworthy SVR systems and provide discounts on the basis of compliant standards. SAIA invited the established SVR firms to join a subcommittee of the private standard-setting association, VESA (Vehicle Security Association of South Africa). The firms accepted the invitation. Netstar wrote a memorandum, copying Matrix and Tracker, proposing the following standards (which the big three already met) for accreditation by the insurance industry:

- The supplier must have been in business for a year.
- Its system must have been fitted in 3,000 vehicles.
- The supplier must have recovered 100 vehicles.

The insurance discount was sufficiently large to make the products of nonaccredited firms unattractive to car buyers. The SVR subcommittee of VESA recommended Netstar's proposed standards, and VESA adopted them.

---

[35] No. Carolina State Bd. of Dental Examiners v. FTC, 574 U.S. ___, 135 S. Ct. 1101, 1111 (2015).

Tracetec was a hopeful entrant into the SVR market. It complained to the Commission. It could not get into the market without meeting the standards, and it could not meet the standards without getting into the market. It impugned the standards as out of proportion to assuring reliability, and claimed they were barriers to entry constructed by the dominant SVR firms to shield themselves from competition. The Competition Commission referred the case to the Tribunal, and Tracetec brought its own case as well.

The Tribunal largely accepted Tracetec's allegations. It found an agreement or concert of the big three SVRs to set unnecessarily demanding standards, raising barriers, preventing newcomers from entering and expanding in the market, and denying consumers lower price, choice, and the benefits of innovation.[36]

The Court of Appeal reversed. It found insufficient evidence of agreement or concert among the car insurers. It stressed the importance of standards to protect against fly-by-night firms that might enter the business but never recover stolen vehicles, and it ignored the effect of the standards in effectively preventing entry. It found that Tracetec's failure to succeed was attributable to its inferior product, not to the standards, that the plaintiff had not carried its burden to prove that the standards were exclusionary, and that for both of these reasons it was unnecessary to examine the excessiveness of the standards. It dismissed the case.

These two perspectives present choices, which we discuss in Section V below.

## 4. Abuse of Dominance

Abuse of dominance violations normally falls into two categories, exploitative abuses and exclusionary abuses. An exploitatively high price is not a competition law violation in some jurisdictions, such as the United States, which has the luxury of not worrying about prices that are too high. It is said, usually with some merit in the United States: the market will take care of the problem. Excessive pricing is a violation in the European Union and most other competition jurisdictions.

The second category is exclusionary abuses by dominant firms. The dominant firm engages in strategies that put roadblocks in the way of the entry and expansion of rivals, often in response to competitive threats. All competition jurisdictions prohibit anticompetitive exclusionary practices, but they differ in what it takes to be anticompetitive. Some jurisdictions such as the United States define "anticompetitive" very narrowly. Defendants usually have efficiency stories to tell about their practices that may squeeze smaller firms, and US courts are usually sympathetic to these stories.

---

[36] The Tribunal noted also that the big three firms sought and got special exemptions for their own new offerings. *See* Competition Comm'n and Tracetec Ltd. v. Netstar, Martrix, Tracker and VESA, 17/CR/Maro5 (2010).

Both categories—exploitative and exclusionary—have particular salience for developing countries. Abuses in these categories hold the real possibility of harming poorer consumers, of marginalizing smaller business and outsiders, and of undermining inclusive development by clogging the channels for advancement by people and firms on their merits.

We have noted earlier that some violations are so complex to prove under standards of developed countries that the violation can almost never be proved, at least not without a team of experts dedicated to the case for years. The Tribunal has implicitly identified two missions of the Tribunal: to make cases triable by simpler rules where simple rules are reasonably good proxies, and to develop jurisprudence that facilitates access by outsiders.

### a. Proving a Dominant Position

A dominant position is usually defined as a position of economic power such that the firm can profitably raise price significantly above its costs for a significant period of time. We have noted that the Competition Act defines dominance, instead, in terms of the firm's percentage of the market. "[A] firm is dominant in a market if... it has at least 45% of that market."[37] The consequence is that, for firms of 45% or more, the analyst moves immediately to the next stage, not pausing long on proof of "power," to determine whether the firm has engaged in a prohibited act. Is the equation of significant market share with dominance helpful or harmful?

The South African choice on assessment of dominance is more aggressive than that of the United States or the European Union. That is, South Africa makes this step in enforcement simpler for the enforcer.

One of the early projects of the International Competition Network—the virtual network of competition authorities that is the main international forum for convergence of law—was to articulate best practices in proving dominance. The strong and unyielding view of the competition authorities of the West was: high market share does not prove dominance. It should not be taken to do so even as a matter of convenience and practicality, for even a firm with a very large share of the market may be constrained by forces of competition. Conflating dominance with high market share—the argument goes—will chill the incentives of firms to win a high share by good works.

The issue of how to prove dominance arose in the International Competition Network. David Lewis, Chair of the South African Competition Tribunal, argued for flexibility. He urged his colleagues from other nations to recognize the fact that some nations such as South Africa have statutes that define dominance by market

---

[37] Competition Act § 7.

share, and he argued that attempts to form best practices in the world should not discount countries' statutory law. He argued that developing countries may not have the luxury to engage in extensive and expensive debates of the experts on the preliminary point (in abuse of dominance cases) of market power. Skeletal facts are often sufficient for a first-level judgment, he argued, and the authorities can then concentrate on the main point of the case: assessing the nature and effect of the conduct. South Africa lost the debate on international standards for proof of dominance.[38] But still, the South African way is a choice that many nations have adopted.[39]

### b. Excessive Pricing

Excessive pricing is a prohibition fraught with contradictions.

Power over pricing is the hallmark of a monopolist. A monopoly firm has the power to raise its price significantly over a competitive price, and maintain it. That high price, which also means lower output, is what economists identify as the problem with monopoly. Namely, a monopoly price means too few resources flow into the market, causing allocative inefficiency.

Should competition law step in to condemn a monopoly price? This turns out to be a complicated issue. Firms' flexibility in pricing, higher and lower, is at the heart of the competition process and is a necessary element of a market system. We want firms to take risks; we do not want to punish them for taking risks and winning the race. If we tightly limit a firm's gains, firms will not invest in markets and ideas in the hope of making gains.

Intervention against high prices creates a host of other problems. How do we know when the price is "too high"? Too high compared with what? Compared with the firm's costs? Compared with a comparable benchmark in a competitive market? Can dominant firms' costs be confidently identified, rationally and in reasonable time, given the complexity of firms' books and accounting and their incentive not to make the discovery job easy for challengers? Further, if the competition authority

---

[38] *See* International Competition Network [ICN], Recommended Practices for Dominance/Substantial Market Power Analysis, ICN Doc. 317 (Apr. 14–16, 2008), http://www.internationalcompetitionnetwork.org/uploads/library/doc31 7.pdf; Eleanor M. Fox, *Linked-In: Antitrust and the Virtues of a Virtual Network*, 43 INT'L LAW. 151, 171 (2009).

[39] Dominance, where it exists, may be more durable in "developing countries and African countries, in particular[.] There are reasons why the durability of dominance is greater. Scale economies are more significant given the smaller size of markets; information is likely to be poorer; and the costs of building brand awareness, advertising, distribution, and marketing may be higher relative to sales. The first movers in many countries are likely to have gained their position either through state support and ownership (even if now privatised) or by being a subsidiary of a multinational corporation that established its footprint under colonial rule." Simon Roberts, Thando Vilakazi, & Witness Simbanegavi, *Competition, regional integration and inclusive growth in Africa*, Chapter 11, *in* COMPETITION LAW AND ECONOMIC REGULATION: ASSESSING MARKET POWER IN SOUTHERN AFRICA 263, 267 (J. Klaaren, S. Roberts, & I. Valodia eds., Wits 2017).

or courts declare a price excessive, is there an appropriate remedy that is not in itself market-distorting or too interventionist? Will the competition authority become a price regulator—without the skills or access to data of a regulatory agency? And in the aftermath of a price-lowering command, who will keep a watchful eye over the offender's prices to be sure that they do not again become excessive? How can a competition authority do all of these jobs?[40]

South Africa has had at least three important excessive pricing cases. The first was *Hazel Tau* and concerned excessive pricing of the cocktail of drugs (patented drugs) needed by individuals with HIV/AIDs in the midst of the horrific epidemic. It also concerned refusal of access to an allegedly essential facility. The price of the cocktail was more than twice above costs and was prohibitive to those who needed the drugs to save their lives. Neither the Tribunal nor the Court ever had the chance to hear the case and grapple with the legal questions and standards because, when required to open their books to reveal their costs, the pharmaceutical companies (GlaxoSmithKline and Boehringer International) settled. Upon settlement, prices fell some 50 percent to 68 percent.[41]

The other two cases are of more recent vintage. Mittal Steel is the corporate successor to state-owned ISCOR, which was the beneficiary of privilege and favors from the government over many years. ISCOR and then (and now) Mittal held nearly 100 percent of the South African steel market and was productively efficient. South Africa imported little steel from abroad because the alternative producers were far away and, since steel is heavy, transportation costs were high. For many years, Mittal charged the low world price in the international market and a much higher price in the domestic market (import parity pricing),[42] with the effect that all South African businesses that needed steel as an input were paying a monopoly premium and were forced to be less competitive in their export markets.

Harmony Gold, a big buyer of steel in South Africa, brought an excessive pricing charge. The case was heard by the Tribunal, which, after hearing voluminous and conflicting testimony, cut through the quagmire. It found: (1) Mittal was superdominant. (2) Its import parity pricing evidenced excessiveness, since it bore no reasonable relation to competitive pricing. (3) Mittal engaged in ancillary abusive conduct by prohibiting its distributors who bought the steel in South Africa

---

[40] These questions are debated in the international community, especially in relation to the huge hikes in the price of pharmaceuticals. The United Kingdom has imposed a high fine of £84.2 million on Pfizer (2016), and the European Union has ongoing investigations.

[41] Competition Commission, Settlement Agreement, Case No. 2002Sep226. *See* Roundtable on: Role of Competition in the Pharmaceutical Sector and its Benefits for Consumers (Submission by South Africa to UNCTAD competition branch) (July 2015).

[42] Mittal was able to command import parity plus a 5 percent freedom-from-hassle price.

(for export) from reselling it into the South African market (i.e., Mittal prevented arbitrage). (4) The circumstances presented an effective self-executing remedy: remove the contract term imposed by Mittal on its own buyer-distributors that limited them to export only. By opening the avenue for arbitrage, more steel would be sold on the South African market and the domestic price would fall. The Tribunal held that Mittal was liable for violating South Africa's competition law.[43]

Look again (above) at all of the pitfalls for banning excessive pricing. The Tribunal's decision avoided every one of them.[44] There was an available benchmark, and there was an available remedy that was virtually self-enforcing.

The Court of Appeal reversed the Tribunal decision and remanded the case. The Court stressed the words in the Competition Act defining "excessive" as "bearing no reasonable relationship to economic value," and held that the Tribunal could not avoid a detailed evaluation of economic and financial evidence in determining economic value. It said: "[E]conomic value is a notional objective competitive market standard, not one derived from circumstances peculiar to the particular firm."[45] Prices ordinarily charged in other markets by the same or cost-comparable firms may serve as a measure of economic value if the other markets are characterized by effective competition in the long run.[46] Other proxies could be used to make a prima facie case; but delving into cost evidence could not be avoided.[47]

Harmony Gold and Mittal settled the case before the remand could be heard—a secret settlement that surely benefited Harmony Gold but not the community or the market.

The next and more recent excessive pricing case is *Sasol*. Sasol, like Mittal, is the successor to a state-owned firm. It got where it was by state privilege and not good works. The products in point were purified propylene and polypropylene. Propylene and polypropylene are used to make hard plastics for a variety of household products such as pails and brooms. Feedstock propylene is a byproduct of Sasol's production of oil fuels from coal. The next best use of the byproduct—which is a factor in the production of fuel—has a very low value.

---

[43] Harmony Gold Mining Co. v. Mittal Steel Corp., 13/CR/FEB04 [2007] ZACT 21 (Mar. 27, 2007), *rev'd*, (70/CAC/Apr07) [2009] ZACAC 1 (29 May 2009). The Tribunal fined Mittal 5.5 percent of its annual turnover. Remedies Decision, 13/CR/Feb04 [2007] ZACT 71 (Sept. 6, 2007).

[44] Not only was there a self-executing remedy, but Mittal/ISCOR had grown to its nearly 100 percent size by acts of the state, not acts of good works. Thus there was no concern that a firm that had succeeded in the market was punished for its success. Moreover, the monopoly, as a practical matter, was incontestable in the foreseeable future.

[45] *Id.* at para. 43.

[46] *Id.* at para. 51.

[47] Mittal argued, among other things, that its low export price did not fully cover allocated costs.

Sasol was the only significant producer of purified propylene in South Africa. It sold feedstock propylene domestically at import parity prices, which was up to 23 percent higher than the prices it charged in the export market.[48] Pursuant to the *Mittal* judgment, the Tribunal set about to reconstruct the economic value of the feedstock. Doing so, it gave important weight to the history of Sasol and the fact that Sasol's past privileges from the state allowed it to obtain the feedstock propylene at a cost that was nearly nothing. It found the price charged to be more than 40 percent above Sasol's costs, and also found it to be more than 40 percent higher than prices in western Europe; and it found excessive pricing.[49]

The Court of Appeal reversed, determining that the proper base price was the actual price the Sasol sister corporation (producer of the byproduct) charged the defendant (Sasol Chemical Industries, or SCI), augmented by the cost of capital and allocated fixed costs,[50] which together would equal "economic value." To give producers breathing room in pricing, it held that a price not in excess of 20 percent over economic value is not excessive. It found that SCI's price was less than 20 percent over economic value and thus not excessive. The past history of Sasol, it said, was irrelevant.[51]

Which was the better view—the Tribunal's or the Court's? Which risk of error or cost should developing countries prefer—the risk that (super)dominant firms might take fewer risks in the future and therefore be less inventive, or the cost of not suing: that South African buyers bear the costs of overcharge and (if they are business buyers) be less competitive in world competition?

In the case of pharmaceuticals, the trade-offs are starker on both sides—chilled innovation that might otherwise have produced new drugs, or unavailability of necessary medicines.

### c. Exclusionary Conduct

Exclusionary conduct may be seen as the centerpiece of a project to integrate efficiency and equity. A dominant firm engages in strategies that tend to exclude outsiders or to marginalize them. The strategies may prevent challengers and upstarts from being effective competitors. Are the strategies efficient and responsive to consumers? Or are they a use of market power to put costs on competitors and set

---

[48] Competition Commission v. Sasol Chemical Industries Ltd., 48/CR/Aug10, para. 18 (2014).

[49] *Id.* at para. 13.

[50] The Tribunal also added an increment for cost of capital and allocation of fixed costs: its estimates were significantly lower than those urged by Sasol and adopted by the Court.

[51] Sasol Chemical Industries Ltd. v. Competition Commission, 131/CAC/Jun14 (CAC), paras. 160, 186 (2015), appeal to Constitutional Court denied.

them back? Or both? Systems of competition law tend to embed presumptions. In the United States, for example, the default presumption is that the dominant firms' acts help consumers and the market. This is a particularly strong presumption if the conduct involves price, product change, or a refusal to deal.[52] According to this view, if competitors complain, one may presume that they are complaining about competition, not its restraint.[53] The South African competition law does not share these presumptions.

We present two cases, *South African Airways* (loyalty rebates) (Tribunal decision, not appealed) and *Nationwide Poles v. Sasol* (Tribunal decision, reversed). The latter concerns price discrimination by a dominant firm, an offense under Section 9 of the Competition Act.

I. SOUTH AFRICAN AIRWAYS. *South African Airways* was a case of loyalty rebates. It was brought under Section 8(d)(i)—inducing a customer not to deal with a competitor. SAA put into effect practices to cause travel agents to shift customers from competing airlines (at a time before internet booking became popular and when agent sales were the dominant mode of sale). Here, for simplicity, we will deal with just one of the challenged practices—the override incentive scheme. This involved contracts between SAA and a large portion of South African travel agents. The agent received a flat basic commission. If the agent exceeded a target tailored to that agent's past performance, the agent received not only the normal commission on the marginal sales but also an override commission back to day one, rand one. SAA's overall average commission rates remained low—often just above a standard 7 percent—since override incentives were spread across all sales, but smaller rival airlines trying to match the value of the SAA offering would have to pay a much higher average commission, often 15 percent or more.[54]

The incentive scheme had the effect of diverting sales from the two domestic competitors (Nationwide and BA Comair) to SAA. Evidence showed a CEO instructing his entire travel agency group to deal only with SAA and not the competitors in order to get the rebate. In another instance, an agent's managing

---

[52] *See* Verizon Communications Inc. v. Trinko, 540 U.S. 398 (2004); *see also* Cascade Health Solutions v. PeaceHealth, 502 F.3d 895 (9th Cir. 2007); *but see* LePage's Inc. v. 3M, 324 F.3d 141 (3d Cir. 2003), *cert denied*, 542 U.S. 953 (2004); ZF Meritor v. Eaton Corp., 696 F.3d 254 (3d Cir. 2012), *cert denied*, Eaton Corp. v. ZF Meritor, 133 S. Ct. 2025 (2013).

[53] *See* Eleanor M. Fox, *We Protect Competition, You Protect Competitors*, 26 WORLD COMPETITION, no. 2 (2003), at 149.

[54] *See* Competition Comm'n v. South African Airways Ltd., (18/CR/Maro1) [2005] ZACT 50, para. 151 (2005). *See also* Helen Jenkins, Gunnar Niels, & Robin Noble, *The South African Airways cases: blazing a trial for Europe to follow?*, Oxera Consulting, Third Annual Competition Conference of the South African Competition Commission, Aug. 14, 2009.

director announced that loyalty to SAA can be "highly lucrative" and that the incentive targets are more important than the consumers. After a period of strong growth, the competitors experienced a period of decline, coinciding with SAA's ramping up the application of its override incentive scheme.

Holding the scheme illegal, the Tribunal found that, because of the override incentive scheme, "consumers are likely to have made wrong choices of airlines, chosen the wrong prices and essentially, it has led to the wrong set of outputs."[55] The case was not appealed.

The Tribunal's decision and reasoning are noteworthy in two respects. First, dominant firm loyalty rebates are in a suspect (singled-out) category under Section 8(d) of the Competition Act and therefore are presumptively illegal without plaintiffs' showing an anticompetitive effect. The Commission went further than the text seems to require to show diverted sales. Second, the Tribunal's approach is positioned between two poles on the "global competition rules" map. Loyalty rebate schemes by dominant firms have been treated as presumptively illegal in the European Union, although they may be justified.[56] The loyalty rebate scheme itself is described as having a "suction effect"; it is likened to a magnetic draw of the customer to the implementing firm.[57] United States law requires a showing of harm to consumers. The harm would normally be framed as: consumers are paying more for air travel as a consequence of the scheme. This is very difficult to prove. If the South African law means to protect against exclusion of or significant diversion of business from smaller competitors who would otherwise have a clear path to sell on their merits, it may not choose the level of proof required in the United States.

11. NATIONWIDE POLES. Nationwide Poles, owned by James Foot, was a small producer of poles for grapevines, which were weatherproofed by wood preservatives. The supplier of the preservative, creosote, was Sasol, a dominant firm. Sasol charged Nationwide a significantly higher price than it charged the big buyers with whom Mr. Foot competed, and it refused to give Mr. Foot the same lower price. The price difference was admittedly not cost-justified. Mr. Foot's business floundered as a result of his high cost of creosote. He sued Sasol for abuse of dominance by reason of price discrimination. Under Section 9, price discrimination by a dominant firm is prohibited if "it is likely to have the effect of substantially preventing or lessening competition." Cost justification is a defense, but as noted, here there was none.

---

[55] *South Africa Airways*, (18/CR/Mar01) [2005] ZACT 50 at para. 252.
[56] *See* Intel v. Commission, C-413/14P, ECLI:EU:C:2017:632.
[57] *See Michelin II*, COMP/E-2/36.041/PO [2002] OJ L143/1 (2001); but compare *Intel, id.*

Mr. Foot, for Nationwide, appeared pro se. But he did not prove that prices would go up in the treated pole market as a result of the price discrimination; he did not think he had to.

The Tribunal held for Nationwide. The opinion revisits the background of the Competition Act and underscores one of its dominant aims—to create a level playing field and equal treatment for small and middle-size businesses. "[I]t is telling that one of the stated purposes of our Act is to ensure the 'equitable treatment' of small and medium-sized enterprises."[58] The act is "punctuated with references to the legislature's desire that the statute should promote market access and equality of op- portunity...."[59] "The Act is clearly concerned to promote market access for SMEs [small and medium-size enterprises] and an important mechanism by which it seeks to so do is by ensuring 'equitable treatment.'"[60] The decision notes that under the South African Competition Act there is no requirement that the defendant's offen- sive conduct causes output reduction or price increase. It observes that fairness is not alien to the act.[61] Thus:

> [104] Mr. Foot effectively responds [to the need to show competitive effect] by demonstrating that he is not merely an individual consumer of creosote who purchases it to coat his fence on the weekend.... What distinguishes Foot from that individual consumer is that he is a competing producer of goods, treated poles, in which the subject-matter of the discrimination, creosote, is a crucial input in his production process and thus Sasol's quantitatively sub- stantial discrimination, persisting year after year, places him and other small customers at an ongoing disadvantage relative to other competing producers of treated poles.

> * * *

> [121] These considerations, apart from dictating a low level of interest on Sasol's part in its smaller customers, also dictate that its focus is on satisfying its larger customers. To some extent this latter purpose is achieved by giving these larger customers a preferential price relative to the smaller players in the pole market. In a market—the poles market—in which entry barriers are, it is common cause, low, the price differential assists in limiting the entry of new and small entrants and their ability to thrive.

---

[58] Nationwide Poles v. Sasol Ltd., (72/CR/Deco3) [2005] ZACT 17, para. 81 (2005).

[59] *Id.* at para. 88.

[60] *Id.* at para. 89.

[61] *Id.* at para. 83.

The Court of Appeal reversed. It rejected an interpretation of Section 9 that would include the equity values catalogued in the preamble to the act, for they are not specified in the text of Section 9. It was not able to conclude that there was a reasonable possibility that competition was significantly prevented or lessened.[62]

## 5. Mergers and the Public Interest

We have noted that the South African merger law requires the competition authorities to consider the public interest and allows them to prohibit or condition mergers whether or not the merger is anticompetitive. In the case of a number of mergers with anticompetitive effects, the Commission has asked the Tribunal to approve, and it has approved, conditions that require the merging firms not to lay off workers for a period of months or years, or to retrain or fund retraining of laid-off workers.[63] Conditions in another case require investment in infrastructure and in black empowerment funds.[64]

By far the most celebrated merger case involving public interest is Wal-Mart's acquisition of Massmart. The merger posed no competition problems. Wal-Mart previously had almost no presence in South Africa. A number of stakeholders, including two ministers, complained, asserting public interests in job security, treatment of workers, and fear of displacement of small suppliers. The Tribunal took a narrow view of its jurisdiction over "public interest," stating: "Our job in merger control is not to make the world a better place, only to prevent it from becoming worse as a result of a transaction."[65] Felicitously, Wal-Mart proposed a package of remedies, most importantly including an investment of 100 million rands (US$7.3 million) to enhance the capacity of the small suppliers so they could potentially become part of the Wal-Mart value chain, as well as including Wal-Mart's acceptance of the current union agreements. The Tribunal examined the adequacy of the package in view of the public interests raised (jobs and small businesses). It found the package adequate and approved the merger.[66]

---

[62] Sasol Ltd. v. Nationwide Poles, (49/CAC/Apr05) [2005] ZACAC 5, at 26 (2005).

[63] *See, e.g.,* Glencore PLC v. Xstrata PLC, (33/LM/Mar12) [2013] ZACT 11 (2013); Press Release, Competition Tribunal, Competition Tribunal approves Glencore/Xstrata merger subject to employment conditions (Jan. 18, 2013).

[64] *See, e.g.,* Gareth van Zyl, *Competition Commission approves R7bn Vodacom-Neotel deal,* FIN 24, June 30, 2015, http://www.fin24.com/Tech/Companies/Competition-Commission-approves-Vodacom-Neotel-R7bn-deal-20150630. In the case of the merger of beer giants SABMiller and Anheuser-Busch InBev, in addition to divestitures, the firms agreed to provide a 1 billion rand fund (US$68 million) for the development of the South African agricultural outputs for barley, hops, and maize and to promote the entry of emerging black farmers, and to continue to source glass bottles, cans, bottle crowns, and raw materials for beer from South Africa. http://www.comptrib.co.za/assets/Uploads/INBEV/Ab-Inbev-SAB-Final-Conditions-PUBLIC-VERSION-signature-document.pdf.

[65] *Wal-Mart Stores Inc. and Massmart Holdings Ltd.,* (73/LM/Dec10) [2011] ZACT 41, para. 32 (2011).

[66] *Id.*

But the complaining stakeholders were not satisfied; they wanted more. Two ministers filed a petition for review, and the union appealed. The Court of Appeal permitted the merger and affirmed many of the Tribunal's conditions, but it reversed as to retrenchments (requiring that the 503 workers laid off in early stages of the merger negotiations be rehired), and most notably it reversed as to the sufficiency of the investment fund. It ordered a study and found the promised fund insufficient to build capacity of the small suppliers. It doubled the amount to be placed in the fund, made the fund a mandate rather than a voluntary undertaking, and set up a process and procedure for stakeholders' administration of the fund.[67] Evidence shows that the fund has facilitated entry and expansion of SMMEs (small, medium-size, and micro enterprises) in agriculture and manufacturing and has contributed to job creation and local procurement.[68]

## V. Choices: Leaning In

### A. INTRODUCTION

From the richness of the South African jurisprudence, we can easily extract choices. In some cases there is no dichotomy within the South African law and the South African choice might be the same as Western world standards. We map here some of the choices, their benefits and weaknesses.

Where we see a dichotomy within the South African jurisprudence, we find the Tribunal leaning in to exonerate the interests of the powerless and the Court taking a more technical juridical path, often on grounds that the language of the law does not permit the social policy overlay.[69]

Is "leaning in" a bias, and is it a bias against efficiency?

Leaning in, as we use it, is a bias in favor of inclusive development. It is one point on a continuum of perspectives. It is integral with a belief that inclusion conduces to dynamism and efficiency.[70] A number of the contemporary US Supreme Court

---

[67] SACCAWU v. Wal-Mart Stores Inc., 111/CAC/Jun11 [2012] ZACAC 6, para. 122 (2012).

[68] *See* Thulani Mandiriza, Thembalethu Sithebe, & Michelle Viljoen, An Ex-Post Review of the Wal-Mart/Massmart Merger Working Paper CC2016/03, South Africa Competition Commission (2016).

[69] Some argue that "leaning in" will protect inefficient firms from competition itself and undercut dynamic markets. *See* Hendrik Bourgeois, *The Chilling Effects of Article 82 Enforcement, in* INTERNATIONAL ANTITRUST LAW & POLICY: FORDHAM COMPETITION LAW 349 (Barry E. Hawk ed., 2009). But reluctance to intervene on chilling-competition grounds has not been the tack of the South African appeals court, which has eschewed the market fundamentalism of the Chicago School. *See Federal-Mogul Aftermarket So. Afr. Ltd.*, (33/CAC/Sep03) [2003] ZACAC 9 (2003); *see also Kumba Resources Ltd.*, (26/CAC/Dec02) (rejecting Chicago School reluctance to intervene in vertical cases). Moreover, the Chicago School assumptions do not fit the South African market.

[70] *See, e.g.*, Wolfgang Kerber, *Should Competition Law Promote Efficiency? Some Reflections of an Economist on the Normative Foundations of Competition Law, in* ECONOMIC THEORY AND COMPETITION LAW (Josef Drexl, Laurence Idot, & Joel Moneger eds., 2008); OLIVER BUDZINSKI, AN EVOLUTIONARY THEORY

Sherman Act opinions tilt in the other direction: they give the dominant firm the benefit of the doubt that what it does is good for markets and consumers. This leaning is commensurate with the belief that a laissez-faire bent conduces to dynamism and efficiency. [71] This age-old debate is part empirics and part belief.[72] As for the empirics, it is surely the case that laissez-faire is a more fitting prescription to achieve market robustness in very free-market economies where firms have grown by their wits and capital markets are efficient, than in economies where the converse facts are true—as in most developing countries.[73]

## B. CARTELS

The anti-cartel principle is strong, and the South African institutions have a commitment to its enforcement.

## C. MARKET DEFINITION

The market definition cases are heavily fact-based, but they do suggest a modus operandi. Market definition often presents choices. If one of two plausible market choices would preserve an option particularly important to the poorer population, an inclusive-leaning competition system would prefer that choice.

*JD/Ellerines* is a helpful example. The two department stores sold financing for furniture (plus the furniture) to low-income people when no one else would give them credit or loans. If, in defining the market, we start with beds or tables and

---

OF COMPETITION (2004), *available at* http://ssrn.com/abstract=534862 or http://dx.doi.org/10.2139/ssrn.534862.

[71] *See* Eleanor M. Fox, *The Efficiency Paradox, in* HOW THE CHICAGO SCHOOL OVERSHOT THE MARK: THE EFFECT OF CONSERVATIVE ECONOMIC ANALYSIS ON U.S. ANTITRUST 77 (Robert Pitofksy ed., 2008).

Before 1977, the US Supreme Court generally took an inclusiveness perspective. Warren Court cases were robustly aligned with inclusiveness. *See* Eleanor M. Fox, *The Modernization of Antitrust—A New Equilibrium*, 66 CORNELL L. REV. 1140 (1981).

[72] *See* Harold Demsetz, *Two Systems of Belief about Monopoly, in* INDUSTRIAL CONCENTRATION: THE NEW LEARNING 164 (Harvey J. Goldschmid, H. Michael Mann, & J. Fred Weston eds., 1974).

[73] *See* John Fingleton & Ali Nikpay, *Stimulating or Chilling Competition*, 2008 FORDHAM COMP. L. INST. 385, 416 (B. Hawk ed., 2009). In South Africa, the factual context may demand an abuse-of-dominance law that is focused on "ensuring wider access to economic opportunities" and that promotes the dynamic and creative role of competitive markets as part of rules-based frameworks for increased economic participation." Javier Tapia & Simon Roberts, *Abuse of dominance in developing countries: a view from the South, with an eye on telecommunications, in* THE ECONOMIC CHARACTERISTICS OF DEVELOPING JURISDICTIONS 357 (Michal Gal, Mor Bakhoum, Josef Drexl, Eleanor M. Fox, & David J. Gerber eds., 2015); *see also* Haroon Bhorat, *Economic Inequality Is a Major Obstacle to Growth in South Africa*, N.Y. TIMES: ROOM FOR DEBATE, Dec. 6, 2013, http://www.nytimes.com/roomfordebate/2013/07/28/the-future-of-south-africa/economic-inequality-is-a-major-obstacle-to-growth-in-south-africa.

"discover" the hundreds of notionally competing alternative suppliers of beds and tables, we miss the point. We might better ask: If JD and Ellerines merge and raise the credit costs of beds and tables to low-income people, would the customers of JD/Ellerines turn to other providers, and who and where?

### D. AGREEMENTS—SETTING STANDARDS

The problem in *Netstar* was that the industry set standards that on their face looked excessively high (e.g., you must have retrieved 100 vehicles). They were a catch-22: you cannot join the industry unless you meet our standards, but you cannot meet our standards unless you join the industry. There was a fact question whether the big three incumbents agreed to these standards among themselves before presenting them to the trade association, but there was in any event a decision of the trade association announcing the standards. There was no need to find any other agreement. Given the insurers' needs (reliability of the firms as trackers of stolen cars), were the requirements excessive? What is the standard for judging whether they were excessively high? Does failure of the plaintiff to prove that specific firms would have entered the market if the bar were not disproportionately high kill the case? (The Court said, yes.) A system concerned with market access for outsiders would not be satisfied with so high a burden to prove that the standards had a negative effect on competition. Industry standards that create significant barriers to entry and that are facially out of proportion to the legitimate needs of the industry are anticompetitive. Their effect in deterring entry can be inferred.

### E. ABUSE OF DOMINANCE

### 1. Excessive Pricing

This is a difficult subject. By the traditional perspective, the problem is extremely complex—we cannot avoid the complexities—and faced with the complexities and the fact that the defendant (dominant firm) has all the facts in its possession, the defendant will virtually always win. The Tribunal would have corrected for this bias when certain special facts coalesced: Mittal was a monopolist. It did not earn its monopoly; the monopoly was handed to it by the state. There were no prospects for its erosion in sight. The domestic prices it charged were significantly above the export prices it charged. Mittal enjoyed years of export business at the competitively low world prices. And a simple cure was in sight: allow arbitrage. The Tribunal cut through the complexities.

Not all arguments supported the Tribunal's approach. (1) The Tribunal considered the world price/domestic price margin to be pure profit, but Mittal insisted that its export price did not cover its full costs. (2) Could the Tribunal approach introduce a slippery slope of price-interventionism? And (3) What to do with the statutory language that defined excessive prices as excessive in view of "economic value"? Was it legitimate to consider the export price to be economic value?

*Sasol*, likewise, was challenging. How should or must a dominant firm price a byproduct? When is the price excessive in view of economic value? The Tribunal would have given weight to the statist, privileged history of the firm and would have recognized the close-to-zero cost of the byproduct. The Court, on the other hand, denied the relevance of history, put a much higher economic value on the input after detailed inquiry into accounting allocations, and, with a nod to the difficulties and perverse incentives created by high-price intervention, declared a safe harbor for prices less than 20 percent above value.

The Court's choice (adding up to a standard very hard to meet) has the characteristic of almost never interfering with the sensitive function of price-setting. The Tribunal's choice has the value of giving effect to both the concerns and the proscription of the Competition Act, and of curing a problem of extremely high pricing that has ramifications throughout the economy and that otherwise would remain a blight.

## 2. Exclusionary Practices

The exclusionary conduct cases present fundamental choices. They require a renewed reflection on the goals of the statute and the goals of the particular prohibitions. What is the reason for the exclusionary practices violations? Is it—as it is said in the United States—solely to prevent price rise or output limitation to the detriment of consumers? (If so, why is the section of the Competition Act worded as it is?) Is it, more broadly, to protect the functioning of the market? to protect market players from uses of leverage and other abuses that distort the market?

The *South African Airways* case presents a model for proof of a loyalty rebate violation where competitors were denied access on their merits and consumers were denied the choice they would have made. South African Airways had, in effect, paid off the travel agents to steer business to SAA by a loyalty pay-off that the agents could not resist and the rivals could not meet. The competitors' loss of business was reciprocal with the consumers' harm (in terms of loss of the choices consumers would have made, and possibly higher SAA prices in the future). There was no hint of price rise or output limitation of air travel.

*Nationwide Poles* is a more difficult case. Dominant firm Sasol denied Mr. Foot the discount on a necessary input that it gave to his big competitors. With the discount, we are told, Mr. Foot and other small firms could compete; without it, they would be forced to leave, or never enter, the market. But Mr. Foot had not proved consumer or market harm. Possibly the big firms were competing effectively against one another (at least no one proved otherwise). Did the statute mean to preserve Mr. Foot's market presence? Or was Mr. Foot merely one small player harmed by the facts of life of the market? The Tribunal thought the statute meant to protect Mr. Foot's competition. The Court of Appeal said no, Mr. Foot had to show harm to competition, and he had not done so.

The Tribunal's posture toward Mr. Foot dovetails with the goals of opportunity and inclusion. But infinite inclusiveness and unbounded equity cannot be a goal of competition law or the law loses all bounds. SAA hurt the market, but Sasol hurt Mr. Foot. Was there any sense in which Sasol also hurt the market?

An option in Mr. Foot's case would have been to shift to Sasol the burden to prove no harm to competition, given that there was price discrimination by a dominant firm that harmed the disfavored firm in its competition and that the higher price was not cost-justified. With a mere shift of the burden, certain hypotheses would suddenly become salient. Perhaps the poles market was not competitive after all and Mr. Foot's competition made a difference to the grape grower/consumers. We know that the big creosote sellers had conspired in the past, enlisting Sasol to raise prices to low-priced moon-lighting micro-competitors—the "twilight treaters."[74] The big sellers wanted the micro-competitors out of the market, and apparently got them out. Were there extra profits that the big sellers wanted to safeguard? And why would Sasol persist in charging "little" Mr. Foot a higher price than it charged its big customers other than to do the bidding of those firms, when Mr. Foot could not absorb the extra-high cost of creosote and thus the discrimination augured a loss of business for Sasol? With a shift of the burden, Mr. Foot would have had a fairer shot, and there would have been a chance to focus on whether the lower price for Foot might have made consumers better off.

Why not judgment for Mr. Foot just because the price to Mr. Foot was discriminatorily high, not cost-justified, and therefore unfair and a barrier to small business, even if there were no harm to competition and consumers? This is a possible tack and maybe the better choice, absent a convincing justification. It could still be acknowledged and considered that a principle of fairness

---

[74] *Nationwide Poles*, (72/CR/Dec03) [2005] ZACT 17 at paras. 122–123; on appeal, *Nationwide Poles*, (49/CAC/Apr05) [2005] ZACAC 5, at 20.

without an efficiency rudder could hurt consumers by disincentivizing low-price initiatives.[75]

In general, exclusionary practices by dominant firms have a distinct impact in keeping new and better products off the market. A rule of law requiring serious regard for the lost competition and innovation of the outsider would align with the goal of inclusive development. The US and EU *Microsoft* cases[76] both took this tack. Exclusionary practices of Microsoft suppressed actual innovative products of rivals—and was meant to do so—and the suppression was done by conduct not on competitive merits. The courts condemned the practices in those cases, but consideration of suppressed innovation by strategies of dominant firms in general is underdeveloped in the law and literature.[77] An inclusive-directed competition law would give serious regard to this side of the equation. The South African law implicitly does so, and is well-positioned to do so in the future.

## F. MERGERS AND THE PUBLIC INTEREST

### 1. Institutional Choices

South Africa made the choice to give authority to the Tribunal and Court to take account of specified public interests. The institutions must examine the effect of mergers on four concerns of public interest: (1) a particular industrial sector or region; (2) employment; (3) the ability of small firms and firms controlled by historically disadvantaged persons to become competitive; and (4) the ability of national firms to compete in international markets. In carrying out this responsibility, the Tribunal and the Court have followed the wise path of separating the issues: analyzing the competition issues first and the public interest issues separately. The quality, expertise, and integrity of the members of both bodies have made this institutional choice work for South Africa. Detailed Guidelines promulgated by the Commission for the Assessment of Public Interest Provisions in Mergers have formalized the task.

---

[75] Chilling price competition is a concern of the US cases. *See* Volvo Trucks North America, Inc. v. Reeder-Simco GMC, Inc., 546 U.S. 164 (2006); Cash & Henderson Drugs, Inc. v. Johnson & Johnson, 799 F.3d 202 (2d Cir. 2015).

[76] United States v. Microsoft Corp., 253 F.3d 34 (D.C. Cir. 2001); Case T-201/04R, Microsoft Corp. v. Commission, 2004 E.C.R. II-02977.

[77] *But see generally* research of Simon Roberts and team at Centre for Competition Regulation and Economic Development [CCRED], University of Johannesburg, which is spearheading work in this direction. Available at http://www.competition.org.za.

## 2. The *Wal-Mart* Choices

In *Wal-Mart*, the Tribunal distanced itself from the public interest issues as far as it could. It is the defender of competition, as it said. It displayed humility about its competence.

The Court of Appeal saw its duties differently. It embraced a model of more involvement in examining and assessing the public interest issues, and it assumed the responsibility of surveillance over the public interest undertakings by the merging firms.

Both the Tribunal and Court embrace transparency, access to the court, and process, and they have shown a strong preference for market-friendly solutions—not domestic supply quotas but funding for capacity-building of the small suppliers who may one day be part of a global value chain.

## VI. The 2018 Amendments and the Future

In early 2017, then President Zuma of South Africa announced that changes would be proposed to the Competition Act. The act states as its purposes: to allow all South Africans to participate equally in the economy, and to provide a greater spread of ownership to historically disadvantaged persons. These aspirations have not been realized. Accordingly, the government committed to bring forward amendments to the act to:

> address the need to have a more inclusive economy and to de-concentrate the high levels of ownership and control we see in many sectors. . . .
>
> In this way we seek to open up the economy to new players, give black South Africans opportunities in the economy and indeed help to make the economy more dynamic, competitive and inclusive.

Minister of Economic Development Patel promised that the plan would include:

> 9. . . . [T]he competition authorities must be empowered to consider these questions proactively or at the request of key stakeholders. . . . Markets plagued by over-concentration and untransformed ownership will be identified, investigated and appropriate measures applied to remedy these market features. These inquiries, and any remedies that result, will target the primary structural impediments to market entry and ownership by black South Africans.
>
> 10. The proposed amendments also will seek to incentivise firms to develop relationships and adopt strategies that would alter market structure, reduce concentrations by encouraging entry of historically disadvantaged South Africans (particularly those who own small and medium-sized enterprises),

reduce barriers to entry, and expand ownership to ensure that more enjoy substantive economic citizenship.[78]

The amendments were adopted in 2018.[79] They tilt the law more decisively toward the left-out population, ease burdens of proof, and expand the role for the minister of economic development. Also, they give the government (apart from the competition authorities) new powers to prohibit deals based on based on national security concerns. In excessive pricing cases, the law shifts the burden of proof. Exercises of buyer power in designated sectors against small business and historically disadvantaged persons (HDPs) are prohibited. Price discrimination by a dominant firm is prohibited where it impedes the ability of SMEs and HDPs to effectively participate. For mergers, the law adds an additional public interest ground: promotion of a greater spread of ownership, particularly to increase levels of ownership by HDPs and workers. Market inquiries may authorize deconcentration of untransformed markets.

South African competition jurisprudence has fully embraced the value of inclusiveness.

## VII. Conclusion

The Tribunal said in *Wal-Mart/Massmart*: "If we are not for competition then who is?"[80] We might say of the effort for inclusive development: If the institutions of competition law and policy are not for the outsider, then who is?

The United Nations, the World Bank, and the International Monetary Fund all call for implementation of the United Nations' Sustainable Development Goals (SDGs), which followed and supplemented the Millennium Development Goals at the turn of the century, to end poverty, build dignity, and empower people.[81] Competition laws and policy are the natural companion of the SDGs: harnessing markets to make them work for the people. Despite huge challenges, the South African competition institutions are trying to do just that.

---

[78] Background Note issued by the Minister of Economic Development, May 25, 2017.

[79] Competition Amendment Bill, Republic of South Africa, B23-2018, published in Government Gazette No. 41756 of 5 July 2018.

[80] *Wal-Mart Stores Inc.* (73/LM/Dec10) [2011] ZACT 41 at para. 115.

[81] *See* Transforming our world: the 2030 Agenda for Sustainable Development, Resolution adopted by the General Assembly on 25 September 2015, United Nations, 21 Oct. 2015. *See also* UNCTAD, A Sustainable Development Review Process, UNCTAD Post-2015 Policy Brief Series, No. 4 (June 29, 2015).

# 6

## REGIONAL ARRANGEMENTS

### Integrating, Coordinating, and Gaining a Voice

## I. Introduction

Regional arrangements occupy a significant part of African competition policy. The arrangements take many forms. The most integrative form is a common market, wherein member states tear down trade barriers between and among them, create supranational authorities to oversee trade and competition, and even create monetary unions. For example, the West African states have formed a common market and monetary union, WAEMU: the West African Economic and Monetary Union. Eastern and southern states have a common market, COMESA: the Common Market of Eastern and Southern Africa. At the informal end of the spectrum and the most grass-roots level, nations' competition authorities cooperate, sharing ideas and methodologies, as the African states do in the African Competition Forum. Moreover, on March 21, 2018, 44 African countries signed the African Continental Free Trade Agreement for a Continental Free Trade Area (AfCFTA), and 27 states also signed a commitment for free movement of persons, thus moving forward the African Union's project 2063 for closer African integration.

Most regional organizations are motivated by benefits in trade (lower trade barriers), not competition (freedom from private firm restraints). Many of the regional bodies are free trade areas, even if they do not go the extra step of forming a

Making Markets Work for Africa. Eleanor M. Fox and Mor Bakhoum.
© Oxford University Press 2019. Published 2019 by Oxford University Press.

more integrated common market. The competition project must fit within the trade mandate, not vice versa. Trade has two components. First, free trade across borders in the internal market, which is made up of the territory of all the member states, and freedom to move business establishments within that area. Second, common bargaining of the regional organization with other nations or regions, usually for reciprocal trading benefits. Member state restraints of trade in the internal market (most of which are prohibited) can include quotas, tariffs, and strategic regulatory requirements of a member nation to keep out neighbors' goods. The competition project focuses on acts of commercial firms, usually private enterprises but also often the state itself when it engages in commercial activities by state-owned enterprises. The competition law is meant to control the power of commercial enterprises and to tear down firm-created barriers to market entry and participation.

By tearing down barriers and seeking to create one common market (often called the internal market), nations incentivize firms to operate more efficiently. By being free to sell across borders without a tax, they can reach greater scale, lower their costs, make their products more available, and even become more competitive in global markets. But the increased competition often whets the appetite of businesses to get protection against it. Businesses often lobby their states to keep "their market" to themselves, free from the competition of "outsiders." State-owned businesses are often puffed up as national champions by privileges such as free loans, and often they are protected by their state from outsider competition. These centripetal forces of protection and nationalism work against the ideal of a common market. Both sets of opposing forces—freer trade and nationalistic trade—are at play in the African free trade areas and common markets.

Despite the challenge, free trade areas and common markets hold much promise for sub-Saharan Africa, both in trade by removing state border barriers (quotas, tariffs, strategic regulation) and in competition. One of the most dramatic contributions a common market can make is integrating the trade and competition disciplines. This is because a huge share of the barriers that encumber African markets and keep them from working for the people are a combination of state restraints (dealt with by trade law or its internal market counterpoint—free movement law) and private restraints (dealt with by competition law). We give examples below. The integration of trade and competition disciplines is underdeveloped in general in the world and is an area of opportunity waiting to be taken in Africa in the African common markets.

For competition policy alone, regionalism can be a vehicle for national competition authorities to pool scarce resources and thereby be better able to challenge restraints by big cross-border firms. It can provide smaller states' competition authorities with bargaining power and can provide states without competition law with the law itself. Through cross-fertilization and sharing of facts (better knowledge of what is happening in the market), the higher vantage point for assessment can reveal a truer picture. For example, the regional view can reveal a market-division cartel that could not be detected at state level. Moreover, regional authorities are not likely to be captured by national champions and national vested interests. Finally, "[t]he strategies of firms are increasingly regional, and as such competition law enforcement needs to transcend the comforts of political borders."[1]

But regional organizations can also be paper tigers or go astray. A robust common competition system might never develop, for reasons of inertia, unwillingness of member states to fund it, or lack of commitment. The worst case, as we mentioned regarding WAEMU, is preemption by the regional authority of all national enforcement and a failure to fill the space with regional enforcement.

This chapter opens with a brief overview of regional coordination in sub-Saharan Africa, and how it may facilitate competition policy. The chapter discusses regional groups that have taken integrated approaches. It explores institutional design, enforcement mechanisms, and the relationship between national and regional laws. Specifically, the chapter focuses on COMESA, SADC,[2] and the EAC[3] in Eastern and Southern Africa, and WAEMU and ECOWAS[4] in West Africa. It then explores more informal networks for collaboration, education, and soft convergence, with particular attention to the African Competition Forum.

## II. Regional Collaboration

Developing states face obstacles in going it alone to free their markets of anticompetitive restraints. Many states do not have the capacity for resource-intensive competition enforcement. They often lack the funding, human capital, and the technology required to investigate potential abuses and to conduct market research. States may not have the enforcement strength or the bargaining power needed to police the behavior of large multinational firms. National governments may be corrupt, they may be unwilling to target the anticompetitive behavior of their own firms, or the state itself may impose restraints on competition. Some states may not have developed or implemented competition law at all. Thus, reliance on national enforcement systems alone is unlikely to be an effective curb on anticompetitive behavior.

---

[1] Thando Vilakazi, *Editor's note: SADC Competition Authorities sign MOU for cooperation on competition issues*, CCRED QUARTERLY COMPETITION REVIEW (June 2016), 2. *See also* Shingie Chizoro Dube & Anthea Paelo, *Prospects for the East African Community Competition Authority*, CCRED QUARTERLY, *supra*, at 3, 5.

[2] The Southern African Development Community.

[3] East African Community.

[4] Economic Community of West African States.

Regional agreements can help overcome these obstacles. Even informal networks of national competition authorities can be agents of cross-fertilization and foster the development of domestic competition policy. Discussions in international fora are invaluable, but they have limits. They are dominated by economically advanced states, and not all of the policies advocated may precisely fit developing countries' markets and needs. Cross-fertilization with like-situated developing countries can help solve real problems and also nurture a distinct developing country voice. Regional agreements can nudge states that do not yet have their own competition policy to develop their own domestic systems and can lead to soft convergence, regional consistency, and a more business-friendly environment.

Pooling resources and sharing human capital can reduce the costs of enforcement. Identifying and challenging anticompetitive behavior can be resource-intensive, and the individual national competition authorities may lack the necessary human capacity and technological capacity. Through regional cooperation, the authorities can join efforts. They can share experts. Regional teams can train newcomers, who can return to (and enhance) their home authorities. Pooled funds can support not only cross-border enforcement but also financial investigations, monitoring, and market studies—which often provide the ground work for detecting and understanding market problems.

Regional collaboration can also increase member states' bargaining power. The united front can provide a more fearsome deterrent to anticompetitive behavior. Size can be critical to policing international cartels, which often target developing countries because they are vulnerable and have little capability of fighting back.

Regional competition authorities have the additional advantage of being removed from domestic political pressures and therefore less prone to capture by national firms. Moreover, given the free-movement competence of free trade areas and common markets, the competition directorate may partner with the free-movement directorate, and together they can curb harmful state measures as well as state-sponsored anticompetitive practices.

However, regional associations often fail to provide the promised benefits. Political realities and institutional weaknesses may intervene. While resource-pooling seems promising, it can result in underfunding domestic systems in order to fund the regional system, or the nations may simply not cooperate in paying their share. The regional system can be preemptive—rare, but it notoriously has happened in WAEMU—chilling the development of effective national competition enforcement. Regional associations can also be plagued with political bureaucracy or pacified through firm or national capture. Uncertainties about jurisdictional overlap between regional and national policies can impede the process. Political and economic disparities between member states can create divergences in enforcement priorities. The engagement of smaller nations can be limited by capital, technology, and human constraints. The unequal capacities of domestic institutions may undermine the coordination required for effective cross-border enforcement. The commitment of larger nations may wane if enforcement conflicts with their national interests.[5]

In sum, incorporating competition policy into regional agreements may be crucial both to enhance economic integration and to foster effective national competition enforcement. However, implementation is often imperfect. Many attempts fail, or simply, the regional association does too little.

## III. Regional Integration in Sub-Saharan Africa

### A. INTRODUCTION

The attraction of regional cooperation has been apparent since sub-Saharan African states began winning independence in the 1960s. Centuries of economic exploitation had left their economies small and fragmented, and many states were still economically and politically dependent upon their former colonial powers. Regional unity and economic integration promised the newly independent states a chance to gain true political independence and economic development. Establishing a regional economic community was seen as a path to overcoming economic dependence on the northern industrialized countries. It was hoped that the creation of a regional market and the development of an efficient industrial sector would reduce the countries' reliance on the export of minerals and the import of industrial products.

African states aimed to create larger markets, diversify their economies, and strengthen industrial sectors. The states considered two approaches. The first option was to create a continent-wide economic and political union. The second proposal sought to move progressively toward a continent-wide market by forming concentric blocs in Western, Eastern, Northern and Southern Africa.

The second approach was more politically and economically feasible. Regional groupings with varying agendas began to emerge. Most commonly, the groups sought to foster trade between member states by progressively eliminating tariffs

---

[5] *See* Thulasoni Kaira, *Challenges of Competition Authorities in Small Countries with Large Neighbours for Successful Regional Enforcement*, discussion paper, 3rd Annual Competition and Economic Regulation (ACER) 2017 Dar es Salaam, Tanzania (14 and 15 July 2017). Small economies are particularly challenged in joining and participating in regional enterprises, given (even more) seriously strained resources, inadequate staff, scarcity of experts, difficulties in handling and reviewing data, lack of capacity to absorb and implement complex analysis, and pressure from oligarchs that frustrates projects to gain connectedness en route to strong enforcement.

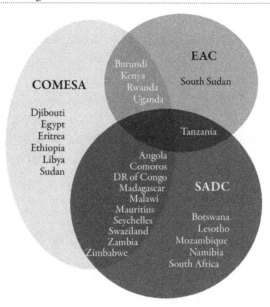

FIGURE 6.1 The Overlaps of COMESA, SADC and EAC.

and nontariff barriers, ultimately planning to create a common market with free movement of goods and services.

Some groups had, and have, different missions. Some are narrowly focused on specific sectors of the economy. For example, the Organisation Africaine de la Propriété Intellectuelle (African Intellectual Property Organization) seeks to harmonize intellectual property filings in West Africa. Most groups are broadly focused on trade, economic development, and regional integration. This chapter focuses on five in the latter category (although there are more), namely: WAEMU and ECOWAS in West Africa, and COMESA, SADC, and the EAC in Southern and Eastern Africa. Taken together, the numerous African regional economic areas are a spaghetti bowl of overlaps. The members and overlaps of COMESA, SADC, and the EAC are shown in the diagram above (Figure 6.1).

## B. SOUTHERN AND EASTERN AFRICAN UNIONS: SELECTED COMMUNITIES

Here we describe the outlines of three major regional organizations in Southern and Eastern Africa: COMESA, SADC, and the EAC. The three include nations at various levels of development, ranging from Burundi to South Africa. We shall turn to their competition regimes below.

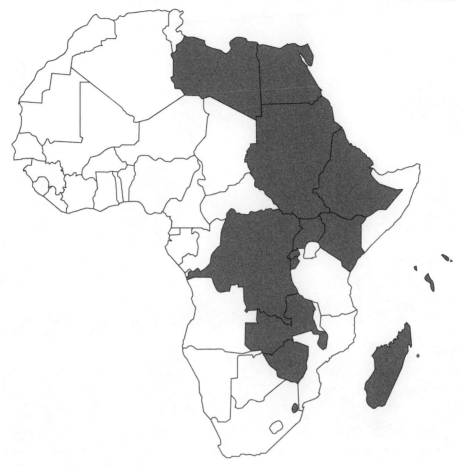

FIGURE 6.2 The Member States of COMESA. (Somalia and Tunisia joined COMESA in July 2018 and are not depicted as such on the map.)

## 1. COMESA: Common Market for Eastern and Southern Africa

The Common Market for Eastern and Southern Africa occupies an eastern strip from Egypt to Swaziland (Figure 6.2). It has 21 member states,[6] with a combined gross domestic product (GDP) of US$700 billion.[7] Like most African regional organizations, it developed as the result of a long process beginning with the independence wave of the 1960s. Discussions surrounding regional economic integration in Eastern and Southern African states other than South Africa intensified in the 1970s when the economic might of then-apartheid South Africa threatened to destabilize its neighbors.

---

[6] COMESA members are Angola, Burundi, Comoros, D.R. Congo, Djibouti, Egypt, Eritrea, Ethiopia, Kenya, Libya, Madagascar, Malawi, Mauritius, Rwanda, Seychelles, Somalia, Sudan, Swaziland, Tunisia, Uganda, Zambia, and Zimbabwe.

[7] The source of the GDP figures in this chapter is the World Bank, 2016.

# 5

## SOUTH AFRICA

### Leaning in Toward Inclusive Development

## I. Introduction

South Africa, still recovering from the dark years of apartheid and still in need of laws and policies to integrate the cruelly excluded majority, has the most sophisticated system of competition law and policy in sub-Saharan Africa. It has a mission to expand economic opportunity and facilitate inclusive development. It is working on this mission in the form of proposed amendments to its competition law as this book goes to press. Despite South Africa's tribulations, its competition system has matured into one of the most outstanding and even pathbreaking in the developing world.

South Africa is a middle-income country with important industry especially deriving from diamond, gold, and other mineral wealth. It has a huge population below the poverty line. The Gini co-efficient is 0.68, making it one of the most unequal societies in the world. South Africa is a country of enormous energy and talent but extensive corruption and crime, and huge governance challenges. It is still fighting to eradicate the vestiges of apartheid, introduced by the Afrikaner government in 1913 with passage of the Natives Land Act and continued and expanded under British colonialism. In 1991, the apartheid laws were rescinded through a negotiated settlement between the state and the African National Congress (ANC), led by Nelson Mandela. The first multiracial democratic elections were held in 1994, when the people overwhelmingly endorsed

Making Markets Work for Africa. Eleanor M. Fox and Mor Bakhoum.
© Oxford University Press 2019. Published 2019 by Oxford University Press.

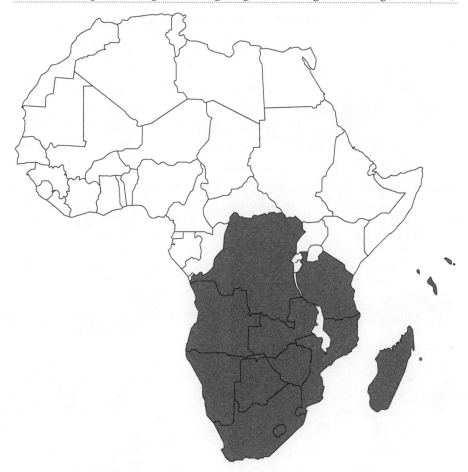

FIGURE 6.3 The Member States of SADC.

the standard and quality of life, freedom and social justice, and peace and security."[9] Specified areas for increased cooperation include infrastructure, trade, investment, and human resources development.

The governing bodies of SADC include the Council and the Tribunal. The Council is responsible for approving and implementing policies and overseeing the functioning of the SADC. The Tribunal interprets the SADC Treaty and adjudicates disputes between member states. SADC is a framework for member states' cooperation. It is not a customs union. It does not have a regional competition law.

[9] SADC, TOWARDS THE SOUTHERN AFRICAN DEVELOPMENT COMMUNITY: A DECLARATION BY THE HEADS OF STATE OR GOVERNMENT OF SOUTHERN AFRICAN STATES (1992).

## 3. EAC: East African Community

The East African Community is composed of six countries in the Great Lakes Region[10] (Figure 6.4) with a combined GDP of US$155 billion. It was formed in the 1960s, building on existing trade agreements among Kenya, Uganda, and Tanzania. In 1977, the EAC collapsed due to disagreements among the nations. It was revived in 1999 with a long-term goal of becoming a political federation. In 2005, the EAC became a customs union. In 2010, it became a common market, establishing free movement of goods, persons, labor, and capital, along with the right of establishment. It began the process of adopting a common currency in 2013.

FIGURE 6.4  The Member States of the EAC.

---

[10] EAC members are Burundi, Kenya, Rwanda, South Sudan, Tanzania, and Uganda.

The prime organs of the EAC include the Council of Ministers, the East African Legislative Assembly, the East African Court of Justice, and the Secretariat. The competition authority is in early stages; it became operative at the end of 2016.

### 4. African Free Trade Zone

COMESA, SADC, and the EAC announced the African Free Trade Association (AFTZ) in 2008. The free trade zone compromises all of their member states.

### C. WEST AFRICAN ECONOMIC UNIONS

The two most important West African regional organizations from a competition perspective are the West African Economic and Monetary Union (WAEMU) and the Economic Community of West African States (ECOWAS). The official language of WAEMU is French. ECOWAS has three official languages: English, French, and Portuguese.

### 1. ECOWAS: Economic Community of West African States

ECOWAS was established by the Treaty of Lagos in 1975. It is composed of 15 West African states including Ghana and Nigeria. Its combined GDP is US$559 billion. Its goal is to create a borderless region with a focus on sustainable development, the free movement of goods and people, and collective security.

ECOWAS has three branches: legislative, executive, and judicial. The legislative arm is the Community Parliament. Members of Parliament are designated by national legislatures. ECOWAS aims to grant universal suffrage, allowing individuals to vote—to make an ECOWAS of people, not an ECOWAS of states. The judicial branch, responsible for interpreting the Treaty of Lagos and relevant regulations, is the ECOWAS Court of Justice. ECOWAS has two primary implementation organs: the Commission and the ECOWAS Bank for Investment and Development.

ECOWAS has two subregional blocks, WAEMU and WAMZ. WAMZ is the West African Monetary Zone. WAEMU comprises the French-speaking states; WAMZ the English-speaking states.[11] WAEMU is a customs union with a common currency. WAMZ is a customs union and proposes to introduce a common currency, the Eco. A goal is for WAEMU's CFA franc and WAMZ's Eco to merge, creating a common currency across West and Central Africa. WAMZ does not have a regional competition policy, but ECOWAS is in the process of setting up a regional competition authority (Figure 6.5).

---

[11] WAMZ member states are the Gambia, Ghana, Nigeria, and Sierra Leone.

## 2. WAEMU: West African Economic and Monetary Union

In 1994, seven Francophone nations in West Africa, which already shared the CFA franc as common currency, signed the Treaty of Dakar and officially formed a common currency and a customs union: WAEMU (UEMOA in French). Guinea Bissau, the only Portuguese-speaking state in the union, joined in 1997. The union's primary objectives are to reinforce the economic and financial competitiveness of member states; converge economic policies; create a common market with a common external tariff, a common trade policy, the free movement of persons, goods, and capital, and the right of establishment across all member states; coordinate national sector policies; and harmonize laws. WAEMU is composed of eight member states (Figure 6.5) with a combined GDP of US$95.21 billion. The structure is more fully defined in Section IV.C, below.

FIGURE 6.5 The Member States of WAEMU.*
*The WAEMU countries are the eight countries that we examined in Chapter 3; namely, Benin, Burkina Faso, Guinea Bissau, Ivory Coast, Mali, Niger, Senegal, and Togo. For a close-up look, see Figure 3.1 at page 20.

## IV. Regional Competition Law and Policy in Selected Communities

A. INTRODUCTION

Competition law and policy in sub-Saharan Africa is diffuse. It exists at national level and also at the level of various regional free trade areas and common markets. It also exists less formally through cooperative interaction of the nations' competition authorities. The regional institutions' competition law is supranational and is especially important for detecting and freeing markets of cross-border restraints, including cartels, monopolistic abuses, and anticompetitive mergers. But there are problems, as we have noted, of insufficient commitment of the member nations and also of overlaps. The overlap problem is recognized and nations are attempting to address it by coordinating if not integrating overlapping regional associations, as we describe below.

Less formally, the nations have formed networks. These serve a different but complimentary purpose to the integrated regional organizations. They coordinate national efforts, for example, when challenging the same merger or cartel; they share information and techniques; and they work toward constructing soft norms or best practices for both substantive law and procedures.

In this section, we begin with the competition policy of the southern and central African associations, of which COMESA is emerging as the most prominent, and we note an effort to merge or coordinate overlapping institutions. We proceed to West Africa with emphasis on WAEMU—both its enforcement and its unique and debilitating stripping the national competition authorities of power. We proceed then to networks, and particularly the African Competition Forum, which spans the continent.

B. SOUTHERN AND EASTERN AFRICA

We return to COMESA, SADC, and the EAC, to describe their competition regimes.

1. COMESA

*a. The Competition Provisions*
COMESA has the best articulated competition law and policy of the sub-Saharan regional bodies. COMESA was established in 1994. The COMESA Treaty provides a framework for the competition law. The institutions necessary for the enforcement of competition law were not established until nearly two decades later. The COMESA Competition Commission and the competition law became operational in 2013. The competition prohibitions apply to anticompetitive practices affecting

the regional (COMESA) market. Member states have the freedom to apply national competition laws in parallel with regional competition laws.

The enabling treaty specifies the basic principles of open and competitive markets. Article 55 prohibits anticompetitive practices by agreement or concert. Article 55 (1) provides:

> The Member States agree that any practice which negates the objective of free and liberalised trade shall be prohibited. To this end, the Member States agree to prohibit any agreement between undertakings or concerted practice which has as its objective or effect the prevention, restriction or distortion of competition within the Common Market.

Just as in the EU Treaty, which is virtually copied by Article 55(1), the COMESA Treaty prohibits agreements that distort competition unless the agreements improve or promote production or distribution or technical or economic progress and consumers get a fair share of the benefits. The COMESA Council may declare that particular restrictive agreements have the enumerated beneficial aspects and that the agreement is authorized, as described below.

Although the COMESA Treaty's competition provisions explicitly prohibit only cartels and other anticompetitive practices *by agreement*, the treaty gives the Council broad authority to "regulate competition within the Member States." The COMESA Council has used that authority to regulate other core anticompetitive practices as well, thus bringing into the competition ambit abuse of dominance and anticompetitive mergers. To do so, it adopted Competition Regulations in 2013.

Article 16(1) of the COMESA Competition Regulations prohibits cartels and concerted practices that affect trade between member states. Firms can file a request for exemption, also called a "Request for Authorisation," with the Commission, which must then weigh claimed efficiencies and other pro-competitive aspects against anticompetitive effects. In the European Union similar authorization procedures were initially required, but the European Commission has relinquished that role. In the European Union, parties are on their own to assess whether agreements are, on balance, anticompetitive.

The COMESA Competition Regulations prohibit the abuse of a dominant position. Article 17 defines "dominant position." It provides that an undertaking holds a dominant position if "it occupies such a position of economic strength as will enable it to operate in the market without effective constraints from its competitors or potential competitors." Under Article 18, an undertaking abuses this dominant position if it falls within one of seven enumerated categories. These include: whether the conduct is likely to restrict entry of any firm into the market; whether it prevents or deters any firm from engaging in competition in a market or is likely to remove any firm from a market; whether it limits production to the prejudice of consumers; whether the conduct exploits customers or suppliers so as to frustrate the benefits of the common market; and whether the firm imposes unfair selling or purchasing prices.

Article 23 empowers the Commission to regulate mergers of a regional dimension. Initially, all mergers in which at least one of the parties operated in at least two member states had to be notified, regardless of the value of the transaction. This overbroad and expensive requirement was much criticized. Amended rules cure the problem by adding a monetary threshold that screens out small mergers, and they reduce what was a very high filing fee. The filing fee is now 0.1 percent of the merging parties' combined annual turnover, capped at US$200,000.

### b. *The Jurisdictional Coverage*

COMESA's Competition Regulations specify that they are applicable to all economic activities "which have an appreciable effect on trade between member states and which restrict competition in the Common Market." The regulations state that COMESA competition law preempts national laws in relation to conduct with effects beyond the state's border, thus leaving to the member states conduct with effects within their borders.

COMESA's competition law applies to mergers with a "regional dimension." Regulations allow member states impacted by a cross-border merger to petition the Commission to allow the merger to be considered under national merger law. The Commission has the discretion to retain jurisdiction or to refer the case or a part of it to a national competition authority. Its discretion may be informed by the effect of the transaction on the national market, the need for effective and consistent merger regulation, the member state's enforcement capacities, and the potential for delay, fragmentation, duplication, and inconsistent rulings.

The COMESA Merger Assessment Guidelines of 2014 clarify what mergers must be notified to the regional authority.[12] If a merger transaction meets the notification requirements, COMESA's regional competition law provides a one-stop shop and preempts the national competition laws.[13] But the member states do not all accept this allocation. For example, although national jurisdiction may not be compatible with the regional rules, Kenya requires merging parties to file notifications in Kenya if its thresholds are met, even if they must also file with COMESA.

---

[12] Merger guidelines point 2.8.
[13] COMESA shares the filing fees with the affected member states.

The competition law bar (the private lawyers) has registered a level of dissatisfaction with the crazy quilt of merger filings and has highlighted lack of predictability, lack of convergence, duplicative filings and filing fees, and prospects for more of the same with merger control by ECOWAS and the EAC in the wings. They suggest that, to attract global investment, the governments should prioritize harmonization of national and regional regimes.

### c. Enforcement and Activity

As of the end of the fiscal year 2016–2017, the COMESA Competition Commission employed three lawyers and 10 economists, plus other staff. Its budget for the year was US$2.1 million. Overwhelmingly, its main activity has been merger review. Between commencement of operations in January 2013 and June 2017, the COMESA Competition Commission had cleared all transactions, 10 with conditions. It had not taken a decision in a cartel case, and had concluded one abuse of dominance case, which did not result in a fine. A contract case with exclusionary clauses is pending. The Commission provides technical assistance to its member states' competition authorities, helping them draft laws and harmonize their laws with those of COMESA and the neighbors.[14]

### d. Merger Enforcement

The merger activity seen by COMESA is driven largely by global businesses investing in the higher growth African economies. Most acquirers come from Europe. Many of the cross-border acquisitions are by South African firms and some by Kenyan firms. The largest number of mergers have been in the financial sector including insurance, banking and investment banking, and the next largest in construction/cement and fertilizers.[15]

The COMESA Competition Commission (CCC) analyzes the mergers filed with it to determine whether the merger is likely to substantially prevent or lessen competition within the common market.

In the last five years there have been three huge megamergers (among others) in cement, chemicals, seeds, and fertilizers whose effects have been thought to fall significantly upon sub-Saharan Africa: Holcim Lafarge (cement), Dow DuPont (global crop protection: agro-chemicals and seeds), and Monsanto Bayer (seeds and fertilizers). These were immensely complicated transactions. The first was a

---

[14] *COMESA Competition Commission, in* EMERGING ENFORCERS 2018, GLOBAL COMPETITION REVIEW (Feb. 26, 2018).

[15] *See* Maria Nkhonjera & Tatenda Zengeni, *Review of COMESA merger and enforcement activity*, CCRED QUARTERLY COMPETITION REVIEW (June 2016), at 6–7.

merger of the two leading competitors in the world in the highly concentrated cement market notorious for cartels. The second also combined leading world competitors, and the third combined a near monopoly supplier of seeds with a leading supplier of fertilizer. The United States, the European Union, and, among others, South Africa (not a member of COMESA), each spent significant time and resources analyzing the mergers for effects within their markets and eventually cleared them with spin-offs and other conditions. Even before the Western authorities completed their difficult evaluations,[16] the CCC issued its decision that the merger, in each case, did not raise competitive concerns within the common market of COMESA. We say a few words about these COMESA clearances.

For *Dow/DuPont*, the CCC published a two-page decision (of September 28, 2016), which provides the competition analysis in two paragraphs: The three-firm concentration ratio in the market will remain the same "as the parties are not among the top three market players in the relevant markets." "The relevant markets are highly contested," therefore "the merger is unlikely to affect the pattern of trade in the Common Market." The United States, the European Union, and South Africa each found significant competition problems posed by this merger of world giants and required divestitures to protect their markets, and South Africa also imposed various conditions such as requiring Dow to make certain seed lines available to third parties for licensing hybrids.

For *Bayer/Monsanto*, the CCC's decision (of June 23, 2017) is also two pages in length. The competition analysis is covered in two paragraphs, one sentence each. The first sentence identifies two relevant markets. The second sentence says the Committee Responsible for Initial Determination (CID) established that the merger is not likely to substantially prevent or lessen competition in the relevant markets or be contrary to the public interest. The United States, the European Union, and South Africa, however, found significant competition problems with this merger that has worried farmers all over the world, a merger that would create in one firm the most extensive portfolio of pesticide products and the strongest global position in seeds and traits. The United States, the European Union, and South Africa ordered divestiture and other conditions to protect their markets.

*Holcim/Lafarge* created the largest cement producer globally and in Africa. The parties to the merger were active in 12 member states, from Djibouti to Zimbabwe, as the CCC decision reports. The CCC cleared the merger without conditions in a two-page decision of November 18, 2014. The competition analysis of the decision

---

[16] These evaluations could have been useful to the CCC.

comprises one sentence, stating: "The CID established that the transaction without conditions would not frustrate the single market objective of the Treaty in that it does not have an appreciable effect on trade between Member States." Further: "The CID determined that the merger does not raise competition concerns. . . ." The CCC accordingly approved the transaction without conditions within the common market, except for Mauritius, which had requested and was granted referral. In Mauritius the merger was a merger to monopoly. Mauritius accepted Holcim's undertaking to sell its local subsidiary. The United States, the European Union, South Africa, and other jurisdictions found serious competition problems and ordered significant divestitures and conditions to cure their jurisdictions' problems.

To repeat, COMESA cleared the huge cement merger on grounds that it did not appreciably affect trade between the member states of COMESA despite the fact that the parties were active in 12 of the member states. Perhaps the authority believed that, if these two market leaders were not competing in a national market, their merger could not affect cross-border trade and there could be no competition problem. But if these two dominant cement producers were not competing in a national African market, that *was* the problem. The big cement producers in Africa are suspected of strategic allocation of national markets. Only regional antitrust is suited to confront this problem. Yet, it appears, not only have the regional enforcers not (yet) taken up the challenge of cross-border collusion, but they may make it worse by allowing the market leaders to merge.[17]

COMESA's merger decisions thus far do not reveal COMESA as a fearsome watchdog in defense of competition in its community. COMESA has expert and dedicated officials, but not enough, and by no means enough staff. Staffing requires funding and funding must come from the member states, which are not generous with their budgets. Perhaps a much larger budget, a much larger staff, and a

---

[17] Thando Vilakazi of the CCRED team of the University of Johannesburg points out, with particular reference to cement and the southern and east African markets:

> Longstanding relationships of coordination between firms, several of which are linked to favourable government trade protectionism and legal cartels, and concentration in key industries within the region [including cement], is likely to have led to the strategic allocation of country markets between firms. There has however not been a competition law case brought against firms at a regional level with a view to addressing conduct which cuts across borders.

Thando Vilakazi, Regional cartels and a review of developments in the cement Industry, paper prepared for the 2nd Annual Competition and Economic Regulation Week, Livingstone, Zambia, March 2016, at 2. *See also* Thando Vilakazi & Simon Roberts, *Cartels as fraud? Insights from collusion in southern and East Africa in the fertilizer and cement industries*, REVIEW OF AFRICAN POLITICAL ECONOMY (forthcoming 2018) (providing factual detail of how the cement and fertilizer companies have manipulated the system by information exchanges through their trade associations, lobbying government, secret agreements, and special exemptions, "while presenting themselves as 'development partners'").

requirement to publish fully reasoned decisions might embolden COMESA to use its injunctive powers against harmful mergers, as well as using fining powers against cross-border hard core cartels. Potentially, the regional community may provide a sturdy platform on which developing countries can stand up to cross-border and multinational restraints.

Regional organizations are best positioned to assess restraints from the viewpoint of the community. If the Holcim Lafarge merger has evils after the divestitures required of it and the clearances granted it, it has them because of cross-border potentialities. These could include the likelihood that, without the merger, each firm would have expanded into the geographic markets of the other, and that the merger creates an enhanced risk of cartelization without detection and of collusive behavior without the need for an explicit agreement. It could also include the likelihood that this bulked-up firm will now find it easier to persuade legislators and executives in countries much smaller than the firm to keep foreign low-priced cement out of its markets, thereby protecting its power over price.

A review of the merger decisions suggests a long way to go to realize the regional antitrust potential. That long path includes greater commitment of the member states to fund the enterprise.

## 2. SADC

SADC does not have a regional competition law. It seeks to foster development of member states' national laws and cooperation among the member states. In 2009 SADC adopted a Declaration on Regional Cooperation in Competition and Consumer Policies. SADC established a Technical Committee on Competition and Consumer Policy to initiate dialogue and cooperation among the member states. In 2016, nine of the member states signed a memorandum of understanding for interagency cooperation on information sharing, coordination of investigation, harmonizing rules and procedures, and undertaking joint research.

SADC's cooperative rather than common market model may be attributable in part to the political and economic differences among the member states. The SADC countries range from Congo to South Africa, and the range itself suggests challenges in adopting common policy. Nonetheless, market research shows that some of the most important markets in these countries such as fertilizer, poultry, cement, and transportation function poorly, and that the same firms are present in the same malfunctioning markets across borders, suggesting that this is a region that would especially profit from common competition policy.[18]

---

[18] *See* Mark Burke, Tamara Paremoer, Thando Vilakazi, & Tatenda Zengeni, Cross-cutting Competition Issues in Regional Industrial Development: African Industrial Development and Integration Research Programme (AIDIRP), University of Johannesburg, CCRED Working Paper, 20/2017.

## 3. EAC

The East African Community comprises six states in the Great Lakes Region of Eastern Africa, all of which have adopted national competition laws. Of these, Kenya and Tanzania have the most developed competition laws. The EAC has a geographic advantage in integrating a region: its member states are tightly linked neighbors.

The EAC adopted a regional competition law to target anticompetitive behavior with cross-border effects within its community. The EAC Competition Act of 2006 calls for a regional competition authority and defines specific offenses. The Commissioners were appointed only at the end of 2016, and little activity on the competition front has yet been reported.

Violations of the Competition Act include concerted anticompetitive practices (cartels, bid rigging, boycotts) and exclusion of competitors (predatory pricing, price squeezing). The law prohibits abuse of dominance, which includes consumer exploitation, discriminatory treatment based on nationality, and unfair prices or trading conditions. Mergers must be prenotified. Mergers that may lead to the strengthening or creation of a dominant position run afoul of the law, unless they are approved on public interest grounds by the EAC Council.

## 4. Overlap among COMESA, SADC, and the EAC and Aspiration for a Tripartite Association

There is considerable overlap in membership of COMESA, SADC, and the EAC. Nine countries are members of both COMESA and SADC: Angola, Congo, Madagascar, Malawi, Mauritius, Seychelles, Swaziland, Zambia, and Zimbabwe. Four countries are members of both COMESA and the EAC: Burundi, Kenya, Rwanda, and Uganda. Tanzania is member of both SADC and the EAC.

The overlap—especially between COMESA and the EAC, because both have competition laws—can lead to conflicts. The considerable shared membership in COMESA and SADC is unlikely to present problems at this time, became SADC does not have a competition law; rather, it facilitates member states' enforcement and cooperation.

The EAC, as noted, while still in early stages, aspires to regional competition law enforcement, like COMESA has. Conflicting decisions and policies, including dual notification requirements, can emerge, counseling cooperation and convergence.

The need to seek convergence and avert conflict on the one hand, and on the other, the important potential to build a union geographically inclusive enough to perceive and combat anticompetitive cross-border strategies of firms larger than countries, has led to ongoing talks of consolidating the three organizations into a common free trade area, possibly as a steppingstone to the emerging continental free trade area.[19] The talks are progressing slowly. Asymmetries of nations may be an obstacle to developing a broad and integrated regional competition culture.

## C. WEST AFRICA

Two regional organizations in West Africa are particularly important from a competition perspective: ECOWAS and WAEMU. As mentioned, WAEMU is a subregional organization within ECOWAS, meaning that every member of WAEMU is also a member of ECOWAS. The overlap of membership can present particular challenges since both organizations seek to establish comprehensive regional competition law.

## 1. ECOWAS

In 2008, ECOWAS adopted a Supplementary Act specifying community competition rules within ECOWAS. The competition authority is not yet operational. It is expected to be established in the Gambia.

The act prohibits all forms of agreements and concerted practices in restraint of trade[20] and the abuse of a dominant position that may affect trade between ECOWAS member states. A firm holds a dominant position, as defined in Article 6, if it has sufficient market share to control prices or to exclude competition.[21] Article 7 prohibits mergers that "shall result in an abuse of a dominant market position resulting in a substantial reduction of competition." The act does not require merger notification, but notification is likely to become the practice. The act exempts mergers that are in the public interest. State aids are prohibited unless exempted for their social character or their contribution to socioeconomic development.[22]

The Supplementary Act specifies the functions and powers of the regional competition authority that will be set up for ECOWAS.[23] The ECOWAS

---

[19] *See* Vincent Angwenyi, *The Tripartite Free Trade Area: A Step Closer to the African Economic Community?*, in EUROPEAN YEARBOOK OF INTERNATIONAL ECONOMIC LAW, at 589 (2016).

[20] The Supplementary Act defines the notion of agreements and concerted practices to include "all agreements between enterprises, decisions by associations of enterprises and concerted practices which may affect trade between ECOWAS Member States and the object of which are or may be the prevention, restriction, distortion or elimination of competition in the Common Market...." Article 5 (1), ECOWAS Supplementary Act, SA 1/06/08, adopting community competition rules and the modalities of their application within ECOWAS.

[21] A dominant position exists when one or more enterprises "possess a substantial share of the market that enables it/them to control prices or to exclude competition." Article 6 (1) of the Supplementary Act. A non-limitative list of abuses is provided in Article 6 (2).

[22] Supplementary Act, art. 8.

[23] *See* Supplementary Act A/SA2/06/08 on the establishment, function of the regional competition authority for ECOWAS.

Competition Authority is to be headed by an executive director assisted by two directors. Unlike WAEMU, the ECOWAS Competition Authority is not structurally part of the ECOWAS Commission. It is an independent authority. However, its directors are directly answerable to the president of the ECOWAS Commission. The ECOWAS Competition Authority has the power to initiate investigations into anticompetitive practices (cartels and abuse of dominant position), conduct inquiries, and impose sanctions. It has the power to grant exemptions (called "authorizations") for anticompetitive agreements if they enhance the competitiveness of SMEs or promote socioeconomic development. It has the power to review mergers.

The ECOWAS Competition Authority may also issue advisory opinions on the interpretation of the community competition rules, conduct market studies, and contribute to the capacity-building of national competition authorities.[24]

ECOWAS's competition law applies only when trade between member states is affected, as contrasted with WAEMU's reach throughout its common market regardless of effect on inter-member-state trade. National competition authorities retain the power to enforce their national competition laws, again, unlike the WAEMU regime. Regional and national competition authorities are required to collaborate when applying the regional competition rules.

Conflicts between the competition laws of WAEMU and ECOWAS may arise, necessitating a collaboration mechanism.

## 2. WAEMU

### a. The Reach of the Competition Law

On paper, WAEMU has one of the most fully integrated and expansive regional competition policies in sub-Saharan Africa.

Articles 88 and 89 of the WAEMU Treaty prohibit anticompetitive agreements, the abuse of a dominant position, and state aids[25] that affect the regional market. Article 90 tasks the Regional Commission with the power to enforce the regional competition rules and to enact new competition regulations. Three regulations came into force in 2003. They cover procedures applicable to

---

[24] *Id.*

[25] State aid is a subsidy by the state or equivalent privilege or benefit conferred by the state, such as tax relief, that is not an investment justified by the market. State aids can distort competition by steering businesses to less efficient firms and are most notorious for privileging national firms and building national champions. In some cases they can create market power in the privileged firms, in which case the body of state aid law is more like competition law and less like (unfair) trade law.

anticompetitive practices,[26] cartels and the abuse of a dominant position,[27] and state aid.[28]

From the start, the Commission and member states disagreed about the distribution of competences. Before implementation of the WAEMU competition regime, some member states had already adopted national competition laws and some, particularly Senegal, had started enforcement, although enforcement was minimal and in many of the countries consisted only of price control, as we saw in Chapter III. The adoption of WAEMU competition law was to threaten the members' competition law initiatives.

The WAEMU Treaty says that the regional competition rules are applicable when competition within the "Union" is affected. The treaty does not hinge jurisdiction on "trade between member states," as is the case in the European Union. The issue of reach of the WAEMU competition law came before the WAEMU Commission. Member states argued that the WAEMU Commission's powers extended only to conduct with effects on inter-member-state trade, leaving to the individual states control over practices affecting their national markets. They suggested that the treaty and WAEMU's powers should be interpreted in line with EU law—the model for the WAEMU Treaty. But the Commission rejected this argument. It held to the contrary that the treaty gave WAEMU exclusive competence both to enact competition regulations and to enforce competition law within the entire union, even preempting national authorities' right to challenge purely domestic conduct with no cross-border effects.

To clarify the matter, the Commission sought an opinion (which is a nonbinding interpretation) from the WAEMU Court of Justice. The Court agreed with the WAEMU Commission. It found that the treaty confers on the Commission the exclusive competence to regulate anticompetitive practices that have an "effect on trade *within the Union*,"[29] and that WAEMU's competence does not depend on the conduct's having an "effect on trade between Member States." Acknowledging the EU approach, the Court of Justice held that the WAEMU legislature purposefully

---

[26] Règlement n° 3/2002/CM/UEMOA relative aux procédures applicables aux ententes et abus de position dominante à l'intérieur de l'Union Economique et Monétaire Ouest Africaine, *available at* http://www.uemoa.int/sites/default/files/bibliotheque/pages_-_reglement_3_2002_cm_uemoa.pdf.

[27] Règlement n° 02/2002/CM/UEMOA du 23 mai 2002 sur les pratiques commerciales anti-Concurrentielles, *available at* http://www.droit-afrique.com/upload/doc/uemoa/UEMOA-Reglement-2002-02-pratiques-commerciales-anticoncurrentielles.pdf.

[28] le Règlement n°04/2002/CM/UEMOA, du 23 Mai 2002, relatif aux aides d'Etat à l'intérieur de l'Union Economique et Monétaire Ouest Africaine.

[29] Avis n° 003/2000: Demande d'avis de la commission de l'UEMOA relative à l'interprétation des articles 88, 89, et 90 du Traité relatifs aux règles de concurrence dans l'Union. http://www.ohada.com/jurisprudence/ohadata/J-02-32.html.

referred to the "effect on trade *within the Union*" and not the "effect on trade between Member States."

After the Court of Justice holding, the member states stopped applying their national competition laws and refrained from reforming them. The preemption not only seriously undermined the development of the national laws, it hindered the development of WAEMU's regional competition law, which was meant to be built on a network of cooperative member states plying their oars for the good of the community. Indeed, under the WAEMU Regulations,[30] national competition authorities are required to cooperate with the WAEMU Commission during investigations, to monitor national markets, and to report potential competition law violations to the Commission. However, forced to abandon their national enforcement, some member states are refusing to comply with the mandate to cooperate.[31] As we saw in Chapter III, within their own nations, the national authorities have been confined to enforcing "unfair competition" law. Not surprisingly, price control (government price-setting) is still a prominent feature of West African states' law.

### b. The Structure of WAEMU

The WAEMU Commission is WAEMU's executive and administrative body. The WAEMU Commission is organized into departments,[32] all under the Office of the President of the Commission. Each department is led by a commissioner. The departments are organized into directorates each headed by a director. The Directorate of Competition, created in 2007, lies under the umbrella of the Department of the Regional Market, Trade, Competition, and Cooperation. This is the directorate that enforces the regional competition law. The Competition Directorate has only a handful of agents working full time on competition matters.

The WAEMU Commission's structural organization is centralized. The president of the Commission plays a central role. On competition law matters, every inquiry, investigation, and enforcement action of the Directorate of Competition must be authorized by the president of the Commission. This formal requirement applies even to simple actions, such as requests for information and communication with parties. The centralized bureaucracy limits the flexibility of the directorate and slows the processes.

---

[30] Directive n° 02/2002/CM/UEMOA relative à la coopération entre la Commission et les structures nationales de concurrence des Etats membres pour l'application des articles 88, 89 et 90 du Traité UEMOA, *available at* http://www.uemoa.int/sites/default/files/bibliotheque/pages_-_directive_02_2002_cm.pdf.

[31] However, Burkina Faso, the Ivory Coast, Mali, and perhaps some others have been cooperating.

[32] There are seven departments within the WAEMU Commission. http://www.uemoa.int/fr/organes-uemoa/la-commission.

WAEMU's Competition Directorate is affected by the scarcity of resources of the West Africa national competition authorities, for the directorate depends on them (or ideally would do so) for leads and cooperation. The member states' competition authorities often have only a couple and usually less than a handful of full-time officials and staff. The limited national resources are devoted to price control and not to supporting the WAEMU Commission in its enforcement actions at the national level.

The Competition Directorate also suffers from lack of procedural powers. For example, it is not authorized to conduct dawn raids. Dawn raids are unannounced entry on a suspect company's premises to find evidence of price-fixing or other serious violation before the evidence is destroyed. This is a common and effective tool internationally. The Competition Directorate does have power to visit suspect companies' offices, but it informs the suspected companies and announces its visit in advance, so firms inclined to dispose of incriminating documents have time to do so.

Complaints by businesses and individuals as a source of leads to illegal conduct are virtually unknown, as one might expect in a culture where loyalty to fellow "rivals" is stronger than expectations that the market can help them. From a practical point of view, the centralized system makes it virtually impossible for complaints by victims of national restraints to reach the WAEMU Commission. Victims' access to the Commission is an issue.

In many jurisdictions a private right of action by victims can fill the slack created by an inattentive enforcer. There is notionally a private right of action in the WAEMU system, but it can be activated only after a final decision on illegality is taken at the regional level. So far, there has been no final decision on anticompetitive practices challenged by the WAEMU Commission, and the requirement that there be one has rendered private enforcement virtually unavailable.

### c. Enforcement

For more than a decade after the competition regulations entered into force, WAEMU has issued no decision on cartels or abuse of a dominant position. As of the time of this writing, the Commission has just issued three decisions. They are not yet published, but one appears from reports to be a cartel case. This is an exceptionally poor record—especially in light of the fact that only WAEMU and not the national authorities can bring competition cases for harms within the union.

Competition-related decisions taken by the Commission have generally dealt with state-related anticompetitive acts. In an interview, Amadou Dieng, former director of the WAEMU Competition Office, noted his initial expectation that private restraints of competition would be rampant in the regional market. He found, however, that state-related restraints overwhelmed purely private restraints and were particularly harmful in undermining market integration of West Africa.[33]

The Commission's competition bureau has devoted significant resources to state and state-complicit restraints. The two cases described below fall into this category, which is: state restraints that seriously harm competition.

*Norme NS 03-072*[34] involved a regulation of Senegal that would keep Ivory Coast palm oil out of Senegal. Senegal adopted this regulation in 2009. It required a maximum of 30 percent fat acid in refined palm oil and prevented the import of all palm oil that did not conform. The measure was taken without approval by WAEMU. WAEMU was in the course of providing a framework for standardization of products, but the framework was not yet effective. As a result of Senegal's measure, West Africa Commodities, a firm that imported palm oil from the Ivory Coast to sell on the Senegalese market, was blocked from competing with the local Senegalese producer of refined palm oil. The Ivory Coast and West Africa Commodities challenged the measure before the WAEMU Commission.

The Senegalese government defended the regulation, saying it was adopted for public health reasons. It argued that since the regional regulatory framework for certification was not yet effective, Senegal could adopt measures unilaterally, and that the regional rules requiring states to abstain from anticompetitive practices were not applicable.

Evidence during the inquiry showed that the Senegalese company *Société SUNEOR*, Senegal's main producer of refined palm oil, had lobbied the government of Senegal to introduce the measure, which, by blocking the Ivory Coast seller, would have granted *Société SUNEOR* a monopoly of palm oil in Senegal.

The Commission held for the Ivory Coast. The regulation violated the principle of free movement of goods in the common market. Senegal was ordered to suspend application of the regulation. The Commission held that public health considerations justify only temporary measures that are coordinated on the regional

---

[33] *See* Amadou Dieng, then Director of the WAEMU Competition Office, International Competition Network Training on Demand, Developing Countries and Competition video, http://www.internationalcompetitionnetwork.org/about/steering-group/outreach/icncurriculum/devco.aspx (at 47 minutes, 35 seconds); also noting that lack of resources, human and capital, is a huge challenge, and that to garner support for the competition project, the debate on competition policy must take place not just among the experts but also at the political level.

[34] Décision n° 007/2010/COM/UEMOA invitant l'Etat du Sénégal à retirer la norme NS 03-072 modifiée et les mesures prises pour son application, *available at* http://www.uemoa.int. Comments on the decision based on Bakhoum, e-competition, concurrences, 2013 (case decided in 2010).

level. Otherwise, states may not take measures that foreclose national markets from competition.

What if there were a real public health threat from the imports? That would not have been an admissible defense by the member states to the national monopoly-conferring measure, but would have been a matter for decision and possibly regulation at regional level.

The WAEMU holding in the palm oil case mirrors EU law. A member state may not keep out imports from within the community to protect its national industry.[35]

In the *ASKY* case,[36] ASKY, an airline company, agreed to place its headquarters and central hub in Togo in exchange for immunities and tax exemptions. As part of the inducement, Togo promised that ASKY's assets would not be seized and that its records would not be searched by any national or regional authority.

Air Senegal complained. Following through on the complaint, the Senegalese government contested the agreement between ASKY and Togo. It argued that the agreement violated the WAEMU Regulation on State Aids, which requires that all aid by a state to a company be notified to the WAEMU Commission and be preapproved. Togo argued that ASKY was immune from the regional competition rules, on grounds that it was a regional company supported by both the WAEMU and the ECOWAS Conference of Heads of States.

The WAEMU Commission rejected Togo's argument. It pointed out that ASKY is a private company incorporated in Togo. Although the WAEMU Heads of State expressed the desire to create a regional airline, they specified no special treatment for ASKY. The community competition rules (including state aid control) were fully applicable. Togo, by signing the agreement, violated the regional competition rules. The Commission directed the government of Togo to repeal the agreement, which it did. Accordingly, Air Senegal was not forced to compete against a privileged firm.

The two cases are good examples of state-related restraints, which occupy a very important place among restraints that seriously undermine competition.[37] The problem is: enforcement against state restraints does not take the place of enforcement against private restraints, which is sorely lacking.

---

[35] *See* Rewe-Zentral AG v. Bundesmonopolverwaltung für Branntwein (Cassis de Dijon), Case 120/78, ECLI:EU:C:1979:42.

[36] Décision n° 002/2011/COM/UEMOA déclarant certaines dispositions de l'accord de siège entre la compagnie aérienne communautaire dénommée ASKY et le gouvernement de la république togolaise incompatibles avec les règles communautaires de concurrence, *available at* http://www.uemoa.int.

[37] *See* Eleanor M. Fox & Deborah Healey, *When the State Harms Competition—The Role for Competition Law*, 79 Antitrust L.J. 769 (2014).

## d. Reform

The WAEMU Commission initiated an ambitious project in 2011: a study on the reform of the institutional enforcement framework of WAEMU.[38] The study identifies the flaws in the enforcement design and makes proposals to correct them. Building on the research by one of this book's authors,[39] the study takes stock of the relevant laws in the member states and WAEMU and makes reform proposals with a focus on the redistribution of competences between the WAEMU Commission and the member states. National competition authorities and various stakeholders such as consumer associations, academics, and sector regulatory authorities were consulted. They welcomed the study and agreed with the general orientation of the reform project to give back to national competition authorities the power to enforce their national competition laws. The study makes these findings and proposals:

The problems:
- As a regional competition authority, the competition directorate of the WAEMU Commission does not have sufficient structural and functional independence to work efficiently.
- The Commission is understaffed and lacks sufficient human resources.
- The procedural framework does not provide the Commission with sufficient leeway to take strong competition enforcement actions.
- The cooperation between national competition authorities and the Commission is ineffective. Since they don't have any decision-making power in application of their national laws, national competition authorities are not willing to collaborate with the WAEMU Commission.
- The national competition authorities are very weak. They lack human and financial resources.
- The centralized and preemptive system is detrimental to the development of the national competition laws and the creation of a competition culture in the member states.

THE PROPOSALS FOR REFORM. The proposed reforms adopt two main components: First, member states should have the possibility to adopt their national

---

[38] *See* UEMOA/Max Planck Institute, Etude sur la révision du cadre institutionnel de mise en œuvre des règles de concurrence de l'uemoa, 20112, *available at* http://etudes.uemoa.int/upload/rapport%20final%20etude%20 uemoa%20pdf.pdf.

[39] *See* Mor Bakhoum, L'articulation du droit communautaire et des droits nationaux de la concurrence dans l'Union Economique et Monétaire Ouest Africaine (UEMOA) (Stampfli, Bruylant 2007).

competition laws. Second, national competition authorities should have the possibility to apply their national laws to practices affecting only national markets.

The following specific proposals were made:

- Limit the regional competition authority's competence to practices affecting interstate trade, and restore the competence of states to regulate anticompetitive practices with purely domestic impacts.
- Create a separate competition agency under the Commission with sufficient human and financial resources for independence.
- Maintain the centralization of the substantive rules with a unique regional competition law regulating anticompetitive practices (cartels and abuse of dominant position).
- Develop the national competition laws and integrate the basic prohibitions of the community law into the national laws.
- Revise the functioning of the national competition authorities and give them more independence and enforcement resources. A directive could provide guidelines on the main aspects that member states should consider when creating or reforming national competition authorities.
- Combine WAEMU's competition competence over anticompetitive practices affecting cross-border trade with state aid.
- Foster collaboration between the regional competition authority and the national competition authorities.
- Broaden the competences of the WAEMU Council on Competition to act as a forum for information exchanges among the national competition authorities, facilitate resolution of conflicts, and advance common enforcement and other projects.

The member states discussed the proposed reforms and approved them at a meeting of the Council on Competition in 2013. Following agreement between the Commission and the member states on the tenets of the reform project, the Commission, in collaboration with the UN Conference on Trade and Development (UNCTAD), set up a panel of experts, who drafted new regulations to implement the proposals.

In line with the basic orientation of the reform project, the draft regulations would initiate decentralization of enforcement. They would give back to national competition authorities the power to enforce their national competition laws with respect to practices affecting their national markets. A cooperation mechanism would be created between the WAEMU Commission and the national competition authorities. The reform project holds much promise. However, the project lost momentum when the then director of WAEMU's Competition Office, Amadou Dieng, who advocated for the reform, stepped down.

## 3. Overlap between WAEMU and ECOWAS

The overlap between WAEMU and ECOWAS creates the potential for conflicting competition policies if there is no integration, but also the potential for efficiencies, coherent competition policy, and strength in numbers if there is integration. Integration of the competition policies of WAEMU and ECOWAS may be difficult to achieve, however, in view of their different relationships with their member states.

The differences have several possible consequences.

*Possible vertical conflict*: WAEMU member states are obliged not to apply national competition laws anywhere within the WAEMU community. ECOWAS member states, on the other hand, are encouraged to enact national competition laws and to create functioning national competition authorities. A WAEMU member could not exercise its freedom under ECOWAS to have and enforce a national competition law without violating its obligations under WAEMU. WAEMU's centralized approach indirectly contradicts and affects ECOWAS's objective to build functioning national competition policies in its member states.

*Possible horizontal conflict*: ECOWAS's regional competition authority is authorized to investigate and sanction anticompetitive practices, issue advisory opinions, cooperate with national and regional competition authorities, undertake studies and publish reports on the status of regional competition, and provide training programs.[40]

Conflicts may arise when the two regional competition authorities operate within the same regional space and have jurisdiction over the same practices involving the same companies. The process of establishing an ECOWAS competition authority is very advanced. The potential of conflicts is very likely when the regional authority of ECOWAS becomes operational.

An agreement can be cleared by one regional authority and prohibited by another. Standards for the assessment of a merger may differ. A potential abuse of dominance may be assessed differently by the two competition authorities. Companies may lack certainty about which regional authority to ask for clearance or exemption. There is also a risk of a dual sanction for an alleged anticompetitive practice.

The conflicts would arise only when the two regional authorities are actively applying their law. When they do arise, the two authorities would doubtlessly seek

---

[40] Supplementary Act on ECOWAS competition authority.

to cooperate, coordinate, and in many instances converge their law much like the United States does with the European Union.

The drafters of the ECOWAS's competition framework have recognized the possible conflicts and challenges, especially with WAEMU, and have tried to anticipate them. Both of the supplementary acts adopting the community competition rules and establishing the regional competition authority contain provisions on cooperation in general and with the WAEMU Commission in particular. Article 13(3) of the ECOWAS Supplementary Act that sets forth the legal ground for collaboration with WAEMU reads: "*In the implementation of the Community Competition Rules, the Regional Authority shall collaborate with the other existing competition agencies (UEMOA)*." This provision is complemented by Article 3 of the Supplementary Act establishing the ECOWAS competition authority, which also requires the regional authority to collaborate with existing regional competition agencies. Article 3 requires the ECOWAS Competition Authority to perform the following functions:

(f) co-operate with national and regional competition agencies in taking measures necessary to ensure implementation of the obligations arising from this Act;

(g) co-operate with and assist any association, intergovernmental organization, or body of persons in developing and promoting the observance of standards of conduct for the purpose of ensuring compliance with the provisions of this Supplementary Act. . . .

Recognizing the potential for conflicts as well as benefits of collaboration, ECOWAS's Supplementary Act anticipatorily requires the regional authority to collaborate and cooperate with WAEMU. The WAEMU regulations do not include reciprocal provisions, but are not inconsistent with them.

In order to alleviate potential conflicts, as a matter of institutional design, it has been proposed that ECOWAS treat WAEMU as a member state when enforcing ECOWAS's competition law.[41] Although in theory this proposal could reduce conflicts, clashes could still occur. WAEMU is not a state. An anticompetitive practice that affects trade between two WAEMU member states would still fall under the jurisdiction of both WAEMU and ECOWAS. Only serious sympathetic cooperation between the two regional competition authorities would avoid jurisdictional conflicts.

---

[41] *See* James H. Mathis & Kamala Dawar, *Is there potential for competition policy in the ECOWAS*, *in* THE EFFECTS OF ANTICOMPETITIVE BUSINESS PRACTICES ON DEVELOPING COUNTRIES AND THEIR DEVELOPMENT PROSPECTS 365 (H. Qaqaya & G. Lipimile eds., United Nations 2008).

For principles for coordination and collaboration we propose that:

- ECOWAS's competition authority should abstain from dealing with cases taking place only within and affecting only WAEMU's geographical space. WAEMU's regional competition authority should have exclusive jurisdiction on cases with effects only within WAEMU's geographical space.
- The better-placed competition authority should deal with the cases affecting both WAEMU and ECOWAS.
- A mechanism for collaboration on cases affecting ECOWAS's space should be adopted.
- An information exchange mechanism should be created at the inquiry stage on cross-border competition cases. This information mechanism would help in allocating cases.
- The authorities should exercise negative comity and not issue contradictory decisions in cases already decided by one of the regional competition authorities. These cases should be treated as res judicata.
- A database should be built allowing information sharing between the two regional competition authorities.

The future of an ECOWAS-WAEMU collaboration and coordination on competition issues is unclear, and whether there will be a merger of the two bodies is uncertain. For the moment the two regional enforcement bodies work in parallel without working towards a goal of merger. A merger would have the virtue of creating a stronger, more coherent regional competition authority in West Africa. But a merger would be difficult to achieve. Both treaties would need amendment. Moreover, the two bodies are very different, institutionally, culturally, linguistically, and socioeconomically, the competition culture being more advanced in WAEMU. At this stage, practical cooperation between the two regional competition authorities is the most pragmatic step.

D. SUMMARY

We have noted many obstacles to success of the regional associations of sub-Saharan Africa. Yet the promise is great, and success may be necessary to bring enforcement up to the level of the violations. If competition culture is sufficiently nurtured, from roots up, if the regional authorities take seriously cross-border and hybrid state-and-private restraints,[42] and if the regional associations become more sympathetic and

---

[42] See Norme NS 03-072, *supra* note 34. The focus on state and hybrid restraints is a staple of EU law and vital to its successes in building an internal market and strengthening the competiveness of its firms.

community-oriented toward one another, then Africa could be en route to creating a meaningful competition competence in the newly created Continental Free Trade Agreement, or at least on the path to more economic coherence, less privilege and cronyism, and more access to markets even in the context of the current motley mix of regional bodies.

However, the record of past regional enforcement thus far is slim. None of the regional bodies has prosecuted a hard core cartel case. None has prohibited an abuse of dominance that had effects on the market. COMESA, the only body with active merger control, has cleared every merger, usually without conditions, even megamergers in markets such as cement, seeds, and fertilizer—markets of presumptive concern. The megamergers equally impact West Africa, and since West Africa has no merger control they do so with impunity. The competition law staffs are too small for the needs of the regions. To meet the promise, big breakthroughs are required.

## V. The Networks

### A. INTRODUCTION

What cannot be done at higher levels may be done at lower levels. Competition law in the world is an example. Approximately 130 nations have competition laws. In the 1990s, observing the patchwork quilts of national competition laws, the synergies between competition and trade, and the value of coherence, policymakers vetted the idea of an international competition law framework within the World Trade Organization (WTO). Through fears of bureaucracy, squeezed space for industrial policy by developing countries, and loss of sovereignty, the project lost traction. Another very different project took its place—the creation, in 2001, of the International Competition Network (ICN) (discussed in Chapter II). ICN became the forum of choice for informal, nonbinding cooperation and convergence of competition law, procedures, and practice. ICN has helped the competition authorities clarify principles and practices and move toward better ones, and has provided a learning venue for younger authorities, who are the recipients of extensive shared experience.[43] It has provided a support network and helped younger authorities stand up to parochialism, privilege, and cronyism at home. The ICN has done remarkable and well-recognized work.

---

[43] *See* http://internationalcompetitionnetwork.org.

There are two hitches. First, despite its efforts to reach out to developing countries' competition authorities and include them on all projects, the voice of ICN is largely the voice of the developed countries. The principles of law expounded as "recommended practices" are principles that have evolved largely from well-working economies without statist backgrounds (plus, in at least some cases, neoconservative ideology). Second, ICN's work is comparative, not international. It does not span oceans, where trade (e.g., export cartels, and state-sponsored cartels) meet competition. It does not treat state restraints that protect a country's borders, nor the vested-interest strategies that preserve those borders. It does not touch the reality of developing countries' weak position in fighting international cartels and mergers targeted at them, and their weak position at the WTO bargaining table to reduce the developing countries' restraints (subsidies and tariffs) that especially hurt them.

Thus, the need for an African voice. An African competition network could fill the gap of identifying uniquely African competition problems and their solutions. It could also, possibly, with time, ease the way for pan-African coordination into one large FTA to advance the larger trade and competition interests of Africa in the world. Indeed, the African Continental Free Trade Area, now in the process of formation, could ultimately be the vehicle for a comprehensive continental competition policy and a comprehensive internal market trade-and-competition policy, pan Africa.

## B. THE AFRICAN COMPETITION FORUM

At the African Stakeholder Workshop in 2010, heads of competition authorities in sub-Saharan Africa formed the African Competition Forum (ACF). The ACF is a network of competition authorities of nations across Africa. Officially launched at its first conference, held in Nairobi in 2011, it envisions "[a] continent where markets become more fairly and competitively contested . . . [;] where competition delivers significant value for consumers, producers and investors."[44] The ACF aspires to "promote the adoption of competition principles in the implementation of national and regional economic policies of African countries, in order to alleviate poverty and enhance inclusive economic growth, development and consumer welfare by fostering competition in markets, and thereby increasing investment, productivity, innovation and entrepreneurship."[45] The ACF has three functional objectives: (1) to

---

[44] Vision statement. *See* jacarandaglobal, ACF in the spotlight: African Competition Forum promotes policy enhancements, https://africanantitrust.com/2014/11/13/acf-in-the-spotlight-african-competition-forum-promotes-policy-enhancements/.

[45] Quotation from Thulasoni Kaira, The Possibility of Establishing an Africa Competition Forum, Presentation prepared for the Workshop on Competition Law and Policy in African Small States, July 26–27, 2010, Windhoek, Namibia.

encourage and assist African countries to adopt competition laws; (2) to help build the capacity of existing and future African competition agencies by providing training, exchange, and funding to mitigate national deficits in human resources, budget, and institutional structure; and (3) to increase the awareness of the benefits of competition laws among governments, the general public, and stakeholders.[46]

A steering committee coordinates ACF's activities. The chair was first held by Francis Wang'ombe Kariuki, Chair of the Competition Authority of Kenya, and passed to Tembinkosi Bonakele, Competition Commissioner of South Africa.

The African Competition Forum has been active and productive. It holds a bi-annual conference and convenes a number of meetings of the steering committee on the sidelines of international conferences of groups with which it cooperates, including ICN, BRICS (Brazil, Russia, India, China, and South Africa) competition, UNCTAD competition, and OECD (Organization for Economic Cooperation and Development) competition. It has working groups, as on mergers and cartels, and holds training sessions often featuring US and EU enforcers who teach or reinforce investigative skills and competitive analysis. It has launched and completed important ground-up research, notably cross-country studies in four important sectors, each involving large multinational incumbent firms and evidence of market impediments: poultry, cement, sugar, and fertilizer. The participating competition authorities were Botswana, Kenya, Malawi, Namibia, South Africa, Tanzania, and Zambia. The results of the studies have led some authorities to undertake investigations and change some policies, and reportedly have increased rivalry in transportation and trading of fertilizer—a key segment in view of the importance of agriculture to economic growth in these countries.[47] The research papers are published in *Competition in Africa: Insights from Key Industries*.[48] The research results in cement and fertilizer plus additional work on telecommunications are incorporated into a World Bank/ACF publication, which concludes that strong competition enforcement in the cement sector and removal of impediments to competition "could save African consumers from overpaying for cement $2.5 billion per year."[49] Also, competitive public procurement in fertilizers would allow farmers to make a decent living. Further the report notes that the telecommunication sector in sub-Saharan Africa is marked by monopolies. The highly concentrated markets translate into Africa's having the highest prices for mobile broadband services in the

---

[46] *See* jacarandaglobal, *supra* note 44.

[47] Foreword, *in* COMPETITION IN AFRICA: INSIGHTS FROM KEY INDUSTRIES (S. Roberts ed., in collaboration with ACF and participating countries 2016).

[48] *Id.*

[49] WORLD BANK GROUP, ACF, BREAKING DOWN BARRIERS: UNLOCKING AFRICA'S POTENTIAL THROUGH VIGOROUS COMPETITION POLICY (2016).

world,[50] but the sector is also characterized by disruptive technologies, which are moving at a fast pace.

Research continues and papers have been completed in sectors of special interest to Africa, including telecommunications, pharmaceuticals, health care, liquid petroleum gas, construction, airlines, energy, transport, and state-owned enterprises.

English is the dominant language of the meetings, workshops, and training sessions. Efforts are being made, within budgetary limits, to adapt and present in French as well.

The ACF has strong potential to provide a base of collaboration and coordination of competition law and policy across Africa and to support a competition voice for Africa in the world.

## VI. Conclusion

Regional collaboration and integration hold much promise for Africa in theory, but practical obstacles loom large. They are especially large in West Africa. In East Africa, COMESA's activity and scope are still unfolding. The persistence of prolific cross-border restraints in the SADC countries could lead to a stronger SADC, and prospects for a meaningful Tripartite Free Trade Area or even larger collaboration exist if there is a will. Just as Europe in the late 1980s challenged Europeans by notionally calculating the "costs of non-Europe,"[51] Africa might challenge Africans by recognition of the costs of non-Africa.

Meanwhile, informally, the African Competition Forum is playing an admirably productive roots-up role in enhancing the capacities of the competition authorities in Africa and providing a shared research base that could help the authorities detect and target the plethora of restraints that undermine growth and development in Africa.

One key to progress will be establishing modalities to deal with the poisonous mix of strategic restraints by the state and vested interests that cross national borders. A second key will be to listen to the voice of Africa, which demands much more attention than it has thus far commanded regarding how to clear the pathways to entry and success of Africans in African markets.

---

[50] *Id.*

[51] The Cecchini Report, THE EUROPEAN CHALLENGE 1992: THE BENEFITS OF A SINGLE MARKET (The European Commission 1998), based on the specially commissioned report, The Costs of Non-Europe.

3

# Roadmaps—A Place in the World

# 7

## PERSPECTIVES FROM FOUR STAGES OF DEVELOPMENT

What Is Needed by the Nations, What Is Needed for the World?

## I. Introduction

What is demanded by localism, especially in developing countries, and what is desired for globalism, especially by industrialized countries? In this chapter we place the local demands and the global aspirations into deeper context. We do this by identifying four clusters based on state of development, and we ask: What is the most fitting competition framework nationally, and what is the most fitting competition framework internationally, from the perspective of each cluster? In this chapter we assess differences, and how the threads can be brought into a healthy synergistic alliance.

Although we identify clusters, in fact there is a continuum. By identifying four points along the continuum, we are able to highlight significant qualitative differences in economies and needs and capabilities that may call for different law and policies.

Three of the clusters are composed of nations in sub-Saharan Africa, and one, for perspective, is composed of advanced industrialized countries. The three developmental clusters are: (1) least developed countries with the most resource-challenged competition authorities, such as Benin and Togo;[1] (2) more developed countries,

---

[1] Benin and Togo are members of the West African Economic and Monetary Union.

Making Markets Work for Africa. Eleanor M. Fox and Mor Bakhoum.
© Oxford University Press 2019. Published 2019 by Oxford University Press.

such as Kenya, Tanzania, Zambia, Botswana, and Mauritius; and (3) a "set" of one—South Africa. South Africa's cohorts in the world include the other BRICS—Brazil, Russia, India and China. The developed countries represent a fourth cluster.

We take an analogy from Isaiah Berlin's *The Fox and the Hedgehog*.[2] We visualize the clusters as three foxes and one hedgehog; it being recalled that the fox sees many alternative conceptions, and the hedgehog has one big idea or picture; thus, legitimate multiplicities (validating pluralism), versus a unified picture that depends on acceptance of one right point of view. The hedgehog in this story is the developed world or at least those within it who advocate a strong view of convergence to "international standards" based on efficiency and consumer welfare. The foxes are: the little (or least developed), the middle, and the big. The task of this chapter is to explore how each cluster views the world of competition law and policy in terms of anticompetitive restraints within the nation and in terms of anticompetitive restraints from the outside world.

In the literature on competition law and policy, the usual approach is to start with the law and policy as it exists in the mature antitrust jurisdictions of the world and to presume that in essence this law fits the world. We start from a different vantage: local context, roots-up. The chapter begins by addressing three sets of questions.

1. What market restraints and abuses hurt the nation and its peoples the most? We limit the category to those restraints and abuses that might usefully be caught and remedied by competition law or addressed by competition policy asserted by the competition authority. We divide the inquiry into two categories: (1) restraints within the nation including those that are state- or local-government generated, and (2) restraints within the world or outsider-generated.
2. What are the available pathways for addressing and these restraints?
3. What are the most significant limitations that might prevent the competition authority from successfully challenging the restraints? And how do these practical limits influence the scope, perspective, and ambition of the developing country's competition law?

The three sets of questions have a normative as well as positive content. What counts as a "most serious market restraint" depends upon what the nation wants from its market system. Only efficiency, or also equity? Only efficiency, or primarily growth and development? Only growth, or inclusive growth? We will see

---

[2] Isaiah Berlin, The Hedgehog and the Fox: An Essay on Tolstoy's View of History (London: Weidenfeld & Nicolson 1953).

that nations representing each set of clusters may have different perspectives. The developing countries want development. They are likely to want efficient inclusive development in order to achieve a combination of growth and a sense of personal freedom and autonomy.[3] The developed nations want competitiveness in the world and global economic hegemony. These differences in value hierarchies are hidden to the Western world. Students learn: markets are for "efficiency," and "efficiency is efficiency" (the hedgehog's view; thus, inclusive development is not admitted as a proper goal of competition law, especially if it might lessen aggregate wealth).

We will see as our story unfolds: the worst restraints confronting the least developed countries and the worst restraints confronting the developing countries are often different in character. Nonetheless, the worst restraints confronting developing countries are seriously market-disabling from any view of efficiency, and the nations having to cope with these restraints are also least well equipped to tackle them, presenting an overwhelming challenge to least developed countries before they can begin to play in a ballpark staked out as good competition law and policy by the developed world.[4] This reality might suggest the need for a more empathetic approach in helping to construct a competition law and policy appropriate to least developed nations, an approach most likely to pull their economy up to a higher level of functionality. It also suggests that huge reforms in governance, rule of law, and the competitive environment in the nation might need to occur before its competition authority can make more than a ripple of difference in enabling markets.

Now we are ready to embark on our inquiry. What are the clusters, and what are their answers to the three sets of questions?

## II. The Clusters

*The first cluster.* The least developed countries are the first cluster. Paradigmatically, the country's markets are not functioning well, often as a result of years without a market economy and a skepticism toward markets. Often the country has a background of a command-and-control economy. Typically, the economy is dominated by state monopolies or recently privatized monopolies in the major sectors—energy, utilities, mining, steel, and the state-owned enterprises (SOEs) are recipients of subsidies, exclusive rights, and a multitude of nontransparent privileges. Otherwise, the formal economy may be owned by a few families, and the informal economy is large. Infrastructure for getting to markets is poor. Education except for the elites

---

[3] *See* AMARTYA SEN, DEVELOPMENT AS FREEDOM (1999).
[4] *See* A. E. RODRIGUEZ & ASHOK MENON, THE LIMITS OF COMPETITION POLICY: THE SHORTCOMINGS OF ANTITRUST IN DEVELOPING AND REFORMING ECONOMIES (2010).

is very poor. Corruption is high and pervasive. Poverty and disparity of wealth are high and systemic. Opportunity and mobility are low. There is a very small pool of talent on which to draw for positions in government agencies (among others). Financial resources are scarce. Political pressures on government officials to favor "friends of the President" are high. The competition authorities are staffed by only a handful of people. They have no chief economist. The courts are slow, inefficient, and often corrupt, and the judges are untrained in market and economic concepts. There is an absence of rule of law; that is, there are not ascertainable principles of law transparently applied. The competition authority spends a critical mass of its time regulating prices. If the authority has a consumer protection function, it devotes a healthy share of its resources to attacking deceptive practices. If it has a "fair competition" function, it devotes a healthy share trying to prevent big firms from bullying small players. Even if the competition authority is not corrupt or captured by the firms that might become its targets, it is frustrated by its impotence to challenge the most serious abusers of economic power.[5]

*The second cluster.* The second cluster has many of the same burdens (and all of the same virtues), but the nations in the cluster have advanced economically to a perceptibly higher level, and the disabilities are somewhat less debilitating. The nations have a qualitatively higher gross domestic product and average income. They have less poverty. They may have a promising growth trajectory. They, too, are starved for resources, but still they are able to assemble competition offices with a critical mass of trained or rapidly learning staff. They may have a chief economist, well trained.

*The third cluster.* The third point on the spectrum is a "group" of one—South Africa. With all of its challenges—corruption, crime, poverty, inequality, and persistent marginalization—the South African competition regime is as close to a gold standard as there is in sub-Saharan Africa. The country has seen a good growth trajectory, although it has been set back in recent years by poor economic and political conditions. It has a strong rule of law. It is facing very serious challenges to both governance and economy, but the people have a strong will to overcome them. It has still not equitably incorporated its historically disadvantaged population into its economic life. But at some (although insufficient) levels, its education system is strong. It is home to a talented and well-trained population. Its business is challenged but stable. Its Competition Commission and institutions are able, motivated, and sophisticated.

*The fourth cluster.* In the fourth cluster are the developed countries, led in particular by the European Union and the United States. They have open economies,

---

[5] *See* THE ECONOMIC CHARACTERISTICS OF DEVELOPING JURISDICTIONS: THEIR IMPLICATIONS FOR COMPETITION LAW (M. Gal et al. eds., 2015).

fairly robust markets, good infrastructure, and good institutions. Their competition authorities have large and well-trained expert staffs. Of course they face poverty, corruption, and political pressure, but these problems are qualitatively less and different. They have a strong rule of law, even as many worry about a surge of selfish nationalism.

## III. Four Perspectives

### A. THE FIRST CLUSTER—LEAST DEVELOPED

Question 1—What are your most significant market problems?

What can the first cluster do and hope to achieve in the realm of competition law and policy to improve the functioning of markets for the good of their people? What restraints need the most attention—with a view to dismantling them? What are the most harmful restraints that keep the markets from working and that are plausible targets of competition policy?

#### a. *Restraints within the Nation*

Restraints most harmful to this most-challenged cluster are state acts and measures and other restraints in which the state or state officials are complicit.[6] State and local government restraints typically squeeze the space for competition on the merits; they block the most productive channels for economic opportunity and mobility—the escape routes from poverty—even while they set the stage for corruption, harming consumers and other users of public goods such as roads, housing, medicines, and food. Public goods, while underprovided and typically the subject of antitrust conspiracies, are also most needed by the poor.

Therefore this cluster is well advised to explore the extent to which their competition law (and not just advocacy) can reach and condemn unreasonably anticompetitive state and local government acts. A first step is to ensure inclusion of state-owned enterprises in the coverage of the law, for anticompetitive conduct of SOEs is likely to be a principal source of harm.

Restraints involving the state come in many sizes and shapes, and some may be venal. A state officer may accept bribes to write procurement specifications that can be filled only by his buddy, or to grease the wheels of a procurement bidding cartel. Or anticompetitive state measures or structures may simply be the product of

---

[6] *See* Eleanor M. Fox & Deborah Healey, *When the State Harms Competition—The Role for Competition Law*, 79 ANTITRUST L.J. 769 (2014), at 783, 804.

unknowledgeable bureaucrats who place blind faith in government boards to control the market.

State-imposed border barriers, including measures barricading goods at the border, are among the worst restraints. For example, because of border restraints, Ivory Coast palm oil may not flow into Senegal and Gambian groundnuts may not move into Senegal except at extortionate prices.

While these problems could be classified as sovereignty and trade questions and not competition problems, that would be a mistake. These are most serious market obstructions, and if they are not removed, the role of the competition authority can be greatly diminished. The area of the competition authority's mandate may be too circumscribed for the authority to make much of a difference. If debilitating state and trade restraints can be addressed in some significant measure, the competition authority has a serious chance of making a difference.

There are, of course, also the traditional egregious harms. These can include serious market-blocking acts of dominant firms and cartels—often involving recidivist culprits, as in cement, sugar, and poultry. Mergers can facilitate cartels and create monopolies. Developing countries, more than developed countries, are likely to be seriously harmed by creation of buyer power and the structure and conduct of exclusion by global value chains, which might exclude the unprivileged masses.

Identifying the restraints that are the most debilitating for the society includes identifying the class of victims. In first-cluster countries, where 50 percent to 70 percent of the people may live below the poverty line and some 70 percent may earn their livelihood from agriculture and are among the very poor, restraints in the agricultural sector that deprive the farmers and small processors of access to markets on the merits are among the worst for their societies.

### b. Restraints from the World

The cluster-one nations are targets for anticompetitive practices in the world. Cartels targeted at them often involve basic and necessary goods and inputs such as fertilizers (potash) for crops, and vitamins. The cartels are illegal in virtually every member of the antitrust family of the world. Yet the first-cluster nations are likely to be harmed without recourse, for the competition authority and the victims nearly always lack the resources to press the case against the offshore offenders, and in any event, they lack the ability to exact penalties sufficient to deter repetitions of the offenses.

Likewise the nations stand to be harmed by the huge multinational mergers that win clearance (often improvidently and almost always with conditions) by the industrialized nations, and whose harms are more severe in the developing world. Markets in cement, fertilizers, seeds, and beer may be impaired—with a special bite in developing countries that are powerless to fend against them. Exclusionary practices by both multinational enterprises (MNEs) and large—often state-owned—domestic firms close off valuable channels for indigenous firms. Western standards are often permissive to dominant and legacy firms, which subtly tighten the vise on economic opportunities for outsiders.

Question 2—What are the pathways to solutions?

The competition authority might be powerless to challenge the most severe restraints—those by the state, or with backing of the state. Possibly, the legislature might grant the competition authority power to challenge some state acts, as a number of jurisdictions have done. Also the agency might be entrusted with power to conduct market studies to locate the worst restraints and impose (or present to a court) remedies for their removal.

As for restraints by foreign firms imposed from abroad, the law can confer effects jurisdiction so that the law reaches offshore actors targeting the nation. Most competition laws do. Meanwhile, in regional common markets (see Chapter VI), the nations can collaborate with neighbors for their common good and, very significantly, can invoke the power of the regional regime to discipline anticompetitive state acts with cross-border effects—a power virtually always included in the law of common markets but virtually always ignored by the enforcers who should use them.[7]

Some of the harms from global restraints could be alleviated by an international regime. A wise international regime would at least require nations to prohibit firms from doing to foreigners what they would not do to themselves; thus it would prohibit world-consensus wrongs such as hard core cartels when they injure (sufficiently directly) anyone in the world. At least, a progressive international framework would require the offenders' countries to aid in discovery of evidence on their soil. Moreover, a helpful regime would take a more aggressive stance against world megamergers that facially will harm world competition, would be quicker to prohibit anticompetitive mergers, and would not be fooled by the merging parties' story that a few spin-offs will restore the heady competition that is lost. But there is no world regime. As for practices by dominant firms that tend to exclude or marginalize firms without power, the nations might wish to question conservative Western standards and to consider sympathetically standards that will open markets while giving due regard to (even) dominant firms' acts that bring new or better products to market.

---

[7] The law of the European Union is the model. *See* Fox & Healey, *supra* note 6.

Question 3—What are the most significant limitations in addressing the major restraints?

We have seen that the most significant restraints emanate from the state, or from vested interests or cronies through the state, or are generated offshore. These are the most difficult market obstructions to topple, because of political pressure and the "wages" of politics, or lack of practical power even if the tools for enforcement are in place. In addition, even for the most widely recognized heinous restraints, the set of characteristics that identify these nations conspires against effective enforcement: the scarcity of human and financial resources; weak institutions; lack of rule of law; no competition culture and distrust of markets. The people are accustomed to price-setting by the state when prices rise "too high"; they expect this intervention; they have no faith that they can sit back and wait for the market to work—in general or after a breakup of cartels. How to move the people from a trust in price control to a trust in markets—when they have had no reason to trust markets? This will be a long process. It will take resources, litigation, and policy-reform successes, well-publicized examples of success, and strong, honest, and determined leadership. Even more so, it will take time, resources, and a favorable climate to challenge the market-strangling government restraints. The multifaceted limitations combine to affect the scope, perspective, and ambition of the competition law and policy that cluster-one nations adopt and try to implement.

## B. THE SECOND CLUSTER—MORE DEVELOPED

Question 1—What are your most significant market problems?

The second-cluster nations are qualitatively more developed, have access to more resources, and have stronger institutions than the first cluster.

Developing a competition culture is still a huge challenge, but it is taking root. The people appreciate how freeing up markets can help them, and the competition agenda is not dominated by price control. This greater appreciation of markets is observable in countries such as Kenya, Zambia, Botswana, and Mauritius.

In the second cluster, the development of a more sophisticated competition law and policy is observable. A great source of learning is peers from other nations. Economically more advanced neighbors provide meaningful lessons and insights. The growing communities of regional associations also provide this function. One example is the training that the South African Competition Commission conducts with other African competition authorities.[8] Another is the training sessions offered

---

[8] *See* Kasturi Moodaliyar, *Competition Policy in the SADC: A South African Perspective*, Chapter 4, *in* COMPETITION POLICY AND REGIONAL INTEGRATION IN DEVELOPING COUNTRIES, at 66 (J. Drexl et al. eds., 2012).

by the University of Johannesburg's CCRED.[9] Much learning comes from the international competition community and much from developed countries, which have incentives to share, explain, and teach their modes of operation and analysis. And learning also comes from within Africa; for example, from the African Competition Forum.[10]

The facility of cluster-two countries for connecting with and learning both from neighbors and from the international competition community is greater than that of cluster-one countries. As expertise in the nation's competition authority grows, the authority's comfort zone with deeper interaction with the international competition community grows, and more interaction occurs.

A critical mass of the competition authorities in second-cluster nations have been peer reviewed by the UN Conference on Trade and Development (UNCTAD) at their request. These include Botswana, Kenya, Mauritius, Tanzania, and Zambia. Participation in UNCTAD's voluntary peer review program signals three positive points that give cluster two a more solid connection with market-based progress: (1) the request for a peer review usually signals a level of competition development in the country and the confidence of the competition authority.[11] (2) The competition authority invariably profits from the process and the outcome. The reviewers typically recommend a variety of reforms, big and small, and the authorities typically attempt to use the recommendations to good advantage, for example, in seeking important new enforcement powers from their legislatures. (3) The nations may be hoisted onto a new track of increasing integration with the world community; an upward spiral of learning, contributing, and developing.

### a. Restraints within the Nation

The kinds of restraints within the nation that hurt the people and economy the most are generally the same as for cluster one, and the structural conditions of the economy are commonly quite the same, with highly concentrated markets often controlled by the state or by a few families or businesses. The likelihood of success in challenging the restraints is somewhat greater, albeit still daunting. Resistance against harmful megamergers approved by the developed jurisdictions is equally

---

[9] Centre for Competition, Regulation and Economic Development, http://www.competition.org.za/about-us-1/.

[10] *See* Chapter VI for a description of the work of the African Competition Forum.

[11] Peer reviews have also included cluster-one countries. For example, Benin was peer-reviewed by UNCTAD in 2007.

daunting, but ability to impose somewhat meaningful conditions or local spin-offs is greater.

### b. Restraints from the World

The restraints in the world that harm second-cluster countries are exactly the same as those that harm the first cluster. Second-cluster countries are somewhat better placed to develop mechanisms to protect themselves—for example, by combining forces against international offenders to get their fair share of compensation for harms. Perhaps at some point they will be strong enough to impose penalties that will create credible deterrence, but that point may be a long way off. Resistance to harmful megamergers approved by the developed jurisdictions is equally impossible, but ability to impose conditions or local spin-offs is greater.

Question 2—What are the pathways to solution?

The pathways are similar to those available to cluster one. Benchmarking is more available. The ability to seek peer review and to implement the peers' recommendations can be an important segue into a more fully market-based competition law.

Question 3—What are the most significant limitations in addressing the major restraints?

The limitations are similar to those of cluster one but less aggravated. Markets are more appreciated. Pathways to development are more solid. Still, the limitations seriously influence the scope, perspective, and ambition of the competition law and policy.

### C. THE THIRD CLUSTER—SOUTH AFRICA

As we move up the development ladder to South Africa, we see that wholly private restraints share more ground with public restraints. There is more space for private-firm competition, although in South Africa any early aspiration for inclusive development of the market was badly set back by apartheid. Still, a large portion of market-related problems derive from state-owned enterprises and their progeny, and fall into the category of abuse of dominance.

Because in South Africa there are more working markets than in the nations of the first two clusters, there is less need to *create* markets before competition can exist. Because of apartheid and its indelible effects, there is a special need to bring historically excluded people into markets.

Question 1—What are your most significant market problems?

*a. Restraints within the Nation*

As in most of the developing world, state-owned entities and their progeny impose and maintain some of the worst obstructions to competition. The constantly reinforced noncompetitive structure of markets remains a challenge.

The fact that South Africa has more well-functioning markets than the first two clusters means that cartel cases and merger cases take a higher place on the agenda, and the case docket may look more like that of the developed jurisdictions. Still, the historical powerful few—the state, its progeny, and the beneficiaries of apartheid—take constant advantage of opportunities to ring-fence the market and make it only somewhat penetrable by meritorious challengers.

Like the first two clusters, South Africa aspires to inclusive development. This means that exclusionary practices, whether by single or joint conduct, may warrant a higher place on the agenda than in the developed world.

Some of South Africa's mandate to help the historically disadvantaged people can be fulfilled by enforcement priorities, thus prioritizing markets with high impact on the poor, such as bread, grain, and cement. The Competition Commission has done this.

*b. Restraints from the World*

The world restraints that hurt South Africa are identical with those that harm the nations in the first and second clusters. But South Africa is in a better position to defend itself against world restraints, through proceedings by both the Commission and private victims. And South Africa is in as good a position as any nation to organize a consortium of injured sub-Saharan African states. This does not diminish the need for home nations of offshore offenders to discipline the offenders at the source (foreign soil); for, still, like pollution, the problem is most efficiently and effectively stemmed at its source.

Question 2—What are the pathways to solution?

The pathways to solution are virtually the same as for cluster two.

Question 3—What are the most significant limitations in addressing the major restraints?

The limitations are severe, but qualitatively less so. Big pockets of power, privilege and corruption, resource limits, and shortfalls in governance chill aspirations. Still, competition culture is diffusing, and the people are learning—through

Commission outreach and good journalism—what competition law and policy can do for them.[12]

## D. THE FOURTH CLUSTER—THE DEVELOPED WORLD, LED BY THE EUROPEAN UNION AND THE UNITED STATES (TWO WINGS OF A LARGE AND DIVERSE CLUSTER)

The fourth cluster is the developed nations. These nations/jurisdictions are industrialized. Some, the United States in particular, have had a liberal economy from the inception. Corporations that have grown to a large size have done so largely by being creative, responsive, and efficient. Markets exist and work; there is not a ground-floor challenge to create markets. The talent pool is deep. Whatever resource constraints exist in the antitrust authorities, they are small compared with the constraints in the developing country clusters. Each of the two federal competition agencies employs hundreds of competition professionals (approximately 600), including dedicated economists who are among the best trained in the world. The judiciary is strong and basically well trained and honest. To be sure, the nation suffers from serious corruption, poverty, inequality, unemployment, lack of mobility, triumphs of vested interests, and dysfunctions in democracy. But still, there are so many healthy markets, such deep incentives to innovate, such feisty pro-consumer and anticorruption activism, and so high a level of rule of law and transparency that the bite of corruption and dysfunction is minor compared with that encountered in developing countries.

The European Union is the other pillar on which we focus in this fourth cluster. Its competition model is the most imitated in the world. The structural market characteristics in the internal market are more diverse than in the United States in view of the fact that the European Union is composed of 28 (soon to be 27) sovereign nations. The great disparities of the original six member states' political economy arrangements, and the European goal of creating one common market, led at the birth of the European Community in 1957 to its reinvention of competition law to constrain state, private, and hybrid anticompetitive acts, to create and open markets, and to purge the markets of vested interests, nationalism, and discrimination. Although the structural disparities between member states are now much reduced, the open-market, nondiscrimination motivations have always been at the heart of the European project.

---

[12] *See* DAVID LEWIS, THIEVES AT THE DINNER TABLE: ENFORCING THE COMPETITION ACT (2012).

The United States and the European Union, along with Japan, South Korea, and a handful of other developed countries (each of which has its own unique characteristics and aspirations), are homes to the biggest multinational enterprises in the world. Multinational enterprises would generally profit from common world rules and standards, especially of the less interventionist variety.

Question 1—What are your most important market problems?

*a. Restraints within the Jurisdiction*

What are the most important market problems that might usefully be caught by antitrust/competition policy? In the United States the answer quickly and commonly given is cartels. While monopolistic practices were high on the agenda until the 1980s, this priority receded in view of a trumping concern that antitrust enforcement would coddle small inefficient firms, protect them from efficient competition, and handicap the "best." The targets of US antitrust are almost entirely private firms, most often pursued for engaging in cartels, with sporadic cases targeting anticompetitive market acts of states (of the United States) entities and local entities. The authorities' clear priority is enforcement against cartels. The authorities also devote resources to competition advocacy against excessive and unnecessary regulation. They do not engage in market advocacy against trade restraints such as antidumping laws, which are entrusted to other hands and regarded as off-bounds for the competition authorities' advocacy.

As for abuse of dominance (monopolization), there is a reluctance to bring such cases for fear that the enforcement will chill hard competition and protect inefficiencies of small and middle-size firms. Abuses by privileged state-owned enterprises are not and have not been a problem because state ownership is minimal.

The EU answer to the question is different. Abuses of dominance, and especially those of state-owned enterprises and, separately, abuses that restrain cross-border competition, are at the top the agenda. The EU law targets even certain state *measures*. In addition, the law reaches all of the usual subjects of competition law: other abuses of dominance, cartels, other competitor agreements, vertical restraints, and anticompetitive mergers. In the last two decades, the European Union has replaced formalistic rules with effects-based rules and appointed a chief economist and a large and expert team of economists, moving the law and the Competition Directorate-General's rhetoric in some respects closer to that of the United States.

The biggest market impediments faced by developed countries, and especially by the United States, have nowhere near the dimensions and gravity of the impediments faced by the least developed countries. The developed countries have basic working markets.

## b. Restraints from the World

What harms derive from acts and conditions outside of the nation or jurisdiction? The answer is very different for developing and developed countries. For simplicity (and because they are the two major models for the world), we limit our answer to the United States and the European Union.

Unlike the developing country clusters, neither the United States nor the European Union is at risk from their trading partners' export exemptions. Both jurisdictions have doctrines of extraterritorial reach of their law, and they have the legal and practical power to apply their law to offshore actors who harm the nation's citizens. Potential offenders generally want to continue to do business in the jurisdiction to which they export (e.g., the United States or the European Union), and so they have the incentive to obey its law.

The United States and the European Union see themselves as harmed by the divergences of laws around the world. These harms include the increased cost of doing business and the possibility that more aggressive foreign enforcement may encroach upon the domestic authority's own enforcement decisions and produce overregulation of (if not "intermeddling" with) domestic firms. Thus, the developed countries have an interest in worldwide harmony of rules and outcomes. The United States and the European Union express their concerns in different ways. The United States wants "its" corporations to be able to do business smoothly around the world, without "excessive" regulation from outside and thus without extra costs that might diminish its firms' performance and undercut incentives to innovate. The European Union concern is often phrased in cosmopolitan terms, fitting to an economic community. Business is transnational; solutions should be transnational.

Both US and EU officials generally agree: the worldwide application of more or less common rules and principles is likely to increase business certainty, decrease overenforcement, and thus increase the flow of business around the world, increasing the size of the world economic pie and diminishing international confrontations that threaten trade wars. A crazy quilt of different rules for different countries is seen as hampering trade, competition, efficiency, and economic welfare.

Question 2—What are the pathways to solutions?

The developed nations have led the effort, especially in the context of the International Competition Network, to alleviate system inconsistencies by nurturing convergence. Moreover, bilaterally, and particularly in cases such as mergers of common interest to the authorities, developed nations have reached very high levels of cooperation with other developed jurisdictions, as well as significant cooperation with other nations.

Question 3—What are the most significant limitations in addressing
the major harms?

For restraints arising within the country or jurisdiction: no significant handicaps
prevent these jurisdictions from addressing the harms. The nations have sufficient
resources. Of course problems exist—in response to particular problems, law is reformed from time to time—but sufficient solutions are available.

For outsider/world restraints and harms: there are challenges, but no serious
obstacles. Extraterritorial application of domestic law is generally sufficient to address offshore inbound restraints; for example, export cartels. As for systems clashes,
wherein one jurisdiction might more aggressively condemn mergers or dominant
firm strategies than another, work is in progress to decrease divergences and increase
the convergences in the world. There are gaps in the law because law is national only
(with a few small exceptions in the World Trade Organization (WTO)). But the
developed nations do not generally view the gaps as their problem.

## IV. Is There a "Best" Competition World Order?

What mode of organization of competition systems of the world would best fit each
cluster? Is it possible to consolidate the perspectives for a world conception?
 We put to one side the possibility of a global competition agreement for the world
centered in the WTO because of its improbability in the foreseeable future. An alternative to a world framework is convergence, implying that the various nations or
at least their competition authorities decide on common principles and procedures.
This section focuses on the project of convergence. Here we begin with the outlook
of the developed world and work back to the outlook of developing countries.

### A. CLUSTER FOUR

What regimes or organization of competition systems would best fit the developed
countries?
 These jurisdictions are highly integrated into world competition and commerce,
and they see their economic futures in these terms, despite some lapses into nationalism. They value convergences toward one set of rules and standards, more or less,
for the world. This is particularly so for the jurisdictions that define the goal of competition law as consumer welfare or efficiency, for in theory there could be one set
of rules and standards most likely to increase aggregate economic welfare or world
consumer surplus, or (more accurately for the United States) proscribe only that

behavior that will decrease these sums. If we apply "sound economics," it is said, we will "get it right." There is one right set of rules (says the hedgehog), and it is ours.[13]

## B. CLUSTER ONE

Would cluster-one countries find it in their interest to embrace a strategy of world convergence of substantive law and procedures? Not likely. They may in many cases choose to follow US/EU laws (the notional standard-setters) when they believe the formulations are good for them, or in order to attract foreign investment, integrate with the world, and increase their chances for growth; otherwise, there are no particular benefits to them from seeking a single antitrust rule. Lack of unity of nations' law does not harm developing countries. The benefits that might trickle down to cluster one countries from the efficiency aspects of a single set of rules in the world would not be perceptible. Moreover, the standard to which the law would be hinged would almost surely be a Western standard that would not always be well fitted to their economies.

But what if we hypothetically endow the cluster-one countries with the power to decree that *their* rules are the world rules. Would they then fight for one set of rules? Not likely. They are not likely to presume that their rules are right for all countries of the world. They see so clearly that different context, conditions, capabilities, and aspirations may indicate different rules and standards. Cluster-one countries want and need development and inclusive development; they need to jump-start opportunity and mobility where enterprise by all but an elite has been stifled, people are poor and jobless, and corruption and cronyism are endemic. It is likely to be obvious to cluster-one countries that developed countries do not want or need the same thing. Thus, the little fox.

## C. CLUSTER TWO

How meritorious is a world convergence project through the eyes of cluster-two nations? The answer is similar to that for cluster one. But cluster-two nations may choose to adopt more of the rules of the mature jurisdictions because they are likely to find that more of those rules are good for them or that the trade-off bargain is worth it.

---

[13] Differences in outcomes occur even with a common set of rules and standards. Nations have different market characteristics. Some have higher barriers than others. Thus the same analysis may yield different results. Still, adherence to common rules and standards would lower the incidence of conflicts.

Through the eyes of cluster two nations, is there one right or best set of antitrust rules and standards? Would they, if they could, decree that their rules and standards are best for the world and the world should adopt them? Again, not likely. They too see clearly, from their experience, the impact of context on law and its application. Thus, the middle fox.

### D. CLUSTER THREE

How meritorious is a world convergence project through the eyes of a middle-income developing country on an upward trajectory; a country with access to expertise but still with huge problems of poverty, exclusion, corruption, business concentration, and privilege? Cajoled convergence still would not be favored. Law that mirrors the West might attract more foreign investment, but South Africa can adopt what it wants of "international" rules and standards while preserving its choices. It understands, for example, that multinational businesses and the nations from which they hail would profit from a general world standard that rejects noncompetition public interest considerations in merger analysis. But South Africa marches to its own drummer. It *has* a public interest standard as well as a competition standard. Its law embeds a unique mix of values and objectives—even though most case outcomes significantly coincide with those of the West.

Through the eyes of marker three (South Africa), is there one right or best set of competition rules for the world? Would cluster-three policymakers, if they could, decree that their standards are best and the world should adopt them? No. The terrains are too different. Cluster three is likely to choose eclecticism. Thus, the third fox.

## V. Constructing the Bigger Picture

### A. WORKING TOWARD WHAT?

We have seen four perspectives, based on four levels of development. We have suggested that the crazy-quilt world needs a "dome,"[14] to loosely guide coherence. It is in the interests of all to nudge the competition systems (and other systems) into sympathy with one another: a planetary order in the universe.

The developing countries' needs suggest a world perspective that would give them the space to work toward their country's development; space for modalities, agendas, and pace of progress that would enable them to raise their peoples' standards of living and integrate the nation into the world economy on terms that will enhance and not flatten the talents of their peoples; a perspective that will include them in

---

[14] *See* Eleanor M. Fox, *International Antitrust and the Doha Dome*, 43 VA. J. INT'L L. 911 (2003).

the global economy and not replace them by the global economy. The combination of developing country needs and developed country aspirations suggests, as a practical matter, a world system with moving parts that both seeks common norms and respects diverse value hierarchies. The object is the synergistic alignment of the developing and developed country needs and aspirations, translated into rules and standards, under a common dome.

## B. LAYING THE LINES FOR SYNERGISTIC ALIGNMENT— THE FIRST STEP

A first step on the path is listening to the four voices or at least the three most distinct: the least developed, the emerging, and the developed. Thus, the first step involves appreciation for the diversity of conditions, values, ambitions, and possibilities for better-working markets with law to constrain its excesses, in view of context.

We leave to the concluding chapter our suggestions for creating pathways to sympathetic alignment. In this chapter we have shown the complex diversity of the developing countries of sub-Saharan Africa, each cluster with its own set of issues, ambitions, limitations, and possibilities for tackling the major competitive restraints that hurt their people. We chart some of our findings below, in Table 7.1. For simplicity, we use three clusters instead of four: least developed, middle-level developing, and developed.

TABLE 7.1

Nations' Needs, Potentials and Priorities, Specified by Stage of Development

|  | *Goals and aspirations* | *Biggest restraints* | *Biggest handicaps in attacking the biggest restraints* |
|---|---|---|---|
| Cluster 1 | Development<br>Lifting up the poorest<br>Inclusiveness<br>Fair opportunity of<br>  outsiders to compete<br>Protection against<br>  abuses of market<br>  power<br>Efficiency | By the state, SOEs, and<br>  "friends of the state"<br>Abuses of dominance<br>  that barricade<br>  markets and<br>  suppress outsiders'<br>  competition on<br>  merits | No resources<br>No trust in markets<br>No markets<br>Poor institutions<br>No power against<br>  the State, MNEs, or<br>  MNE mergers |
| Clusters 2–3 | Development and<br>  competitiveness, and<br>  all above in Cluster 1 | State, hybrid, private<br>Also as above | Much of the above<br>  but to a lesser degree |

TABLE 7.1

*(Continued)*

|  | *Goals and aspirations* | *Biggest restraints* | *Biggest handicaps in attacking the biggest restraints* |
|---|---|---|---|
| Cluster 4 | Efficiency Competitiveness Economic hegemony For EU, also: level playing field, openness of markets | US—cartels EU—the state abuse of dominance cartels | No serious obstacles |

|  | *May or must the competition authority consider public interest, including jobs, sustainability of SMEs?* | *Does the competition authority have the capacity for sophisticated economic analysis?* | *In light of scarce resources, capacity level, and public interest mandates, are different rules for developing and developed countries legitimate?* |
|---|---|---|---|
| Cluster 1 | Yes, usually | No | Yes |
| Cluster 2–3 | Yes, usually | Yes | Yes |
| Cluster 4 | US, EU—No | Yes | US—No |

| *Biggest priority/ mandate/concern:* | *1) Create and open markets* | *2) Avoid too much enforcement because it might chill effective competition* |
|---|---|---|
| Cluster 1 | Yes, high urgency | No, the contrary |
| Clusters 2–3 | Yes, urgent to open markets to outsiders | No, the contrary |
| Cluster 4 | US—No EU—Yes | US—Yes |

## VI. Conclusion

We derive three major conclusions.

1. Cluster-one and cluster-four countries are so far apart in terms of
   a. the most serious market restraints that must be addressed before competition can work,

      b. the character of the market, of institutions, and of governance, and

      c. resources, experience, capacity, and expertise of the competition authority

that one can hardly imagine competition law standards equally fit for the first and the fourth clusters, even if standards designed for each would bear a large resemblance to one another.

2. First-cluster competition authorities face extreme challenges. The good that the authorities can do for markets is tightly circumscribed under current conditions. They *can* do good, particularly in advocacy, to call attention to the worst restraints, and their role can be vital to the future of markets and growth in their country, but they alone cannot lead their nations out of economic dysfunction, stagnation, autocratic governance, weak institutions, and other persistent ills that set the economic environment. The competition authorities are cabined by their systems.

3. The most appropriate global conception is a framework that facilitates the synergistic alignment of the several autonomous threads of rules and standards. This does not impugn the project of convergence. Quite the contrary, common norms are necessary to the concept of a unifying dome overhead and to coherence in the world. Such a framework will give space to developing countries and indeed to all countries to develop, grow, and continually adjust their laws to their markets. A formula for competition law in the world based on industrialized economies in which markets generally work well and exclusion of the masses is not an inherited problem can effectively leave behind more than half of the world.

# 8

# BETTER LAWS FOR AFRICA

## Pro-Development, Pro-Inclusion, Pro-Outsider

## I. Introduction

The African nations face an array of challenges: war and peace, life and death, human dignity. Harnessing markets for the people is a piece of these grand challenges. If the people have a fair opportunity to engage in the mainstream of economic life, they can support themselves and their families, they will gain autonomy, they are less likely to be driven along terroristic paths of alienation, and they are more likely to live lives of dignity. In this chapter we address how markets can be made to work for the people by better competition law and policy.

## II. What Inclusive Development Means for Competition *Law*

### A. SETTING THE STAGE

Competition, it is said, is good for all of the people, and in a strong sense it is. But many people conclude that it helps the well-off more than the less well-off, and many question whether it helps the less well-off at all.

Markets entail rival market players. The market environment, as compared with its alternatives (such as command-and-control by the state), produces more and better goods and services and innovation and offers the best opportunity to people to be part

Making Markets Work for Africa. Eleanor M. Fox and Mor Bakhoum.
© Oxford University Press 2019. Published 2019 by Oxford University Press.

of the system and thus to make one's own livelihood; access to markets empowers. But still, the claim is made that market competition even as policed by antitrust law makes the rich and enabled better off at the expense of people without power. Is this true?

The claim has resonance. Competition law as applied today in many countries is guided by the goal of increasing (or more accurately not diminishing) *aggregate* economic wealth or *aggregate* consumer surplus. This means, taking all buyers and their purchases together, do they gain or do they lose from a certain merger or market strategy? Since better-off consumers have more votes than poor consumers (more rands, shillings, or euros to spend), the aggregate wealth standard naturally favors the better off. People who have less money have fewer "votes" in the economic marketplace.[1] If in addition a jurisdiction *presumes* that the practices of dominant producers are efficient and that their strategies are pro-competitive (wealth-increasing) even when they destroy small rivals, again, the law tilts in favor of the better established and the better off. Can the competition laws of Africa correct this bias? Can they do so in a way that will help and not hurt the poorest consumers? What would the competition law look like if it were written by Africans for Africa, and by Africans who are not the elite? What would a pro-outsider, pro-inclusive development antitrust policy value?

A pro-outsider, pro-inclusive development antitrust policy would value a free and open marketplace without privilege or favor. This set of values is especially critical for nations and market players without economic power and especially for those populations in societies ruled by a few privileged families or firms or by autocrats. Clogging the channels with privileged actors especially hurts the outsider and keeps the poor poor. It reinforces a two-tiered economy and can constantly increase the wealth and inequality gap.

Within the framework of the overarching aim to harness competition for the outsider (people without power), constrained by practical realities of the structure of

---

[1] Maximizing aggregate total wealth or consumer wealth is not always in the interests of the poorer population and outsiders, although it can be. *Compare* Ronald Dworkin, *Why Efficiency?*, 8 HOFSTRA L. REV. 653 (1980) (embracing utilitarianism, which is effectively one person, one vote), *with* Richard Posner, *The Ethical and Political Base of the Efficiency Norm in Common Law Adjudication*, 8 HOFSTRA L. REV. 487 (1980) (embracing wealth maximization—which is effectively one dollar or peso or ruble or rand, one vote). *See also* John Rawls, A THEORY OF JUSTICE 150–161 (1971), arguing that justice requires maximizing the utility of those who are worst off.

As wealth maximization implies, the wealthier you are, the more weighted consumer sovereignty you have. Wealth maximization serves a function in terms of the GDP and the competitiveness of nations, but concern for distribution of wealth and opportunity is likely to have greater legitimacy for the nonpowerful and the unendowed. Distributional goals can be relevant to competition law choices; for example, in deciding whether to prefer freedom to discount or freedom of firms to protect against free-riding distributors by prohibiting discounts.

business, governance, and society, we address the basic questions that confront everyone who drafts and applies competition law in the developing world.

## B. THE SCOPE OF THE COMPETITION LAW:
### THE STATE-REGULATED SECTORS

It has often been observed that undue anticompetitive state acts[2] are more damaging to competition than anticompetitive private acts, because the power of the state cannot be eroded even by creative, competitive firms. State and crony control have a freezing-out effect; good ideas for the marketplace by members of the uncredentialed masses are likely to die an unheralded death.

An antitrust law that prohibits harmful state restraints is not the norm in the world, but it is a growing trend. The subject of anticompetitive and unduly harmful state restraints and what to do about them is increasingly on antitrust agendas.

Competition laws can be drafted to reach abusive anticompetitive state acts and measures, and competition *policy* (pro-market efforts other than law enforcement) can help reach the rest.

One of the authors studied 33 countries and the European Union to determine the extent to which national competition laws may invalidate unreasonably anticompetitive state and local restraints.[3] The study found it to be common practice for competition laws to cover state-owned enterprises (although with exceptions) and that a critical mass of the laws reach significantly further to invalidate anticompetitive state-granted privileges and barriers to trade within the nation, and even to invalidate public procurement rules that are not neutral but give preferences. This extra reach of competition law is particularly common in countries with a history of state control over the economy and state intervention in it, for that is where the discipline is needed most. For example, cases are cited in which post offices are prevented from blocking entry of new forms of mail delivery, ports are prevented from monopolizing ferry services, provincial water providers are prevented from requiring users to buy water pipes from cronies, government procurement agencies are prevented from writing specifications to fit their friends' capabilities, and local administrations are barred from barricading highways against lorries delivering goods from neighboring

---

[2] States need freedom to act in the interests of their citizens. Legitimate state acts might have anticompetitive byproducts, and we would not want an antitrust law to challenge the normal byproducts of governance. "Undue" is a marker to signify a class of acts that are excessively and unjustifiably anticompetitive.

[3] *See* Eleanor M. Fox & Deborah Healey, *When the State Harms Competition—The Role for Competition Law,* 79 ANTITRUST L.J. 769 (2014). *See also UNCTAD Research Partnership Platform Publication Series: Competition Law and the State—Competition laws' prohibitions of anti-competitive State acts and measures* (2015), *available at* http://unctad.org/en/Pages/DITC/CompetitionLaw/ResearchPartnership/TheState.aspx.

provinces.[4] An article derived from the study proposes seven principles, which we list in the footnote.[5] The principles are useful tools for developing countries that are struggling to open their markets to the people. Without these tools, state measures and acts can strangle the space for competition on the merits, and thus for economic opportunity as well as consumer welfare.

## C.  EXEMPTIONS AND OTHER NONCOVERAGE

A good pro-development competition law would minimize exemptions, although it would allow them when necessary to help small stakeholders become more efficient and effective.[6] Exemptions often include agriculture, banking, other regulated industries, intellectual property, and acts by the state.

Often in poorer developing nations, up to 70 percent of the people work in agriculture. There is a particular need for a competitive market in agriculture, both for producers and consumers. The farmers need access to inputs at a competitive price and they need markets for their goods. But the farmers may be exploited by big agribusiness and multinational buyers, who are often part of a global value chain. A broad exemption for agriculture would leave the agricultural markets prey to power, and miss the chance to use competitive opportunities to improve the lives of the poor.[7]

---

[4] *See* Fox & Healey, *supra* note 3, at 781–783.

[5] (1) The competition law should cover state-owned enterprises. (2) The competition law should cover state officials who facilitate illegal cartels or bidding rings by rogue conduct outside of the course of their duties (such conduct being especially notorious in procurement). (3) Where the law allows a state action defense to a challenge to anticompetitive private acts, the defense should be narrowly drawn. It should not be admissible when asserted by private actors who can easily obey the competition law. (4) Some laws allow collective lobbying to procure government action. Lobbying defenses should be narrow. The defense should be lost if the competitors use fraud or deception to solicit government action. (5) The competition law should empower the competition authority to challenge unduly anticompetitive state measures, or provide a mechanism for the authority to identify such measures and trigger their challenge. (6) If the jurisdiction is a common market or a system that adopts the principle of federal supremacy, the EU standard should be adopted. State measures that frontally undermine competition, such as a command to competitors—"form a cartel and allocate quotas"—should not be allowed to override competition law. (7) Moreover, as in the European Union, and as is critical in common markets, jurisdictions should integrate trade and competition restraints, and let them fall into the precipice between the two bodies of law.

[6] *See* Competition Act of 1998 § 10(3)(b) (So. Africa) (amended 2000) (authorizing the Commission to grant an exemption for an anticompetitive agreement or practice if it allows small and middle-size business or historically disadvantaged persons to become competitive).

[7] Small farmers could, however, be helped by targeted exemptions for their cooperatives. Small stakeholder collaboration in a number of competing joint ventures normally would not harm competition and should not need exemption, but farmers may wish to have the comfort of a safe harbor. *See* Alexander Italianer, Director General for Competition, European Commission, Conference on Antitrust Guidelines in the Agricultural Sector: Co-operating to Compete—The New Agriculture Antitrust Guidelines (Mar. 4, 2015).

Exemptions for the banking industry can also be harmful. Notoriously, in developing countries with large masses of poorer people and a small percentage of elite who own most of industry, unconnected individuals with talent and good ideas cannot get business loans; but if they can and do, they risk falling into traps of exploitation.[8] (They may default and be placed in bankruptcy.) State laws often limit property ownership to males. This means women have no collateral to secure a loan. Poorer entrepreneurs, and especially women entrepreneurs,[9] are a risk that banks avoid. A combination of competition law and property law reform, and selective government support, are needed to open access to capital. A banking exemption from competition law that leaves regulation to a regulator often captured by the banking business can entrench economic power and exacerbate a spiral of disempowerment.

Regulated sectors may present a challenge to developing economies. All jurisdictions have to make decisions about the relationship between sector regulation and antitrust. The decision is complicated because, on the one hand, overlap of the two regimes costs resources, and on the other hand, an antitrust exemption for firms in the regulated sector removes the best watchdog and increases the risk that the regulated firms will "capture" the regulator. If Mexico had relinquished all authority over the Telmex/Telcel giant (owned by the then richest man in the world, Carlos Slim) to the telecom regulator COFETEL, the public would never have seen the halving of cell phone prices, which followed the settlement of a monopoly abuse case prosecuted by a persistent Federal Competition Commission of Mexico under the stewardship of Eduardo Pérez Motta.[10]

Some, but not most, competition laws exempt intellectual property or aspects of it. Helpfully, most exemptions do not extend to *abuse* of intellectual property (IP) rights. A full exemption can be particularly harmful in poorer countries whose people are plagued by diseases whose treatment requires high-priced drugs. The ability of competition authorities to prevent abuses that result in extraordinarily high drug prices is vital for the poor and middle class.

Much of modern technology, including that used in computers, smart phones, and other mobile phones, incorporates intellectual property. Access to information and communication technologies is critical; it means access to business opportunity, at home and in the world. A growing body of literature shows how mobile

---

[8] *See* Keith Epstein & Geri Smith, *The Ugly Side of Microlending*, BLOOMBERG BUSINESSWEEK, Dec. 12, 2007, http://www.bloomberg.com/bw/stories/2007-12-12/the-ugly-side-of-microlending.

[9] In Kenya, for example, women make up the vast majority of farmers yet struggle to obtain loans from banks because of property laws depriving them of title to land. *See* http://www.dw.com/en/women-take-over-kenyas-farming-sector/a-16716322.

[10] *See Let Mexico's Moguls Battle*, THE ECONOMIST, Feb. 4, 2012. Authority over telecommunications was later taken from the competition authority by legislation. Federal Law on Economic Competition 2014, art. 5.

phone technology enables the flow of market information and facilitates financial transactions in cottage industries and to isolated entrepreneurs, such as fishermen who can now get on-the-spot information as to where they can sell their catches. And migrant wage earners needing to transfer money to their families simply and fast can now do so through M-Pesa.[11] Keeping modern technology within the reach of the middle class and the poor is a job for competition policy.

Foreign restraints. A good deal of harm to competition is perpetrated by foreign firms acting offshore. Foreign and multinational firms often price-fix into the most vulnerable countries, where they might ply their harm with impunity. It is especially important that developing countries' laws reach these acts, but not all do. There are many examples that underscore the importance of extraterritorial jurisdiction. Examples include the world vitamins cartels, the cargo and fuel oil cartels, and the Canadian/Russian potash export cartels. All of these cartels have seriously injured individuals in poor developing countries and have undermined these nations' prospects for engaging in the world economy.

The potash cartel is a notorious example of an offshore cartel targeting, among others, developing countries with no practical power to resist. Potash is a major ingredient in fertilizer. Fertilizer accounts for a large part of the cost of crops. When farmers in sub-Saharan Africa pay monopoly prices for this input, tens of thousands of farmers are deprived of even the smallest profit from their crops; their families can starve; businesses, which could succeed on the merits if the competition "coast" were clear, are crippled.[12]

D. PROCEDURE

When poorer individuals suffer anticompetitive injury, can they get justice? Often, they cannot. Systems tend to disfavor the poorer population. Especially in poorer countries that are run by connections, not merit, the poor lack access to the system of justice.

This means that, for antitrust harms, it is especially important to open the channels for legal recourse to compensation. The two obvious channels are: government lawsuits to exonerate the rights of the victims (and the public), and private lawsuits by victims themselves or on their behalf. In some jurisdictions when the competition authority sues violators, it may or must obtain monetary recovery to be

---

[11] See OECD, Policy Roundtables: Competition and Poverty Reduction, Oct. 4, 2013; Oumy Khairy Ndiaye, *Is the success of M-Pesa empowering rural women?*, 18 FEMINIST AFRICA 156 (2013).

[12] For the effect of the potash cartel in India, *see* Frederic Jenny, *Global potash trade and competition*, THE ECONOMIC TIMES, Nov. 25, 2010.

distributed to the victims. But this is not usual. In many jurisdictions, private actions are allowed, but even so, in many places they are available only after the competition authority wins its case. Moreover, in many jurisdictions that are under the political thumb of autocratic governments or that simply lack the resources or stature to stand up to powerful offenders, the competition authority does not bring the cases that should be brought. In many jurisdictions there is no provision for collective actions (joining together the many small victims), lawyer fees contingent on success, or other vehicles that make private actions affordable, and there are no procedures or possibilities for obtaining the evidence that the plaintiffs need in order to win their cases. In some jurisdictions there are prohibitively high burdens not only for proof of the offending conduct but also for showing that the conduct caused injury to the plaintiff, and by how much.

To help poorer victims and others whose losses are a fraction of court costs, jurisdictions can incentivize people to bring proceedings on their behalf. This implies class or representative actions: collective actions. While the collective action mechanism can be abused by unscrupulous lawyers, the need for collective actions outweighs the costs. Most lawyers are not unscrupulous, and abuses can be contained by good institutional design.

## E. FORMULATING AND APPLYING THE SUBSTANTIVE LAW

Is there a pro-development view of best substantive principles of antitrust law?

As we have seen in Chapter V on South Africa, there *are* principles and perspectives that are more, rather than less, friendly to people without power.

In the antitrust community, we all want robust, efficient, dynamic markets, with players who are inventive and creative. Dynamic markets are good for the poor and the outsiders. Indeed, competition on the merits benefits outsiders more than insiders as long as there is no "insider track." A good competition law would lean against power.[13] Below, we discuss pro-development principles within this framework. The principles do not protect inefficient firms *from* competition; they protect competition. Some might argue for a fairer distribution of opportunity at the expense of efficiency, but we do not reach that question. So much can be done that is not being done within the range of efficiency, and that is the space we occupy.

Below are eight areas or issues in which there is a pro-development perspective that fits precisely with the objective of making markets work more efficiently. Indeed, an outsider perspective is likely to produce more efficient markets than do

---

[13] This proposition is complicated by efficiencies, because certain acts and transactions that produce productive efficiencies also produce market power.

rules based on presumptions that dominant firm conduct and big mergers in general are efficient.[14]

1. *Discounting.* Poorer people need goods and services at lower prices. This should go without saying. The freedom of sellers to discount is therefore especially important to the poor. Discounting has obvious efficiency properties. Established firms are often tempted to suppress discounting, sometimes in the name of preserving professionalism (minimum fees for engineers, doctors, or dentists); sometimes in the name of protection against free riding (the discounter, supposedly, will "free ride" on full-pricers' investments in service and undermine efficient provision of service). A pro-development perspective would give more weight to freedom to discount than to business' attempt to preserve professionalism or discourage free riders.[15] For example, a developing jurisdiction might prefer a per se or presumptive rule against resale price maintenance to an indeterminate rule-of-reason analysis that assumes a branded good needs to quash low prices to preserve its high-priced distributors' incentives to invest.

2. *Market definition choices.* Market definition is a construct. It may help us understand whether a firm has market power. Often there is more than one good candidate for "the market." As we note in Chapter V, in two cases among others, the South African Competition Tribunal faced the problem of market definition when interests of the poor were at stake. In one case, a narrow and distinct market would have protected the poor from loss of a product they needed, namely, low-priced furniture *on credit.* In another case, a narrow market (capitated managed health care) would have triggered development of a promising niche for reducing the cost of low-end health care insurance, thereby bringing masses of the poor into health care coverage for the first time. In each case, the Tribunal opted for the choice that would most help the poor population. (In the health care case, the Tribunal's decision was reversed.)[16] A pro-development perspective would choose pro-poor options.

3. *Leveraging, foreclosure, and access violations.* In numerous cases, especially abuse of dominance cases, the decision maker is faced with the choice between more market access for those without power and more freedom for firms with power. The

---

[14] Irwin M. Stelzer, *Some Practical Thoughts about Entry, in* How the Chicago School Overshot the Mark: The Effect of Conservative Economic Analysis on U.S. Antitrust (Robert Pitofsky ed., 2008).

[15] Regarding resale price maintenance, compare the dissenting opinion of Justice Breyer in *Leegin Creative Leather Products, Inc. v. PSKS, Inc.,* 551 U.S. 877 (2007), giving weight to the value of discounting, with the majority opinion of Justice Kennedy, disregarding the value of discounting.

[16] *See* Medicross Healthcare Group Ltd. v. Competition Commission, 11/LM/Mar05 (2005), *rev'd,* 55/CAC/Sept05 [2006] ZACAC 3 (2006). *See also* David Lewis, Thieves at the Dinner Table: Enforcing the Competition Act 100–112 (2012) (describing the *J.D. Group/Ellerine Department Store* and the *Prime Cure/Medicross* cases).

US and EU *Microsoft* and *Intel* cases involved this choice. Which choice would produce a more efficient and dynamic market? Economics does not answer the question. The answer depends on assumptions as well as on the particular facts and context. Freedom of outsiders to contest markets on the merits and not to be frozen from important outlets by a dominant firm's use of leverage is a prescription that favors those without power.[17] This, as opposed to a presumption that the exclusionary act is efficient,[18] would be the developmental choice, all other things equal.

4. *"Efficient" foreclosures*. In a constant stream of cases, a feisty challenger appears on the dominant firm's horizon, and the dominant firm becomes concerned. It might lose its power. It decides to offer its big customers loyalty rebates. If they stay loyal to the dominant firm and thus do not stray to the attractive newcomer, the dominant firm will give them a handsome reward at the end of a period. In the West, there is an emerging rule of law that may require the plaintiff to prove that the foreclosed competitor was "as efficient" as the putative predator; if not, there may be no violation.[19] Consider, for example, the case of Intel/AMD wherein dominant Intel gave its key customers loyalty rebates after its smaller competitor AMD launched a better chip. Under the strong view of the "equally efficient" competitor requirement, the loyalty rebate would be legal regardless of its effect on competition if AMD were judged not as efficient as Intel.[20] Without such a safeguard, its supporters say, the law would protect inefficient competitors.

The "equally efficient" requirement is a poor way to screen out bad cases, especially in poorer jurisdictions dominated by entrenched monopolies. Loyalty rebate programs are often devised by dominant firms threatened with competition in order to stave off the competitive challenge. The inventive challenger typically has higher costs than the monopolist. In poorer developing countries, there may not *be* an equally efficient challenger. Moreover, the dominant firm strategy may devastate all possible challengers, and entry or re-entry is typically more difficult and less likely to occur in developing countries. Capital markets work poorly, and new entrants are seldom sitting on the sidelines. The market is not likely to correct itself.

Competition law should protect *the market*, not weak competitors, but the "as efficient competitor" test is not needed to protect the market. For example, after

---

[17] Every case has its context; there is a basic background question regarding the state of a nation's competition law. In the 1980s, the US law was recalibrated in favor of freedom of firms to act because the law had gone too far to proscribe transactions that could not have harmed competition and might have been efficient.

[18] *See, e.g.*, Commissioner Joshua D. Wright's dissent in McWane, Inc., FTC Docket No. 9351 (Jan. 30, 2014), majority *aff'd*, 783 F.3d 814 (11th Cir. 2015).

[19] *See, e.g.*, Cascade Health Solutions v. PeaceHealth, 515 F.3d 883, 905 (9th Cir. 2007); Konkurrensverket v. TeliaSonera, Case C-52/09 (Feb. 17, 2011). *But see* ZFMeritor v. Eaton Corp., 696 F.3d 254 (3d Cir. 2012), *cert. denied* (2013).

[20] *Cf.* Intel v. Commission, ECLI:EU:C:2017:632 (equally efficient competitor can be a factor).

the plaintiff shows that the dominant firm's strategy (such as exclusive contracts) significantly forecloses rivals from entry or expansion in a concentrated market, the dominant firm could be required to justify its conduct by business needs or prove that prohibition of the conduct would make consumers worse off. Defendants can always defend that the smaller rival's own ineptitudes caused its injury, but that is a far cry from requiring it to be equally efficient in order to establish a cause of action.

5. *Excessive pricing violations.* Excessive pricing violations are a challenge, as we have explained in Chapter V. Agencies may not wish to second-guess the ups and downs of a single firm's pricing decisions. Yet most developing countries' laws prohibit excessively high prices, and their courts or commissions may be called upon to determine when prices are excessive. This is typically a complicated question. Poorer jurisdictions may need a relatively simple rule in order to be able to prove a violation. They do not want a Promethean rule that chills normal price fluctuations, and they do not need one.

In the South African *Mittal* steel case (also discussed in Chapter V),[21] Mittal, the successor to the state-owned and historically privileged firm ISCOR, was the only significant steel company in South Africa. It was superdominant. Its size was the result of state policy. Its nearest competitors were located across oceans, and shipping costs were high. Mittal sold steel to domestic buyers at import parity price (what the distant overseas competitors would charge), while it priced its exports at the much lower world price. This strategy handicapped Mittal's South African customers' competitiveness in world markets. Mittal sold large volumes of its steel for export only, and its contracts prohibited the export-destined steel from being sold on the South African market.

On the above facts and in view of an available nonintrusive (and creative) remedy, the South African Competition Tribunal found that Mittal had violated the competition law by excessive pricing. The remedy was: Mittal would be forbidden to bar the export-designated steel from sale in South Africa. As we recounted above, the Appeal Court reversed. It held that the plaintiff was required to prove that the South African domestic price was substantially above Mittal's cost. It presented several possible scenarios that would have made a prima facie case for violation. If the plaintiff met the requirements, the burden of going forward would shift to the defendant.

The Tribunal's solution would have made a potentially unmanageable case manageable. Its formulation and remedy were both pro-market and pro-outsider. The Appeal Court believed that the statutory language required a more complex inquiry. But that is beside the point here, for nations need not adopt complexity-creating

---

[21] Harmony Gold Mining Co. v. Mittal Steel Corp., Case 13/CR/Feb04 (South African Competition Tribunal 2007), *rev'd*, 70/CAC/Apr07 (Court of Appeal 2009).

statutory language. This very language was changed by amendments to the South African Competition Act.

There is a current spate of obscenely excessive drug pricing around the world, and competition authorities have filed challenges.[22] The world problem underlines the need for seizing simple paradigms where we find them.

6. *Buyer power.* Suppliers in poorer developing countries are more likely than suppliers in developed countries to be victims of exploitative buyer power. Developed countries may decide to confine their competition laws to consumer welfare goals; but poorer developing countries might find this too narrow and static a measure and might prefer to take account of all market harms, not just consumer harms. Small farmers are particularly vulnerable to harm from monopolistic purchase and distribution practices and to harm from mergers that create buyer power, as has been documented in Zambia and the Ivory Coast,[23] and to buying cartels, as in cotton and tobacco in Malawi.[24] Huge seed and fertilizer mergers illustrate the point.[25]

Jurisdictions in which most jobs and businesses are in the agricultural sector may especially need to take buyer power seriously.

7. *Intellectual property.* The world is in the throes of IP/competition battles. Patent protection of intellectual property is notoriously broad and often unrelated to the goal of inventiveness. At least in many cases, the poorer population is likely to be better served by more competition and less protection of intellectual property. This is so in the two areas of current debate: pharmaceuticals and generic competition, and information technology.

As for pharmaceuticals, the poorer population is in great need of cheaper medicines. Generic prices are exponentially lower than brand prices. In a current

---

[22] *See* Shingie Chisoro Dube, *Excessive Pricing in the Global Pharmaceutical Industry*, CCRED QUARTERLY REVIEW (Dec. 20, 2017).

[23] *See* Thula Kaira, *The Role of Competition Law and Policy in Alleviating Poverty—The Case of Zambia*, at 133 (exploitation of out-grower farmers by ginners in Zambia, at 150–157), and Bruno Dorin, *From Ivorian Cocoa Bean to French Dark Chocolate Tablet: Price Transmission, Value Sharing and North/South Competition Policy*, at 237 (exploitation of cocoa farmers by chocolate makers in Côte d'Ivoire, passim and 306–310), *in* THE EFFECTS OF ANTI-COMPETITIVE BUSINESS PRACTICES ON DEVELOPING COUNTRIES AND THEIR DEVELOPMENT PROSPECTS (Hassan Qaqaya & George Lipimile eds., UN 2008). *See also Promoting Pro-Poor Growth: Agriculture*, Annex 3. A1, Spotlight on Global Value Chains—Does It Mean Shutting Out Small Producers? (OECD 2006).

[24] *See* Maxton Grant Tsoka, Competition Scenario in Malawi, for CUTS International (2006), *available at* http://www.cuts-ccier.org/7up3/pdf/CRR-Malawi.pdf.

[25] *See* joint letter of July 26, 2017, from the American Antitrust Institute, Food and Water Watch, and the National Farmers Union to Andrew Finch, Acting Assistant Attorney General, analyzing how the merger of Monsanto and Bayer could harm competition, consumers and farmers. http://www.antitrustinstitute.org/sites/default/files/White%20Paper_Monsanto%20Bayer_7.26.17_0.pdf.

spate of litigation, brand owners bring infringement actions against generic entrants who challenge the patent's validity. The parties to the infringement litigation announce a settlement in which the brand owner agrees to pay millions of dollars or euros to the generic firm to stay out of the market for a term of years. This is called "pay for delay" or reverse payments, since we would normally expect the alleged infringer (the generic) to pay the brand owner damages for the infringement if there is one, and that no money at all would pass hands if there is no infringement. Both the EU and the US competition agencies have been aggressive against pay-for-delay agreements, while allowing legitimate settlements.[26] The EU court has adopted a rule of presumptive illegality for pay-for-delay agreements, thus easing the plaintiff's burden.[27] The EU court rule is sympathetic to generic entry, and generic entry is normally helpful to development.

Communication and information technologies are also caught in the storm of controversy between more IP protection or more competition law protection. Holders of patents (legally) agree to standards. This means that the standard-setting agreement will confer market power on the technology essential to work the standard. So the participants further agree that if they hold patents essential to work the standard, they will grant licenses for a fair, reasonable, and nondiscriminatory fee. Holders of essential patents, such as the patent allowing a smart phone to connect to a web service provider, typically sue for injunctions against infringers who are willing and ready to pay a reasonable fee, but they have not yet finished negotiating the fee. In Europe, the very suit for injunction against the infringer who wants to license but has not reached terms may be an abuse of dominance.[28]

Here, too, the outsiders (and those who need to use the information technology (IT) networks) need competitive markets more than they need greater property protections. As we have noted above, access to communication and information devices is uniquely empowering, and empowerment is critical to development.

Still, the law must protect incentives to invent. If developing countries excessively appropriate pharmaceutical patent rights, the inventing firms will have less incentive to invest in cures for diseases unique to these countries. These investments are risky, especially when the scope for return on investment is limited. Pro-development formulation of rules of law must consider the trade-offs between low prices of IP and access to IT, and incentives to invent.

---

[26] The principal US case is *FTC v. Actavis, Inc.*, 570 U.S. 756 (2013).

[27] Lundbeck, Ltd. v. Commission, Case T-472/13, ECLI:EU:T:2016:449 (General Court 2016), on appeal to the Court of Justice, Case C-591/16P.

[28] *See* Huawei Technologies Co. v. ZTE Corp., Case C-170/13, ECLI:EU:C:2015:477.

8. *Simpler rules and more presumptions.* For poorer developing countries, human resources and capital resources are scarce. The competition authorities do not have teams of lawyers and economists ready to identify and analyze reams of documents and construct scores of models and studies. Where simpler, reasonably accurate rules exist, less well-financed authorities need them. Some simple rules are available. For example (as we suggested above) resale price maintenance by firms with market power can be presumptively illegal unless justified, as in the European Union and much of the world.[29] The *Mittal* rule of the South African Tribunal regarding import-parity pricing by superdominant firms is also a simple rule with low costs of error. A per se rule or at least presumptive rule against hard core cartel agreements is widely accepted. Some per se or presumptive rules can be constructed in the other direction; for example, per se legality for simple sustainable low-pricing.

Many rules and regulations of the mature antitrust jurisdictions are too technical and too complex to suit poorer, resource-starved jurisdictions. These poorer jurisdictions should be encouraged to experiment, and, transparently, to construct simpler rules and standards fit for their capabilities and contexts.

\* \* \*

All of the above suggested choices of rules or standards have strong efficiency properties. The choices are pro-inclusive development. They serve the interests of consumers or at least do not disserve them.

## F. INSTITUTIONAL DESIGN

Institutional design is a basic choice for every jurisdiction. There are three dominant structural alternatives: (1) a competition agency that prepares cases and brings them to court; (2) a competition agency that prepares cases and brings them to a prosecutor who re-evaluates them and decides whether to bring them to court; and (3) a competition institution that includes the prosecutorial and first-level decision-making function. The last option normally includes a board, commission, or tribunal that decides the cases. The board, commission, or tribunal may be more or less independent. It usually includes some mix of lawyers, economists, business people, and others, such as consumer representatives. Typically, its decisions may be appealed to the courts. The courts may have powers of de novo review, or duties of

---

[29] *See* Treaty on Functioning of the European Union [TFEU] art. 102, OJ C 326 (Dec. 13, 2007); Competition Act art. 21 § (3)(d) (Kenya); Anti-Monopoly Law art. 14 (China); Competition Act of 1998 § 5(2) (South Africa) (as amended). *But see* Leegin Creative Leather Products, Inc. v. PSKS, Inc., 551 U.S. 877 (2007), overruling the per se rule against resale price maintenance.

deference on fact-finding and policy perspective, while retaining authority to decide questions of law.

Institutional design within common markets entails an overlay above the national systems. Design of common markets is highly relevant to Africa because of the common markets already formed and being developed. The European Union provides an excellent model. The member states of the European Union may apply their own competition law, and, where inter-member-state trade is involved, they *must* apply EU competition law and may apply their own competition law as well, as long as it does not conflict with EU law.[30] In matters of cross-border effects, the European Union takes the lead. In mergers of community dimension, the EU law alone applies, subject to a minor exception where the effect is largely national. In matters involving member state measures that have a transborder EU effect, EU competition law intervenes aggressively against privilege and power, and if the restraint is not caught by the competition law, it might well be caught by the free movement law; the provisions on competition and on internal trade work hand in hand. Moreover, the member states and the "center" have a network, the European Competition Network, to coordinate actions at the horizontal level. Thus, there is a high level of information exchange and coordination, and a common voice and action at Community level.

The European Union has given extraordinary voice to the common interests of the member states. If each member state alone would have to wage its own competition battles against the world, it would very often be weak and ineffective. This is a lesson for Africa.

In Africa, a unique design was adopted by the West African Economic and Monetary Union (WAEMU), the common market and monetary union in Francophone West Africa. The regional union does all competition enforcement for this West African common market. The member states have been deprived of competition enforcement authority, even for restraints solely affecting their internal markets.

The WAEMU centralization of authority has not worked. It has sucked the life out of national authorities such as in Senegal, which was a promising enforcer before the WAEMU edict.[31] Nor has WAEMU been able to step in and do all of the jobs that the West African national enforcers would normally do. It is constrained by

---

[30] They may apply their national abuse of dominance law even if it goes further than EU abuse of dominance law.

[31] *See* Daniel P. Weick, *Competition Law and Policy in Senegal: A Cautionary Tale for Regional Integration?*, 33 WORLD COMPETITION, Issue 3, 521–540 (2010); Advisory Opinion 3/2000/CJ/UEMOA (27 June 2000) (ruling that WAEMU member states cannot maintain their national competition laws because of the disruption it could cause to WAEMU in creating a unified market). http://www.ohada.com/imprim_juris. php?article_juris√432.

scarce resources and not surprisingly does not have sufficient omniscience. Member nations of WAEMU are trying to retake national antitrust enforcement authority, but the road looks long and not promising.

As to the three choices of national institutional design, all have their benefits and costs.[32] The first option—the competition agency brings cases directly to court—depends for its success on fair, efficient, and noncorrupt courts whose judges have a reasonable level of expertise. Some of these qualities are likely to be missing in many developing countries. The second choice—the competition agency brings cases to a prosecutor—entails another level of basic evaluation before a case can be brought,[33] and in many developing countries a fair amount of special interest pleading occurs en route to prosecution. Moreover, in some jurisdictions,[34] court cases must be brought criminally, and there is no room for noncriminal enforcement. This is a great drawback, for there are a multitude of possible offenses that do not and should not rise to a criminal level, and the agency needs to establish legal rules and standards to govern conduct in these areas. The third option—a board, commission, or tribunal—is the best fit for most developing countries, and indeed appears to be the form most often selected.[35]

Within each model, there are many design choices to be made. Should the system allow criminal enforcement or should it be civil only? Does it allow private actions in court, and can they be self-starting or do they depend upon successful agency action first? What remedies may be ordered, and are they sufficiently strong so that the competition law has bite? What functions other than competition law enforcement are entrusted to the agency? Market studies?[36] Advocacy?[37] Consumer protection? Sector regulation, such as energy and telecommunications? What is the relationship between the competition authority and the sector regulators? Are there any rules of preemption or exemption? What are the options for settlement? These are legitimate questions of design as to which there is much experience and literature.[38] Nations

---

[32] *See* Eleanor M. Fox & Michael J. Trebilcock, *The GAL Competition Project: The Global Convergence of Process Norms, in* THE DESIGN OF COMPETITION LAW INSTITUTIONS: GLOBAL NORMS, LOCAL CHOICES (Oxford 2013).

[33] Law No. 3 of 2005 on the Protection of Competition and the Prohibition of Monopolistic Practices (Egypt) (2005).

[34] *E.g.*, the Competition Act of Kenya before recent amendments.

[35] *See* William E. Kovacic & Marianela Lopez-Galdos, *Lifecycles of Competition Systems: Explaining Variation in the Implementation of New Regimes*, 79 L. & CONTEMP. PROBS. 85 (2016) for an evaluation of existing trends in competition institutional design.

[36] Power to conduct studies of markets that appear not to be working well is important. The studies may produce valuable information that may lead to prosecution or legislative remedies. *See* LEWIS, *supra* note 16, at 287.

[37] A mandate for advocacy is likewise important. *See* Simon Roberts & Trudi Makhaya, *Expectation and Outcomes: Considering Competition and Corporate Power in South Africa under Democracy*, REV. AFR. POL. ECON. 556–571 (2013).

[38] *See* Fox & Trebilcock, *supra* note 32; Kovacic & Lopez-Galdos, *supra* note 35.

choose what is likely to work best for their systems. But whatever they choose, there are certain essential qualities for a good and legitimate system: transparency, independence,[39] accountability, due process, trustworthiness and honesty of the officials and staff, absence of conflicts of interest, and good leadership with effective delegation and sharing so as to build institutional continuity. The nations need a system that performs with reasonable efficiency, and as to which every respondent called to account can say: I was treated fairly; I got a fair and impartial hearing based on an appreciation of the facts and application of the rule of law.

## III.  What Inclusive Development Means for Competition *Policy*

We have just considered competition *law*. We turn now to competition *policy*, which may be implemented through advocacy by the competition authority and others, such as the World Bank.

Competition advocacy is the last of the triumvirate addressed by this chapter—the first being scope of the law, prominently including competition law *enforcement* against state acts and measures; the second, competition law enforcement in general, the law and its institutions. The third—advocacy—rounds the circle: there are numerous state or hybrid anticompetitive measures that unreasonably block markets, causing special harm to the poor or poorer populations; acts or measures that are beyond the purview of the competition law. These may be targets of advocacy—advocacy to identify the barriers and restraints; to muster the evidence, to offer analysis, and to identify allies to work with, for removal of the restraints. We have already described how restraints of this sort are particularly damaging, excluding, and disabling to the people of developing countries.

We consider advocacy in two categories: first, advocacy against restraints by and within a nation's own government, and second, advocacy to improve the international environment so as to protect against or seek to correct international and foreign restraints that harm the nation.

### A.  ADVOCATING AGAINST RESTRAINTS BY AND WITHIN THE NATION

At the outset of this chapter we identified excessively restrictive state restraints and the extent to which some competition laws reach them. A far larger set of state restraints may be unwise and anticompetitive but not facially excessive and out of

---

[39] Independence from control of the government can be relative. Virtually all agencies experience some attempts of high officials to interfere.

proportion to a legitimate governance task, and in any event not covered by the competition law. If a legal challenge to obstructive state restraints is possible, it might be brought under free movement or commerce clauses (free trade within the nation's internal market) or World Trade Organization (WTO) agreements. If not, the best tool is persuasion, and an effective program of persuasion is based on groundwork, facts, analysis, and a sense of what is politically possible.

A critical avenue for advocacy concerns the country's regulatory laws. Regulation (while often important to public welfare) can be excessive and harmful to consumers, and may block entry to worthy entrepreneurs. Often the harmful restraints are procured and supported by vested interests. The International Competition Network (ICN) has launched a project under the aegis of ICN's Advocacy Working Group to identify methodologies for assessing the pro-competitive and anticompetitive aspects of specific regulations.[40] This project promises to be a first step toward developing a template for identifying unwise anticompetitive regulation and then advocating to repeal or limit it.

A second important target is state-owned monopoly boards for buying and selling commodities, which typically not only squeeze the sellers and exploit the buyers but squeeze out entrepreneurial opportunity. The pyrethrum board in Kenya, described in Chapter I, is a good example both of the problem and the competition policy challenge.

A third important target for competition advocacy is national trade laws, such as antidumping laws. These measures typically are procured by vested interests. Even so, as an example from Tanzania shows, "the market" can sometimes win.[41] Fortunately for developing countries, their competition authorities tend to have much more authority to advocate against protectionist trade laws within their governmental system than do competition authorities in some mature developed nations.[42] This authority is vital. Without it, the most critical connections may never be made (e.g.,

---

[40] Available at http://www.internationalcompetitionnetwork.org/working-groups/current/advocacy.aspx. *See also* OECD Competition Assessment Toolkit, http://www.oecd.org/daft/competition/competitionassesmenttoolkit. htm, providing a method for identifying unnecessary regulatory restraints on the market.

[41] In Tanzania in 2009, the Fair Competition Commission faced a press campaign by the leading cement producers to impose duties of 35 percent on imports of cement. The cement firms urged that the duties would save existing jobs (in inefficient plants) and would save the nation's economy. But the high import duties would have blocked Tanzania's purchases of cheaper and better quality cement from Pakistan and India. Countering the industry campaign, the Tanzanian competition commission publicized the high cost of the duty. It would cost the people huge sums in road construction and housing, in consumer prices, in jobs, and in economic opportunity. The Chairman of the Competition Commission won the ear of Tanzania's president, who refused to impose the duties. As told by Godfrey Mkocha, when Director General of the Fair Competition Commission of Tanzania.

[42] In the United States, the antitrust agencies do not lobby against trade laws, which are entrusted to the US Trade Representative.

the connections between the state and vested interests in harming the market),[43] and the most articulate market advocates—the heads of the competition authorities— may be silenced in the fight against the most harmful restraints.

## B. ADVOCATING FOR A MODEST INTERNATIONAL OBLIGATION

The poorer developing countries are the most vulnerable targets of international restraints that hold back the economic growth of their countries. Despite frequent exhortations from the West that it wants the peoples of developing countries to be enabled to help themselves, in the world trading arena the Western countries pick and choose their targets of liberalization. Often, they cling to protection and subsidy where it hurts developing countries the most.[44] The West hands out more money in aid to developing countries than the developing countries' people would generate for themselves and their families if the West dismantled its tariffs, antidumping laws, and subsidies.[45] The West proclaims that export cartels from their nations' shores are not *their* problem; the victims can sue the offshore cartelists in the victims' jurisdictions. But the poorest nations have no resources or practical power to do so. This is a game that should not have to be played. As in pollution, stemming the offense at its source is the most efficient solution.

These problems suggest a positive agenda of advocacy. The European Union has proposed a helpful framework,[46] which could have been implemented in the context of the WTO (but has not been) and can also be conceived as a stand-alone project. In the spirit of the EU proposal, countries can and should have regard for the harms they cause, especially to developing countries, and especially when developed countries' nationals are the violators of clear, shared principles of antitrust law, such as the law against hard core cartels. If current national statutory limits are an obstacle, the

---

[43] Eleanor M. Fox, *World Antitrust: A Principled Blueprint*, Festschrift Für Wolfgang Fikentscher (1998); Merit Janow, *Private and Public Restraints that Limit Access to Markets, in* MARKET ACCESS AFTER THE URUGUAY ROUND: INVESTMENT, COMPETITION AND TECHNOLOGY PERSPECTIVES (Paris: OECD 1996).

[44] *See* passage, *Hypocrisy of the rich, in* MARTIN WOLF, WHY GLOBALIZATION WORKS 218 (2004). *See* Andres Martinez, *Harvesting Poverty*, N.Y. TIMES, Aug. 4, 2003, http://www.nytimes.com/ref/opinion/harvesting-poverty.html?pagewanted=all. *See* Timothy A. Wise & Biraj Patnaik, *Destruction of US credibility at WTO: It is hypocritical of the US to give price support to its farmers while denying it to the world's poorest farmers*, http://www.livemint.com/Opinion/JPi4078XnwziAnsbzTHgrJ/Destruction-of-US-credibility-at-WTO.html#ref=newsletter.

[45] WOLF, *supra* note 44. *See* Jasmin Malik, *U.S., EU Cotton Subsidies Cost Africa $250 Million a Year, Says New Report* (Nov. 19, 2010), *available at* http://www.ecouterre.com/u-s-eu-cotton-subsidies-cost-africa-250-million-a-year-says-new-report.

[46] Working Group on the Interaction between Trade and Competition Policy, WTO, *Communication from the European Community and Its Member States*, WT/WGTCP/W/184 (Apr. 22, 2002). The Working Group has been disbanded.

developed countries can and should revise their laws, extending jurisdiction so as to make hard core export cartels from their shores illegal.[47]

We can draw inspiration from an environmental convention: the Basel Convention on the Control of Transboundary Movements of Hazardous Wastes and their Disposal.[48] Under the Basel Convention, if a signatory country prohibits the import of hazardous wastes, all other signatories must make the shipment of hazardous wastes to that country illegal. The trading nations could adopt this model for hard core export cartels, which are the hazardous wastes of antitrust.

Also regarding cartels aimed at outsiders, the developed countries could amend their antitrust laws to provide jurisdiction for the discovery of documents and testimony from suspects and others privy to the facts of the outbound cartels. This could include subpoena power when the developed country's citizens are the alleged victimizers of developing countries.

The antitrust family of nations has gone a long way to cooperate with one another on enforcement. The developed nations robustly cooperate with one another. The Organization for Economic Cooperation and Development (OECD), ICN, and the UN Conference on Trade and Development (UNCTAD) are important forces and fora for cooperation. Regional fora in Africa, Latin America, and Asia and the BRICS likewise facilitate cooperation, as do multitudinous bilateral agreements, but the bilateral agreements are largely between developed country pairs. Cooperation is particularly needed by poorer and developing countries, which face extraordinary scarcity of resources and whose poor populations are often the targeted victims. Extra steps in this direction—among closely connected and like-situated developing countries, as in the Southern African Development Community (SADC),[49] and among developed and developing countries—hold promise to help the poor and to contribute to inclusive sustainable development.

## IV. Conclusion

This chapter has explored the core and bounds of competition law and policy in terms of the values of inclusive development and eradicating poverty. It argues:

1. We envision competition law and policy in sub-Saharan Africa as a pro-outsider and inclusive development policy. Access to markets, free from

---

[47] *See* Eleanor M. Fox, *Testimony Before the Antitrust Modernization Commission, Hearing on International Issues in Washington, D.C.* (Feb. 15, 2006), *available at* http://www.AMC.gov; *see also* Special Committee on International Antitrust, ABA Antitrust Section, The Special Committee's Report 83–90 (Sept. 1, 1991).

[48] Mar. 22, 1989, 1673 U.N.T.S. 125.

[49] The Southern African Development Community. *See* Chapter VI.

artificial restraints and vested interest privileges, empowers outsiders and tends to enhance mobility, fostering inclusive development. Lower prices of necessities obviously help the poor. To be sure, competition law and policy and the markets they support cannot do all of the work. Other necessary conditions prominently include directly providing food, health, education, housing, infrastructure, access to capital, good governance, and rule of law. All of these conditions and policies need to be pursued in global partnership. All are a part of an interdependent virtuous circle.

2. There *is* a pro-poorer/pro-development perspective on competition *law*, procedurally and substantively. It would require the competition agency to: (1) target state and hybrid restraints that create a stranglehold on markets, and draft the law with these targets in mind; (2) assure procedural vehicles to make the justice system accessible to the poorer and outsider populations; (3) adopt simpler but sound rules, lest we create a paradox that antitrust is a luxury for the well-off; and (4) within the range of possibilities for efficient and dynamic markets, lean pro-outsider.

3. There *is* a pro-poorer/pro-development perspective on competition *policy*. It would require the agency to: (1) develop programs to identify and advocate against excessive and unnecessary anticompetitive state restraints, especially those that create a stranglehold on economic opportunity; (2) advocate for world norms to oblige nations to stem and rectify the antitrust harms they cause; and, of course, (3) prioritize restraints in markets most essential to the daily lives, health, and well-being of the poorer populations.

# Conclusion

We have seen an array of countries in sub-Saharan Africa, from small and very poor with price control as the sole competition policy, to middle-class South Africa with a well-developed competition law system that controls mergers and monopolies, launches market inquiries, and engages in the international dialogue. We have examined the larger picture of markets, competition, and the world, and the ongoing projects of regional integration and their prospects. We have considered both competition *law* and competition *policy*, examined substantive legal principles that fit various stages of development, and reflected on the tension between law tailored to a country in its political and developmental context, and "international standards" developed by the industrialized world and favored by foreign investors.

Here, we make a few concluding observations. First, we draw lessons from the chapters on specific nations and the regional agreements to which they belong.

1. West Africa (Chapter III): The nations are thus far very limited in their competition law and policy, and thus very limited in making markets work for the people. Urgently, they need to reverse the preemption of national competition law by the regional organization WAEMU and then develop national laws and policies, benchmarking with peers. Even now, the national authorities have room to develop themselves as the voice of open markets for the people, identifying what most needs to be done to unleash the creative

Making Markets Work for Africa. Eleanor M. Fox and Mor Bakhoum.
© Oxford University Press 2019. Published 2019 by Oxford University Press.

economic energies of their people and make goods and services available especially to the poorest.

2. Eastern and Southern Africa (Chapters IV and V): Much potential is being developed, and, in some cases, very well. The problems in fighting corruption, cronyism, and vested interests and opening the space for participation on the merits by the left-out population may sometimes seem insurmountable, but valiant heads of agencies are fighting back, often successfully. The agencies are sometimes overwhelmed by must-do obligations such as review of all filed mergers and all complaints. They need to reserve precious time and resources to be proactive against the most egregious restraints. Yet the officials are often heroic in perceiving the worst restraints and launching plans to correct them, whether by law enforcement, advocacy, or other persuasion; often against the odds in the wake of corruption and the practical realities of politics.

3. Regionalism and cooperation (Chapter VI): So many of the worst restraints that hurt and hold back the people are supranational in origin—hard to detect and hard to challenge by a national agency. Moreover, many competition problems involve state measures to reserve their markets for their nationals. Regional economic organizations are in theory well positioned to surmount these problems: to detect and stop cross-border cartels, hybrid state/private restraints, and harmful multinational mergers. But this is hard work and has not yet been done. Not even has the groundwork been laid. Enforcement is needed and is the promise for the future. The European Union is the model. Like all else, the project requires funds and expertise, which are scarce.

Informal collaboration among the national competition authorities is a complement to regional enforcement. It is very important, for cross-fertilization, convergence, and cooperation. The African Competition Forum is doing this job well.

We turn to a more general set of conclusions.

1. Context is critical. The virtues of responding to context can overwhelm the virtues of adopting international standards. Stable law grows from roots. Technocrats who offer help must first appreciate the cultures, including the political landscape and the existing and possible institutions. International standards are good and helpful, but as a benchmarking input. A prominent example regards antitrust economics: developing countries face very high barriers to market entry and expansion combined with histories of colonization and mass exclusions. To be sympathetic to their needs, developing

countries' competition laws must be tougher than Western law on conduct that systematically excludes people without power or connections.

2. There is no good substitute for freeing up markets to work for the good of the people and for the growth of the economy. But the pioneers in this task in Africa must face and overcome a widely held negative view of markets: that they work only for multinational enterprises, their managers and investors, and other elites, and that free markets produce a new economic colonization. This is a one-sided picture. Nations and their peoples gain from better and cheaper products, transfers of technologies, building out infrastructure, the jobs that investment brings, and the opportunities to engage in the economic enterprise. Still, the pioneers must reckon with a germ of truth. Markets and antitrust can get captured by powerful business and cronyist governments. Even if markets are not technically captured, an antitrust policy that systematically prefers efficiency of entrenched business to entry and expansion of entrepreneurs and upstarts perpetuates a two-tiered system of market competition: a top tier of mostly foreign enterprise, and a secondary tier of mostly indigenous people, many of whom must operate in the informal economy. Developing country law can push back, and it can develop pro-people antitrust. As people come to understand that markets can be in the service of the people rather than in the service of giant corporations, the mistrust of markets may soften.

3. There is a virtuous agenda for the competition authorities, even though success requires overcoming overwhelming forces of corruption, cronyism, and bad governance. The agenda is: Number one: observe, and be creative and proactive. What are the restraints in your market that hold your people back? Where are the barriers? What is strangling the markets, squeezing the space for people to participate on their merits and not letting the markets work? Find them and challenge them, within the bounds of the possible and pragmatic. Some of the efforts called for will be advocacy, such as convincing legislators to abolish monopoly commodity boards, fighting skewed government procurement specifications written to match the capabilities of the president's cronies, and supporting breakthroughs for access to capital for people without connections. Priorities, of course, include enforcement against cartels, harmful mergers, and monopolistic practices, including enforcement against SOE offenders. Positive enforcement action may require recalibrating principles of competition law to give due attention to entry and special regard to people from the poorest populations. Priority efforts include collaboration and coordination with neighbors' competition authorities across national borders. In the future we may see the

emergence of strong regional organizations that enforce regional competition law across borders, that prohibit harmful megamergers, that integrate the disciplines of trade and competition in Africa, and that become a voice for Africa that can begin to approach the voice of the West. But how will this promise be realized? Business as usual will not do. Change and commitment are required.

Sub-Saharan Africa requires the foxes before the hedgehog,[1] to see the possibilities from many angles and to take the opportunities. The best strategies are not always found in a prewritten script for development or for the world.

*How We Made It in Africa* is an online publication. A post proclaims: "How African companies are taking business away from multinationals."[2] The post names well-known multinationals that have recently entered the African market, and then reports new data showing that big international brands "are losing ground to local opposition." It catalogs local winners: South Africa–based mobile telecommunications company MTN, Kenyan FMCG manufacturer Bidco, Angolan beverage company Refriango, and Moroccan banks Attijariwafa, BMCE, and Banque Populaire. How is this happening? It is happening, the post explains, because local firms have a stronger commitment to local markets. They have on-the-ground-experience; they know the local culture and have strong industry connections. They have a better grasp of what the local consumers want. They are comfortable with informal business relationships and flexible in decision-making, and do not have to wait for a go-ahead signal from distant decision makers.[3] In all of those ways, local business is better positioned to compete than the foreign multinational rivals.

These stories do not just happen. Behind every local company that made it or might make it in the marketplace, there are barricades to be hurdled. Overcoming the hurdles is a daunting task in countries often run by autocratic governments and vested interests that profit by keeping others down and out. But that task—pulling down the barricades and being the voice for pro-people markets—is the competition authorities' job and society's hope.

---

[1] *See* reference to Isaiah Berlin, Chapter VII.

[2] Dinfin Mulupi, *How African companies are taking business away from multinationals*, HOW WE MADE IT IN AFRICA, Nov. 14, 2015, https://www.howwemadeitinafrica.com/how-african-companies-are-taking-business-away-from-multinationals.

[3] *Id.*

# Appendices

OVERVIEW

The following data provide generalized descriptions of sub-Saharan African countries using several popular indices that measure factors such as income inequality, government corruption, human development, democratic agency, and ease of doing business. This note provides a brief description of the indices used. It is followed by visual and analytic displays of the data comparing the sub-Saharan African countries, the regional average, and select comparator countries.

INDICES

*Gini Index*

The Gini coefficient is the statistical measure representing the wealth distribution and inequality within a nation. The more unequal the distribution, the closer the number is to 100; perfectly distributed income would result in an index score of zero.

The data come from the United Nations, and most of indices derive from data collected from 2010 to 2015 (Figure A.1).

*Corruption Perception Index*

This index, prepared by Transparency International, ranks countries by their perceived levels of corruption as determined by expert assessment and opinion surveys. Corruption is broadly defined as the "misuse of public power for private benefit." 100 represents a very clean government, while 0 is the most corrupt. For measure, Denmark is consistently given a score of 90, while the United States, ranking at number 18, scores in the mid-70s (Figure A.2).

Making Markets Work for Africa. Eleanor M. Fox and Mor Bakhoum.
© Oxford University Press 2019. Published 2019 by Oxford University Press.

*Human Development Index*

The HDI, indexed by the United Nations, is a summary measure of average achievement in key dimensions of human development, including health, education, and standard of living. Health is assessed by life expectancy. Education is measured by mean years of schooling. Standard of living is measured by gross national income per capita. The sub-Saharan African average is .523—the lowest of all regions (Figure A.3).

*Democracy Index*

The UK-based Economist Intelligence Unit creates the Democracy Index to rank countries based on the strength of their democracy. Countries are scaled from 0 to 10, using 60 indicators that generally measure pluralism, civil liberties, and political culture. Those numbers then are categorized into four broad groups: Authoritarian Regime, Hybrid Regime, Flawed Democracy, and Democracy (Figure A.4).

*Ease of Doing Business Index*

*Doing Business*, a World Bank Group publication, measures regulations affecting 11 areas of business life. For 2017, 10 factors were included: starting a business, obtaining construction permits, accessing electricity, registering property, receiving credit, protecting minority investors, paying taxes, trading across borders, enforcing contracts, and resolving insolvency (Figure A.5).

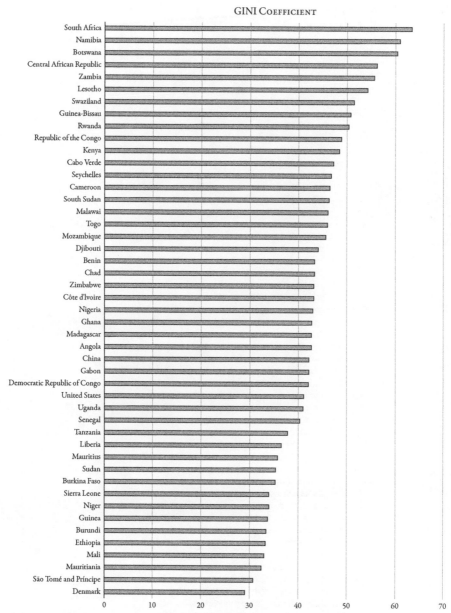

GINI COEFFICIENT

FIGURE A.1 GINI coefficient (inequality index) for sub-Saharan African nations with the US, Denmark, and China as comparators. 0 is perfect equality.

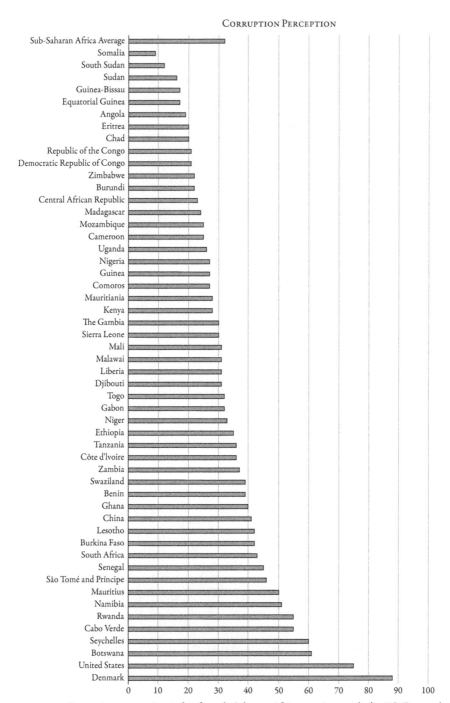

FIGURE A.2 Corruption perception index for sub-Saharan African nations with the US, Denmark, and China as comparators. 100 is very clean government.

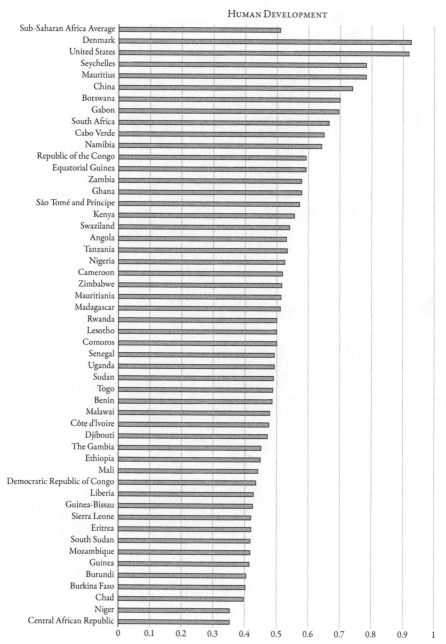

FIGURE A.3 Human development index for sub-Saharan African nations with the US, Denmark, and China as comparators. 1 is very high achievement.

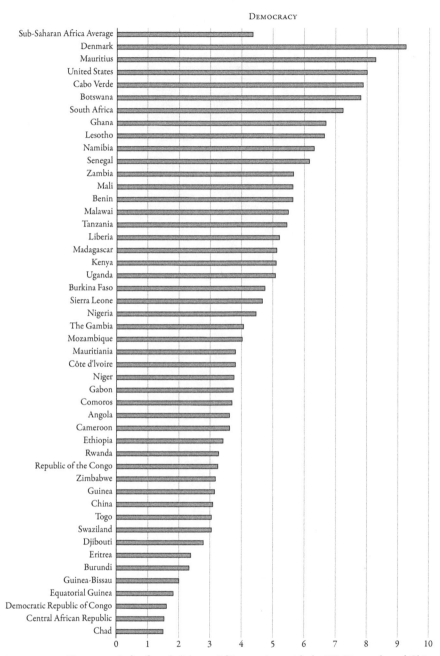

FIGURE A.4 Democracy index for sub-Saharan African nations with the US, Denmark, and China as comparators. 10 is very strong democracy.

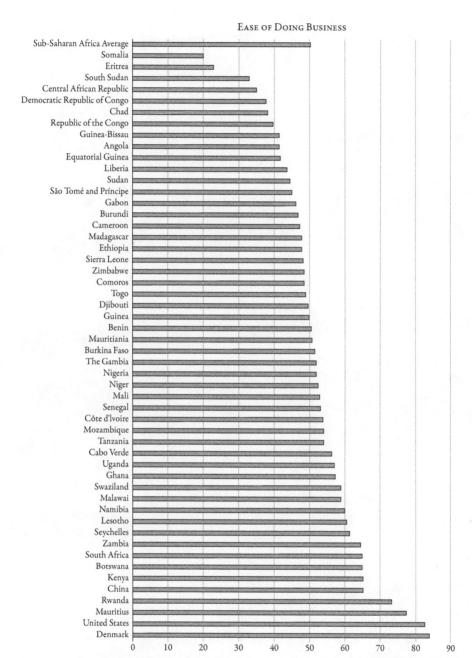

EASE OF DOING BUSINESS

FIGURE A.5 Ease of doing business index for sub-Saharan nations with the US, Denmark, and China as comparators. 100 is great ease of doing business.

# Index